RON HOWARD

From Mayberry to the Moon . . . and Beyond

BEVERLY GRAY

Rutledge Hill Press™
Nashville, Tennessee

A Division of Thomas Nelson, Inc.

www.ThomasNelson.com

Published by Rutledge Hill Press, a Division of Thomas Nelson, Inc., P.O. Box 141000, Nashville, Tennessee, 37214.

Library of Congress Cataloging-in-Publication Data

Gray, Beverly.
  Ron Howard : from Mayberry to the moon — and beyond / Beverly Gray.
    p. cm.
  Filmography as an actor (p.   )
  Filmography as a director and producer (p.   )
  Includes bibliographical references and index.
    ISBN 1-55853-970-0 (hardcover)
  1. Howard, Ron. 2. Motion picture producers and directors—United States—
Biography. 3. Actors—United States—Biography. I. Title.
  PN1998.3 .H689 G73 2003
  791.43.'0233'092—dc21   2002153251

Printed in the United States of America

03 04 05 06 07—5 4 3 2 1

TO MY FAMILY

my severest critics,
most trusted supporters,
and best friends

Contents

Acknowledgments

I could never have finished a project of this magnitude without help from many quarters. I deeply appreciate the contributions of Kelly Cutts, Selise E. Eiseman, Charles W. Fries, Noela Hueso, Wendy Madnick, Ron Magid, Gary Mednick, Judith Merians, Donie Nelson, Naomi Pfefferman, Jerry Purvis, Henry Seggerman, Gail Shenbaum, Ashley Wrobel, and especially Jim Clark, founder and guiding spirit of *The Andy Griffith Show* Rerun Watchers Club. Through the magic of the Internet, I located an international group of friendly and knowledgeable *Happy Days* fans, among whom John Dagley of Melbourne, Australia, and Arianna Bianchi of Milan, Italy, have been particularly obliging. And of course I owe a large debt to everyone I interviewed for this biography.

My research into Ron Howard's early years was hugely facilitated by Pee Wee Cary, director of the Stephens County Historical Museum in Duncan, Oklahoma. I would also like to thank the following for giving me access to their archives and collections: Albert L. Ortega; Holly Jones and Jeni Rosenthal at AP/World Wide Photos; Beverly Hills Public Library; Burbank (California) Historical Society; Burbank Public Library; Scott Baillie at Celebrity Archive Corporation; Anthony Sullivan at Getty Images; John Burroughs High School; Los Angeles Public Library; Amy Garawitz at the Museum of Television and Radio; Santa Monica Public Library; the UCLA Arts Library.

The Margaret Herrick Library of the Academy of Motion Picture Arts and Sciences was my home base for many months. Donovan Brandt helped me find what I needed among the vast resources at Eddie

Brandt's Saturday Matinee. At the University of Southern California, my questions were answered courteously and efficiently by Justin Wilson and Peter Pampusch of the School of Cinema-Television and by June Hudson in the office of the registrar. For assistance above and beyond the call of duty I must single out Mark Quigley, reference and outreach coordinator for the archive research and study center of the UCLA Film and Television Archive.

James Robert Parish deserves special thanks for sharing his vast knowledge of the publishing world and for never allowing me to rest on my laurels. My agent, Stuart Bernstein, has been wonderfully diligent on my behalf; his words of wisdom and good cheer always prove to be *eggs-actly* right. At Rutledge Hill Press, Larry Stone has been a model of cordiality and common sense. I also appreciate the help I've received from Rutledge Hill's Jennifer Brett Greenstein, Christy O'Flaherty, Bryan Curtis, Terri Woodmore, and especially Geoff Stone.

Within my circle of family and friends, I'm grateful to everyone who has provided encouragement. My husband, Bernie Bienstock, has been my personal tech support system ever since the day a computer moved into our home. My son, Jeffrey, cheerfully accepted the duties of a research assistant. My daughter, Hilary, was living in Beijing, China, throughout the writing of this book. Nonetheless, she read every word of my text and gave me the benefit of her always-perceptive comments, in spite of eccentric keyboards in far-flung Internet cafes. Heartfelt thanks to all of them.

Introduction

Sizing up Ron Howard should be as easy as pie. After all, everybody knows him. At least, we think we do. He has been coming into our living rooms for the past forty years, first as lovable Opie Taylor on *The Andy Griffith Show* and then as perennial teenager Richie Cunningham of *Happy Days*. Viewers too young to have caught his act the first time around have discovered his homespun charm through reruns. Others fell in love with his screen image as early as 1959, when he was first featured on network television. Baby-boomers, in particular, can chart the passage of their own youth in terms of Ronny Howard roles. During their childhood years, he was a plucky little boy. When they began moving out into the world, he was gingerly exploring life in high school and college. Now that Ron Howard is a full-fledged adult, with a family, a receding hairline, and a major career as a Hollywood film director, it's no wonder that many of us still feel a sense of connection.

So familiar is Howard that members of the media tend to make sweeping generalizations about him. Some praise him as an "American genius," while others dismiss him as little more than an overgrown Boy Scout. Kirk Honeycutt, film critic for the *Hollywood Reporter*, sees in Howard's directing career the results of "a life [lived] entirely within the cocoon of Hollywood." The general view is that Howard, as a highly successful product of the Hollywood studio system, naturally gravitates toward the kind of filmmaking that upholds the system's strengths, by relying on star power, a high technical gloss, and the assurance of mass appeal through a predictably upbeat ending.

Honeycutt's use of the word "cocoon" is apt, because throughout

Howard's years in show business, the protective cocoon has been a recurring motif. *Cocoon* is, of course, the title of the 1985 film that moved Howard into the big leagues as a director. But even back in his acting days, his best-known roles could be said to cocoon him from the harsh realities of life. The happy hamlet of Mayberry was a cocoon of sorts, as was the whole nostalgia-fueled environment in which Richie Cunningham of *Happy Days* moved toward adulthood.

But this is only one side of the picture. He's a lot more complicated than he seems.

I spoke to Ron Howard on January 29, 1999, while researching my book, *Roger Corman: An Unauthorized Biography of the Godfather of Indie Filmmaking* (Renaissance Books, 2000). He and I had a cordial, unhurried chat about the legendary low-budget filmmaker, who was both my former boss and the man who gave Howard his first directing gig.

When it was time to choose my next biographical project, I found myself intrigued by Howard's own long career. No one else in Hollywood has so emphatically made the jump from child star to direc- tor. And his iconic status from his days as Opie and Richie continues to resonate, even while he directs award-winning motion pictures. Part of his appeal for me was that, in his journey from Opie to Oscar, there has never been the slightest whiff of scandal. As one veteran observer of the Hollywood scene told me, "I have never heard a bad thing about Ron Howard. Never." Not that I was looking to write about a saint—but part of the challenge of a biography of Ron Howard would be locating the human core within the pristine image.

My great hope, of course, was that Howard would give my project his blessing. But I was hardly surprised when, speaking through his publicist, Howard politely announced his decision to keep his distance from this book. He said he felt himself to be in midcareer and not ready to participate in a long-range assessment of his accomplishments.

Howard's reluctance to get personally involved fit my conception of him as modest and self-effacing, as a star who has never wanted a star's notoriety. But to ensure the accuracy of my work, I tried making contacts within Howard's company, Imagine Entertainment, taking pains to spell out my credentials and my good intentions. Some of my overtures were simply ignored. I was taken aback, however, by several telephone conversations with Howard's colleagues who expressed outrage that I would consider writing about Howard without his formal consent. I tried to explain that Ron Howard is known and admired all over the globe. Celebrity confers many privileges, both material and emotional, and the downside is that being in the public eye includes being subject to public scrutiny.

What impressed me about Howard's associates was how personally they seemed to take my writing plans. Evidently, they regard it as their mission to protect Howard from any intrusion by the outside world. I admire their dedication and see it as one more sign of the loyalty Howard inspires. But in examining his career, I did get help from a variety of sources. Many of Howard's old friends, former teachers, coworkers, and costars gave me a picture of his early life. To fill in the more recent years, I was lucky to find actors who have appeared in Howard productions and crew members who have worked on his sets. A few asked that their names not be used, and I have honored these requests. All were emphatic in stressing Howard's graciousness, intelligence, and talent for collaboration.

To supplement the nearly three dozen interviews I conducted, I turned to the archives and discovered a treasure trove. Howard has been speaking to the press since he was six years old. These vintage articles, along with later radio and television appearances, gave valuable insights into Howard's personality. *Ron Howard: From Mayberry to the Moon . . . and Beyond* explores the fascinating contradictions that mark his life: how he manages to be public and private, brave and cautious, small-town boy and big-city success story.

To think of him as "Opie" is far too simple. The cute kid has grown into a man who defies easy labels as he sets out to make Hollywood movies on his own terms.

PART I

The Early Years

CHAPTER 1

Small Steps

(1954–1960)

"He's the most determined person that I have ever met in my life. I think he gets this from his dad."
—JEAN HOWARD

LITTLE RONNY HOWARD WAS AMERICA'S KID BROTHER. Bright-eyed and gap-toothed, with a shock of red hair that seemed made for Technicolor, he quickly came to exemplify the American virtues of innocence, optimism, common sense, and good humor. In the second half of the twentieth century, when life in America was becoming ever more complicated, Ronny seemed to dwell in a world apart. His signature roles as Sheriff Taylor's son on *The Andy Griffith Show* (1960–1968) and as young Winthrop Paroo in *The Music Man* (1962) conveyed the fantasy of growing up in a better place and time. Whether fishing with Pa in the imaginary hamlet of Mayberry, North Carolina, or joining the marching band of Professor Harold Hill in River City, Iowa, young Ronny inspired in his fans a feeling of nostalgia for a simpler past, as well as hope for the future.

As Ronny passed through his teen years, he shortened his first name, slicked down his hair, and earned his driver's license. In the role of Steve Bolander, a recent high school graduate much like himself, he spent an unforgettable night cruising Modesto, California, in 1973's *American Graffiti*. Then came a seven-year stint (1974–1980) on *Happy Days*, a candy-coated view of adolescence set in suburban Milwaukee, in which he played perennial nice guy Richie Cunningham. Through these and other roles, Howard was embraced by audiences who saw in his wholesome image a reflection of what American life ought to be.

One key to Howard's success as a child actor was that he seemed an integral part of the American scene. He could play a California whiz kid or a Manhattan youngster mourning his mother's death with equal conviction, but his best roles often brought him close to the soil. Included on his long list of credits are many youthful farmers, home-steaders, and country boys. Although he was reared in the workaday Los Angeles suburb of Burbank, California, Howard's roots are in the American heartland. Oklahoma-born, he can trace his ancestry back to early settlers, including two great-grandfathers who rode in the Oklahoma Land Run of 1893. He also feels a deep emotional attach-ment to his kinfolk and their values. As a young actor, Ronny Howard often played roles in which he searched for—or quietly grieved for—a missing parent. In real life, however, he enjoyed sturdy family ties. There's no question that Ronny, like all show biz kids, was subject to the caprices built into the Hollywood system. But unlike many of his peers, he had the support of parents who were remarkably down-to-earth. It is with them that this story begins.

Duncan, Oklahoma, is in the southern part of the state, midway between Oklahoma City and Dallas, Texas. It lies along the old Chisholm Trail, the path taken by Texas cowboys driving their cattle north through Indian Territory to the railroads of Kansas. In 1872, a Scotsman named William Duncan purchased a store close to the trail. When he learned that the Rock Island Railroad was planning a north-south route through the area, he determined to relocate near the depot. He completed his second store in 1890, at what is now the corner of

Seventh and Main in downtown Duncan. This historic location was only a few doors away from where Ronny Howard's maternal grandparents would later open Speegle Meat Market.

By the time the first passenger train pulled into Duncan's depot on June 27, 1892, a small community had developed. As a local newspaper would later put it, "A Trail, A Rail—A City!" Some early arrivals founded businesses that served the cowhands; others opted for ranching and farming, with cotton and wheat as the principal cash crops. A major jump in Duncan's fortunes came with the discovery of oil around 1918. Though Duncan's farmers suffered during the Dust Bowl era of the 1930s, oil booms led to sporadic periods of growth. In 1954, the year Ronny Howard was born, the population was about twenty-two thousand. It remains the same today.

Within Duncan, members of the Speegle clan have long played a prominent role. Ronny's great-grandmother, Mrs. W. T. Speegle, was a pillar of the community, active in social and church circles. The next generation included Mr. and Mrs. W. A. Speegle, better known as Butch and Louise, who were the proud parents of Ronny's mother, Jean. Jean Frances Speegle, born on January 31, 1927, attended Emerson Elementary School and Duncan Junior High School. By the time she entered Duncan High School, there was no question that this effervescent young lady was going places. She appeared in the junior class play, was society editor of the school newspaper, and held offices on the student council. In her senior year (1944–45), she served as editor in chief of the school yearbook, and was elected student council president. It's hardly surprising that the junior class named her "Outstanding Senior Girl."

After graduation Jean enrolled in Oklahoma College for Women. But the state of Oklahoma was not big enough to contain her ambitions. By October 1946, she had been accepted into New York City's American Academy of Dramatic Arts, famous for launching the careers of such luminaries as Spencer Tracy and Lauren Bacall. On the evening of February 10, 1947, however, Jean left a dance class and stepped into the path of a speeding truck. The collision left her with a brain concussion, a broken arm and shoulder, and a pelvis shattered in three places. She lay unconscious for ten days in a New York charity hospital, because the wallet containing her

identification was lost in the accident. At last she was put on a train for
Oklahoma City. An ambulance carried her to Duncan, where doctors
warned her worried family she might never walk again.

But Jean, always a fighter, beat the odds. On Easter Sunday, she sat
up for the first time since the accident. By May 15 she was walking, and
soon afterward she was ready to resume her life. For the time being, she
chose to stick closer to home. In the fall, she entered the school of
drama at the University of Oklahoma, where she played major roles in
a host of student productions. Her crowning achievement was the
female lead in *Winterset,* Maxwell Anderson's prize-winning poetic
drama inspired by the controversial execution of anarchists Nicola
Sacco and Bartolomeo Vanzetti. *Winterset* was performed on the
Norman, Oklahoma, campus March 18–19, 1948. Jean, who had dyed
her strawberry-blond hair black for the occasion, played the tragic role
of Miriamne, an idealistic young slum-dweller. A writer for the campus
newspaper, *The Oklahoma Daily,* began his rave review by saying,
"Last night an audience wept." He had especially high praise for the
final love scene between Jean's "tender little tenement girl" and the tor-
tured young man seeking vengeance for his father's death.

The campus reviewer also singled out one of the supporting players:
"Harold Beckenholdt, as the half-wit hobo, molded a minor part into an
important role." Beckenholdt, born in 1928, was a tall, lanky Oklahoma
country boy who remembered the Dust Bowl all too well. He had caught
a glimpse of a better world when local merchants, hoping to lure farmers into town, began screening free movies on Saturday nights. At age
seventeen, Beckenholdt walked off his parents' farm, bent on becoming
an actor. Fellow student and future television star Dennis Weaver first
introduced him to Jean, and he renewed the acquaintance in 1948 when
they toured together in a children's theatre troupe, Penthouse Productions.
By this time, she was calling herself Jean Allan, and he had adopted the
stage name of Rance Howard.

Much Howard family lore stems from these bus-and-truck productions of *Cinderella* and *Snow White.* Ron Howard remembers hearing
how "they only had four dwarves, so my father would occasionally get
on his knees and put a beard on and be another dwarf." Most of the

time, however, Rance would play Prince Charming to Jean's fairy tale princess. Years later, Rance told a hometown newspaper that Jean "had a great smile and a warm and wonderful personality. . . . She was full of vitality, and I just really fell in love with her."

The long theatrical tour provided the backdrop for their courtship and honeymoon. The wedding took place on October 5, 1949, in the ballroom of the Brown Proctor Hotel in Winchester, Kentucky. A local Methodist minister conducted the double-ring ceremony, at which the guests and attendants were mostly fellow actors. Though the festivities were kept simple, an account in a Duncan newspaper notes that the bride was beautifully dressed in "a floor-length gown of rose pink taffeta." This was Jean's Cinderella costume, stripped of its sequins for the occasion. The marriage that began on that day, between the determined young woman and the dreamy farmer's son, would survive and flourish for more than half a century.

Once their commitment to Penthouse Productions was over, the young couple settled in New York City and started looking for acting jobs. Jean appeared in an off-Broadway staging of *The Passion Play*. Rance, though never losing his boyhood dream of starring in cowboy films, scrounged for minor parts on stage and live television, and once even worked as a doorman at the Roxy Theater, a renowned movie palace. But his blond good looks and deep, resonant voice seemed to promise better things. A big break came when he was cast as a sailor in the national touring company of the 1948 Broadway hit, *Mister Roberts*. Henry Fonda, who had created the title role in the World War II comedy-drama, headlined the tour as well. Then *Mister Roberts* finished its run, and Rance was drafted.

Even while serving a three-year hitch in the Air Force, Rance continued to act, and tried his hand at directing. A clipping from that era shows Rance and Jean among those entertaining at an Optimists Club gala near Chanute Air Force Base in Rantoul, Illinois. While Rance was stationed in San Antonio, Texas, the Howards' first child was born. Because Jean had chosen to have their baby in the cozy confines of her hometown, she moved into her parents' rambling brick house at 1010 W. Chestnut Street to await the big moment.

Ronald William Howard first saw the light of day on March 1, 1954. His proud relatives were soon circulating a birth announcement written in the form of a playbill. It proclaimed "in response to numerous demands" a new comedy-drama, "Life Begins At 9:03 A.M.," with its world premiere at Duncan's Lindley Hospital. The cast of characters included Jean Howard as the Patient Mother and Rance Howard as the Distracted Father. Ronald W. Howard was listed as the show's leading man, and was also credited with providing sound effects. A Production Note pointed out: "In the first scene, the star appears in the nude, creating quite a sensation."

Jean once told an interviewer that although she and Rance were very pleased to have a baby son, they did not alter their career goals on his account: "He lived in our world with us." This meant that young Ronny quickly found himself among theatrical folk, and before long he too was getting into the act. His early start would eventually become Hollywood legend. At the time of *Splash,* Tom Hanks joked that Howard "has seen absolutely everything that can possibly happen on a movie set, because the man started doing it three months before he was born." Pat Morita, who appeared as Arnold on *Happy Days,* insists with a straight face that "Ronny Howard's little poop-poop was on the very first Pampers commercials. . . . That's how far back his career goes."

In fact, Ronny's first screen appearance came at the ripe old age of eighteen months. His father, then still in the Air Force, wangled a thirty-day leave to play the bad guy in a Grade-C Western called *Frontier Woman.* At one point the filmmakers needed a crying baby, and Ronny—watching from the sidelines in his mother's arms—was elected. The novice actor was given a little Indian tomahawk to play with. When it was suddenly snatched away, he began to wail. It was the first, though not the last, time that Ronny showed he could cry on cue. He doesn't count this as his professional debut, however, because he didn't get paid. He was not to lose his amateur standing until his fourth birthday.

In the meantime Ronny enjoyed his parents' theatrical endeavors. When Rance began spending summers as an actor and resident director at Baltimore's Hilltop Theatre, he cast Jean and two-year-old Ronny as his wife and son in a production of *The Seven Year Itch*. The son's part was no more than a walk-on, but at least one Baltimore critic was charmed, proclaiming that "Ronny stole the show." Even when not needed on stage, Ronny liked hanging around rehearsals, soaking up the actors' dialogue. His ability to memorize lines, and to deliver them with feeling, was to pave the way for his own big break. At age two and a half, he had learned a comic scene from *Mister Roberts*. When he played the irrepressible Ensign Pulver at social gatherings while his father took on the Henry Fonda role, he was always assured of hearty applause. In 1958 while Rance was auditioning for a major MGM film called *The Journey*, he discovered that director Anatole Litvak needed a small boy to fill out the cast. On a whim, he praised his son's acting skills and was invited to bring almost-four-year-old Ronny in for an interview. The *Mister Roberts* scene got him the part. It also got him two tickets to Vienna, Austria, for himself and his mother. Because Rance had already been cast in a small role, this seemed a once-in-a-life-time opportunity for a family trip to Europe. Forty years later, Ron described his parents' thinking: "We'll take the money and we'll put it in a separate fund for college, and he never has to do this again."

To Rance, the decision seemed more complicated. The experience, of course, might be a great adventure for young Ronny. On the other hand, moviemaking could put adult pressures on a small child. Rance recalls that "we debated about whether we had a right to force show business on a little kid, but here was a chance to see Vienna. So why not? Later we told ourselves, 'Well, it didn't seem to screw the kid up any.'" As for Jean, she seemed thoroughly content to put her own ambitions on hold for the time being. Shortly before their departure, she told a local reporter she was dropping out of acting "to let the two men in the family make their mark."

The Journey, released in 1959, was an ambitious drama about the aftermath of the failed Hungarian Revolution. It was also a clear attempt to reignite the spark that Yul Brynner and Deborah Kerr had brought to the screen in the 1956 blockbuster, *The King and I*. *The Journey* revolves around the fate of sixteen international travelers trapped at a Hungarian inn by Russian soldiers, led by the suavely menacing Major Surov (Brynner). Kerr plays an elegant British aristocrat with secrets to keep. The other key player in the film's offbeat romantic triangle is Jason Robards, making his motion picture debut. (Thirty years later, Ron Howard would direct Robards in *Parenthood*.)

Ronny's part in *The Journey* is small but crucial. His role is the younger son of an American couple, played by E. G. Marshall and Anne Jackson, who are emotionally torn by the hostilities erupting all around them. Though he's kept at a distance from the film's most brutal skirmishes, Ronny is present for several potentially life-or-death confrontations. During a tense bus ride he playfully sticks out his tongue at some Russian soldiers; later he whimpers in Anne Jackson's arms as she defiantly tells her fellow travelers, "I don't care who lives and who dies as long as my family's okay."

Ronny's character, Billy Rhinelander, has only two lines in the film, but one of them is supposed to help viewers understand his family's travel plans. Today Howard admits that his boyish diction could have used some work: "I watched *The Journey* a couple of years ago, and I couldn't even understand what I was saying." Still, he remembers his time on the set with great pleasure: "I got to use a Soviet tank as my jungle gym. [Also] Yul Brynner taking a shot glass, which I didn't know was made of edible sugar, and devouring it before my eyes." Ironically, in the finished film Rance cannot be spotted, and his name does not appear in the credits. But his son, as a highly visible member of a polished ensemble, had made an auspicious acting debut.

Once the Howards returned to New York, they faced a decision. Rance's bread-and-butter work was in live television, but by 1958 most of the cowboy and detective shows were being produced in and around Los Angeles. Ron Howard recalls that "like the Okies a couple of decades before us, we loaded up the car." In their trusty '52 Plymouth, the three Howards rumbled across the country, stopping to visit Duncan and the farm where Rance grew up. Their route, which also took them through the Painted Desert and the Petrified Forest, perhaps inspired Ron's own later love for driving trips. (As a husband and father, he has enjoyed piling his wife and kids into their oversized car, along with a stack of peanut butter sandwiches, and heading for the open road.) But for Ronny's parents, the road trip was serious business, because at journey's end they would need to establish a life in a new place.

Upon reaching California the Howard family settled not in Hollywood but in nearby Burbank, just north of the Hollywood Hills in the San Fernando Valley. Burbank, which began as a large *rancho* deeded to early settlers by the Spanish authorities, was incorporated as a city in 1911. The 1920s brought the founding of Lockheed Aircraft Company, destined to become Burbank's biggest employer. The city also attracted fledgling movie studios, led by Warner Bros., which was soon flying high on the strength of its first talking picture, *The Jazz Singer* (1927). Ultimately Disney Studios too found a home in Burbank, with Universal Studios not far away. Burbank boomed during and after World War II, reaching a population peak of ninety thousand in 1957, the year before the Howards arrived. Civic boosters claim that in this era one fifth of the movies filmed in the United States came out of Burbank. And since this was when television first caught on with the American public, the production facilities at Burbank's NBC Studios were humming.

Burbank's close connection to the movie industry is suggested by its street names, which include Warner Boulevard, Bob Hope Drive, and Screenland Drive. The family rented an apartment on Hollywood Way, and went to work. Rance soon appeared on episodes of popular television series such as *Bat Masterson* and *Perry Mason*. Because Ronny was now a movie veteran, and because cute kids dominated the sitcoms of the era, the Howards set aside their scruples and signed him with an agent. As Rance acknowledged, being on the set was like "a wonderful game to him. . . . It would be, possibly, a good way for him to earn money for his college education. And of course that would take a big burden off our shoulders."

Ronny's first television show, at age four and a half, was a segment of *Playhouse 90*. He also was part of a group of children in a comic

"Freddie the Freeloader" sketch on *The Red Skelton Show*. During rehearsals, Skelton happened to spot him enthusiastically devouring fried chicken. Skelton quietly warned the boy that he was actually eating fried cat. Unfazed, Ronny shrugged, "Well, I guess I just like fried cat," and went on chewing. Skelton was amused and gave him a few lines in the show.

The *Red Skelton* appearance led to more comedy roles, on such popular series as *Dennis the Menace* and *The Many Loves of Dobie Gillis*. Ronny was also featured on one of his favorite Westerns, *Johnny Ringo*, as a boy who must point out his mother's killer in a crowded courtroom. In "Walking Distance," an early *Twilight Zone* episode that aired on October 30, 1959, he played marbles with Gig Young but refused to accept him as a grown-up version of his neighborhood playmate, saying, "You're not Marty Sloane. I know Marty Sloane, and you're not him." In the *Twilight Zone* credits, he was listed, not for the last time, as "Ronnie" Howard. This was carelessness, because he spelled his screen name "Ronny" until officially shortening it to Ron at the time of *Happy Days*.

Because five-year-old Ronny could not yet read, his father taught him his lines. Rance also imparted lessons in basic acting technique that stood Ron in good stead throughout his career. He still remembers his dad telling him, before his *Red Skelton* appearance, "Really look at him in the eye and really listen to what he's saying. Don't just wait for your line; really listen. And then your line will just come naturally."

These lessons proved invaluable when Ronny filmed a pilot based on cartoonist Crockett Johnson's well-known character, Barnaby. The show, known as "Barnaby and Mr. O'Malley," aired on December 20, 1959, as an episode of *General Electric Theatre*. It concerns a small boy who has, or imagines he has, a fairy godfather. Bert Lahr starred as O'Malley, a godfather never quite sure of his own magical powers, and Ronny was Barnaby. He was not billed on-screen, but the program's host, future President Ronald Reagan, ad libbed a special thank-you to "little Ronny Howard." The fallout was immediate. *Variety*'s review devoted a paragraph to his achievement: "In the title role, Ronny Howard played with authority and awareness. The moppet cavorted between fantasy and reality as though such behavior was most normal." And his agent's phone started ringing off the hook.

Among the members of the viewing public, Burbank resident Phyllis Cohen was especially impressed by Ronny's performance. Because she had a child enrolled at Burbank's Robert Louis Stevenson Elementary School, Cohen participated in the Stevenson PTA Playhouse, which performed original comedies for the student body. The day after the airing of "Barnaby and Mr. O'Malley," she enthused to a friend at a Stevenson Playhouse audition, "Last night I saw the most adorable kid in a TV show. He's going to be a star!" Her friend replied, "Meet Jean, his mother." Thus Phyllis Cohen was introduced to Jean Howard. They were to become neighbors when the Howards moved to a house on Burbank's Cordova Street. And Cohen's chance remark became the start of a warm, enduring friendship between the two women.

Four months later, the Howard family made a weeklong visit to the folks back in Duncan. Ronny, newly turned six, was considered a local celebrity, and a reporter from the *Duncan Banner* asked him to sit for his first-ever interview. He wiggled, squirmed, and sometimes groped for the right words, but his father, typically, would not let him be anything less than a professional. Whenever reporter Elizabeth Sandlin turned to Rance for responses to questions, he would demur, saying, "No, I want Ronny to answer them."

Ronny told Sandlin about auditions, rehearsals, and attending school on the set. He also revealed that his little brother Clinton, born on April 20, 1959, had show business aspirations. Said Ronny, "He went for the interview when he was seven months old. But he didn't get the part. They wanted a baby who could feed himself and had two front teeth." Clint, alas, couldn't even sit up at the time, so his acting days would have to wait.

When Sandlin asked about his own plans, Ronny expressed the hope that "Mr. O'Malley" would be turned into a series. "It's a fantasy," he reported, "and I like fantasies." But if that didn't work out, the young actor had other irons in the fire. It seems he had just appeared on Danny Thomas's popular television show, *Make Room for*

Daddy, as the son of a small-town Southern lawman. His on-screen father, Sheriff Andy Taylor, was played by Andy Griffith, a North Carolina–born stage actor who was starting to make a name for himself in Hollywood. Thomas and producer Sheldon Leonard planned to spin off Griffith's character into a series of his own, and Ronny was invited to join the cast.

Soon after Ronny's conversation with the *Duncan Banner*, "Mr. O'Malley" disappeared into the shadowy vault reserved for failed television pilots. *The Andy Griffith Show* made its CBS debut on October 3, 1960. The rest is history.

CHAPTER 2

Home Sweet Home

(1960–1968)

*"Life around Mayberry was kind of idyllic.
There were certain moments and scenes that
I could relate to, but it was pretty much
another world . . . a better world."*
—RON HOWARD

THROUGHOUT THE EIGHT YEARS OF ITS RUN, MILLIONS
of fans cherished *The Andy Griffith Show* as a matchless example of
folksy Americana. Although it made little impression overseas, this
chronicle of the mythic town of Mayberry, North Carolina, developed
a huge following in the United States. In its last season, ending April 1,
1968, the show topped the Nielsen ratings charts, making it the most
watched program on American prime-time television. Spin-offs
included *Gomer Pyle, U.S.M.C.,* which completed its own six-year run
in 1970, and the shorter-lived *Mayberry R.F.D.* Meanwhile, the original series lives on in syndication, attracting new generations of fans.

Today, more than forty years after a tall man and a small boy first
ambled down to the fishing hole in the famous opening sequence, the
series still warms many hearts. *The Andy Griffith Show* Rerun
Watchers Club maintains a vibrant presence on the Internet, and other

Web sites are also devoted to the Mayberry phenomenon. One fan site has even compiled selected episodes into a Bible study curriculum. Mayberry-themed merchandise continues to attract customers. *Aunt Bee's Mayberry Cookbook*, featuring down-home recipes connected with the show, appeared in 1991 and proved so popular that two sequels soon followed. (Jean Howard's contribution to the first volume was "Opie and Leon's Favorite Buttermilk Pie," in honor of the characters her sons played on the show.) And a 1961 recording of the show's soundtrack, complete with Earle Hagen's whistled main theme, was reissued on compact disc in May 2000.

The Andy Griffith Show has even found a place in everyday conversation. A bureaucrat who approaches his job with more zeal than competence may be compared to Andy's overeager deputy, Barney Fife. And young Opie Taylor, the role played by Ronny Howard, remains a national touchstone for youthful innocence. In the July 19, 2001, edition of Mell Lazarus' syndicated comic strip *Momma*, the title character is unable to sleep because she's fretting about her bachelor son's love life, so she turns on her television set to watch a late-night rerun. In the final panel, she still can't sleep, now "worried sick about Opie going fishing all by himself."

The name "Opie," which Griffith borrowed from a bandleader popular in his own youth, has stuck with Ron Howard to this day. On school playgrounds he found it a burden, especially when other kids learned to rhyme it with "soapy" and "dopey." Later, in his teen years during the turbulent Sixties, he sometimes was called "Opium." On October 9, 1982, Eddie Murphy compounded the problem during an episode of *Saturday Night Live* when he addressed Howard, the show's guest host, as "Opie Cunningham." By joining the names of Howard's two most famous television characters, Opie Taylor and *Happy Days'* Richie Cunningham, Murphy created a new name that countless smart alecks have since used in Howard's presence. Howard has always tried to take the razzing in stride. He once said that "my initial reaction every time I hear 'Opie' is a little tightening in the gut. I'm not Opie. But I'm smart enough not to slug anybody."

Still, the mature Howard can recognize the nickname as a source of affection as well as derision. He's even used it on movie sets as a unique incentive device. While directing *How the Grinch Stole Christmas* (2000), he rewarded animal trainer Roger Schumacher for solving a thorny production problem by telling him: "That's an excellent idea, Roger. That earned you one Opie." Schumacher was thereby entitled to one use of the taboo word in his boss's presence, though he never pressed his luck by exploiting his rare privilege.

But none of this was on Ronny Howard's mind on February 15, 1960, when the almost-six-year-old assumed the role of Opie Taylor on Danny Thomas's highly rated family comedy, *Make Room for Daddy*. The series was built around Thomas's on-screen alter ego, a sometimes brash New York nightclub entertainer named Danny Williams. Danny's life normally unfolded in Manhattan, where he tried to cope with his family as well as his own short fuse. But in this particular episode, he is caught ignoring a stop sign while driving through a small North Carolina town. The arresting officer (Andy Griffith) first seems an easy-going yokel, but he turns out to be more than Danny can handle, thanks to an unbeatable combination of quick wit and homespun wisdom.

In one scene witnessed by an increasingly nonplussed Danny, the sheriff's son, Opie, loudly laments the demise of his pet turtle. Poor Wilfred met his fate when Mrs. Bolliver stepped on him in Mayberry's ice cream parlor. Opie's demand for swift justice—"I want you to arrest her, Pa, and we'll give her a fair trial and hang her!"—brings forth Sheriff Taylor's gentle explanation about the need to accept grief. As he puts it, "We have to learn to live with our sorrows, boy. I learned when you was just a leetle-bitty speck of a baby, when I lost your ma. Just like you lost Wilfred here." To which the wide-eyed little boy replies, "You did? Who stepped on Ma?"

When this episode was spun off into a full-fledged series, the blending of comedy and truthfulness became its hallmark. Though *The Andy Griffith Show* was often extremely funny, Griffith and the producers took pains never to settle for cheap jokes. Rance Howard, who was on set almost daily to supervise Ronny and teach him his lines, had far more input than most stage parents because the creative team respected his acting background and his basic common sense. It was he who suggested that the show diverge from the usual sitcom formula, with a kid getting laughs at the expense of his parents. Child actors such as Rusty Hamer, who played Danny Thomas's young son on *Make Room for Daddy*, typically specialized in wisecracks and put-downs. Rance's bold idea was that humor could also be found in a father-son relationship based on mutual respect, with the father imparting life lessons and imposing discipline when needed. Years later, Griffith acknowledged that the bond between Sheriff Taylor and Opie in many ways mirrored Rance and Ronny's real-life connection.

Throughout the run of the series, Rance continued to serve as Ronny's coach and mentor, stressing preparation and professionalism. He taught the difference between true acting and mere performing, making it clear that "in order to say a line, you had to have the thought first." Rance helped spare his son the plight of many kid actors once they outgrow their cute juvenile tricks. Rance himself sometimes played small roles on the series, and wrote one episode, "The Ball Game," which aired during the show's seventh season. That story, about what happens when Andy calls Opie out at home plate during a championship game, was based on an incident that briefly rocked the Howard household.

On the set, Rance let Ronny know that his position was not a privileged one. Cast and crew were warned not to coddle him, tease him, or ply him with gifts. Ronny rarely stepped out of line: Don Knotts, who costarred for five years as Barney Fife, has hailed him in his autobiography as "the best-behaved child I ever worked with." Occasionally, however, he was tempted to act his age, and when he did, Rance felt compelled to step in. Ron still remembers the day he got spanked in front of everyone. He readily concedes that his father was right: "I was clearly getting away with something, trying to exploit the situation. The fact that we were not only in public but on the set—boy, everybody got quiet. My dad always did three quick swats right on the butt, and they never hurt as much as they just stung, but it was more the idea." Ron has taken to heart what Rance told him then, that no matter who was watching, "I have only one job and that's to be your father and that's to teach you right from wrong. And nothing about that job embarrasses me." Those who wrote and produced *The Andy Griffith Show* were quick to apply this dynamic between Rance and Ronny to the scripted relationship between Andy and Opie Taylor. The result was the deep emotional attachment between father and son that still heartens viewers today.

Some early reviews of *The Andy Griffith Show* were not clear about the program's long-term chances. But they applauded the talents of the cast, including Ronny Howard. *Variety* called him "a scene-stealer of the first magnitude." Fellow cast members were in awe of his abilities. George Lindsey, who appeared in the show's fourth season as Goober Pyle, said, "He's one of the best actors, not child actors, but one of the best actors I've ever worked with. . . . You loved to do scenes with him 'cause he always knew his part. And he was always as good as you were in a scene." Griffith recalls a poignant interlude from the first season, in which Ronny surprised everyone by bursting into real tears. When questioned, he explained that the tears flowed naturally after he remembered the death of his pet dog. Griffith was impressed: "That's Method acting!"

The Andy Griffith Show gave Ronny the latitude to come up with tears on his own, but some of his later experiences were quite different. On one movie set a director threatened to beat him if he didn't cry on cue. (He was not intimidated by this heavy-handed approach: "My dad was there, and I figured my dad would punch him out if he tried something.") In other ways too, the Mayberry experience was unique. From the first, Ronny was treated as a professional with a creative contribution to make. He was free to suggest script changes, though there was no guarantee that his input would be embraced. One day, when he was about seven, he politely objected that a kid his age wouldn't say a particular line as written. Director Bob Sweeney listened to his variation, then adopted it for the scene. Instead of simply moving on, Ronny stood beaming, savoring the moment. He proudly announced to his grown-up colleagues, "That's the first suggestion of mine that you ever took." Whereupon Griffith deadpanned, "Well, that was the first suggestion that was any damn good. Now let's go back and do the scene."

Everyone who worked on the *Andy Griffith* set considered it special, says Keith Thibodeaux (known professionally as Richard Keith), who played Little Ricky on *I Love Lucy* from 1956 to 1957. After *I Love Lucy* ended in the wake of its stars' divorce, Thibodeaux was hired to fill the occasional role of Opie's school pal, Johnny Paul Jason. The two series were both shot at Desilu Studios in Hollywood, but were polar opposites in terms of atmosphere on the set. *I Love Lucy* had featured volatile personalities, and there was added pressure because it was taped before a live audience. Thibodeaux remembers that *The Andy Griffith Show* "had the liberty to be a little bit more laid back. In the makeup department room they would be playing checkers and chess and strumming the guitar. Andy would be back there singing old songs from North Carolina. . . . And myself being a Southern boy, it was like going back home for me."

The easy spirit on the set did not mean that cast and crew were lackadaisical about the task at hand. In this, Griffith set the tone. He prized efficiency, though he had made clear from the get-go that Hollywood hysteria was not his style. Today Howard speaks of Griffith's balance between dedication and joy as a model for his own on-set behavior: "There was a lot of laughter on the set, and at the same time, hand in hand with that laughter, was very good work being done on a consistent basis. Anything less than 100 percent effort would just never fly—not because he would start yelling, but because simply that wasn't the way we worked on the show. . . . There was a feeling of, 'Hey, here's what we're doing, and therefore it's important. People are gonna watch it. It represents us and let's do it right.'"

Rance has pointed out, "You just couldn't have found a better climate, better atmosphere, and better surroundings for a boy Ron's age." He and Jean were hugely relieved to see the cast and crew develop into a close-knit family, with Andy in the role of favorite uncle. As most of Ronny's kinfolk still lived in Oklahoma, real uncles were in short supply. Years later, Howard noted, "I didn't have a lot of relatives when I was doing the show, so [the cast] became a family to me." In 1962 this television family expanded to include Ronny's little brother, Clint, who was still three when he filmed his first of four appearances as Leon, the silent tyke in the cowboy suit. Publicity photos of the day and the Howards' home movies show the brothers touring the set together, with Ronny cordially showing Clint the ropes.

From the start, the two boys had vastly different personalities. Howard Morris, who played the unforgettably loony Ernest T. Bass, also directed Ronny in several episodes, and years later performed under Ron's direction in *Splash*. Morris admires how Ron, even as an adult, has looked out for his brother's welfare: "That's to be respected." Morris remembers all too well Clint's inclination to walk on the wild side, commenting, "Yeah, he had a mouth!" Clint's natural audacity made him vastly different from Ronny, who was, in Morris's terms, "not shy, just a respectful person." Under Rance's tutelage Clint would prove to be a capable actor like his big brother. But although major roles would eventually come his way, he did not have the benefit of the full *The Andy Griffith Show* experience. He was, after all, only an occasional visitor to Mayberry, while for Ronny it was home away from home.

In March 2000 during a cable tribute to *The Andy Griffith Show*, Michael Farkash of the *Hollywood Reporter* summed up why the program was so attractive to its original audiences: It "was what many Americans wanted America to be in the troubled early days of racial activism and the Vietnam War. Mayberry was a place to hide from the real world, if only for a half-hour at a time."

If the show provided a temporary refuge for the American public, for Ronny Howard it was a cozy cocoon. He has said, "It really was kind of like living in a small town, and having the run of that town." But Mayberry's charm was not simply that it captured the slower rhythms of rural life. It was a protected environment, perfect in its sense of order and simplicity. George Lindsey pointed out that "Ronny was totally safe." So thoroughly had he captured the hearts of cast and crew that they would not have tolerated anyone treating him badly. For young Ronny, Mayberry meant friendship, family, baseball, fishing, Christmas, the Fourth of July, and tidy solutions to every problem: all the best things in life rolled into one. No wonder that Howard admits, "I used to cry every year when the show went on hiatus."

Still, as much as Ronny loved Mayberry, he was eager to explore the world outside the bubble. At the heart of Howard's career has always been a tension between caution and daring, between the impulse to cling to the familiar and a willingness to leap into the unknown. Fittingly, one of *The Andy Griffith Show*'s most beloved episodes touches on these themes.

"Opie the Birdman" opened the show's fourth season. It was September 30, 1963, and Ronny was nine years old. The episode begins with Barney giving Opie a slingshot. Though he is supposed to aim only at tin cans, Opie accidentally shoots and kills a bird nesting in a tree near his house. One of the episode's most touching moments comes as he tearfully begs the bird to return to life: "Fly away! *Please* fly away!" Instead of punishing his son, Andy gently makes him see that his misdeed has robbed three baby birds of their mother. At the show's midpoint, Opie is busily taking on the care and feeding of the three, which he has named Winken, Blinken, and Nod.

Soon the three little birds outgrow the cage where Opie has been keeping them safe from the cat. But although they are reaching maturity, he cannot bring himself to turn them loose. Again Andy steps in with some folksy wisdom. The birds' mother, he says, would have "let 'em go, let 'em be free, let 'em be on their own, like it's intended to be." Ultimately Opie comes to recognize that wild birds are meant to have their freedom. In an echo of his earlier line to the dead mother bird, he urges the three to take to the sky: "Please fly away! Please!" The episode ends with father and son sitting on their porch in a mood of quiet triumph. The birdcage may now seem awfully empty, but as Andy points out, "Don't the trees seem nice and full?"

This episode has much to say about fathers and sons, guilt and redemption. But it also sets up the key polarities of safety and freedom. Opie's inclination is to confine the small birds, keeping them safe from harm. Yet there's more to life than hiding inside a protective cage. Birds need to spread their wings. And so, sometimes, do growing boys.

Which is why, perhaps, Rance was so adamant about giving Ronny a life outside show business. On June 2, 1963, Rance told the *Kansas City Star* that "as his father, my biggest problem—and sincere dedication—is to see that he leads a normal life. No private school or other special privileges for Ronny; he fights his own battles as an average kid at a level with other average kids." Once Ronny enrolled in a Burbank neighborhood school, he was indeed forced to fight a few battles. Because of his television obligations, much of his schooling occurred on the set, which meant he attended Stevenson Elementary for no more than three months each year. Of course his celebrity status aroused some resentment among the other children, and Ron admits that "all through elementary school, there used to be at least two weeks worth of fights when the year started." Fortunately, he was agile, and his fondness for television wrestling shows taught him some useful moves. Eventually he'd blend into the student body, until the next time the series required his presence.

His passion for sports helped him gain acceptance among the neighborhood kids. Early on, Rance and Jean made clear to the producers that Ronny must be able to participate in Little League baseball. So shooting schedules were built around him: he did not miss a single game because of work, and his parents were loyal fixtures in the stands. Another of the Howards' contract stipulations was that Ronny never be required to make personal appearances for the show. This proviso shielded him from overwhelming fan adulation and allowed him more time to focus on baseball cards, dinosaurs, monster models, and a host of other boyish interests. For a while, he even had a paper route, just like the other youngsters on the block. All these activities helped him remain matter-of-fact about fame and fortune: "When I was little, kids would come up to me at school and ask what it was like being on TV. And I always remember my dad saying that it was just like having a paper route—you still have to get up early and learn your way around."

In a household where hard work was valued, young Ronny clearly enjoyed earning and saving money. When he was nine years old, he explained to interviewers that his allowance was twenty-five cents a week, and that he was paid twenty-five cents more for mowing the lawn. In addition, "I'm in business for myself. I collect bottles and turn them in for refunds—sometimes I get as much as eighty-seven cents." He confided to one reporter that he had just spent $37.50 to purchase his first U.S. savings bond. He also had a contingency fund: nine silver dollars, all dated before 1900. Said Ronny, "It's for an extra-desperate emergency. If somebody in the family really desperately needs money, then I have nine dollars I could give them."

Though Ronny took pride in the dimes and quarters accumulating inside his little tin bank, he was of course earning a great deal more. The size of his assets first dawned on him in 1966 when L. A. Dodgers stars Sandy Koufax and Don Drysdale were holding out for then-staggering sums that topped $100,000. He told one reporter, "I remember reading that—it was in headlines in the sports page every day—and sat down and figured out what my salary was going to be for the thirty-four shows we were going to do that year. And it came to $105,000." Ronny was making as much as the Dodgers' top pitchers, and he was only twelve.

He never saw his paychecks. His income was socked away until his eighteenth birthday, except for the 5 percent fee his parents allowed themselves for managing his career. The Howards were so worried about losing any of Ronny's money that, instead of investing it, they deposited it directly into his bulging bank account. To some extent their handling of this huge nest egg was governed by California law, which safeguards the incomes of child actors. But it was also a matter of the Howards' personal fiscal standards. Rance felt strongly that the family should live on his earnings, rather than his son's, because "when kids become the breadwinner, they're quick to realize their power over the family and have a tendency to exercise it." Fortunately he continued to land modest television and film roles, striking a careful balance between the time he spent on *The Andy Griffith Show* set and the hours he dedicated to pursuing his own career.

Because Rance and Jean were more interested in their son's well-being than his earning potential, they turned down possibly lucrative offers. One entrepreneur wanted to launch an Opie line of boys' clothing, but the deal would have required Ronny to travel to visit department stores. For the Howards, that was out of the question. Still he was not wholly shielded from commercial endeavors. Sitcom stars in that era were often obliged to shill for the sponsor's products. One early *Andy Griffith* episode, the hilarious "Manhunt," opens with Andy,

Opie, and Aunt Bee gleefully, if not quite tunefully, singing a jingle for Post cereals. At the end of this show, the capture of an escaped convict segues directly into a kitchen table scene in which Andy tells his son that he could not have rounded up this dangerous criminal without a bowl of Post Raisin Bran for breakfast. Similarly, commercials for JELL-O products are woven into some of the later episodes. Ronny also appeared as Opie in a number of print ads, as well as in comic books and coloring books inspired by the show. So from a young age, Howard learned to be comfortable with modern merchandising practices. Perhaps this helped shape his future direction as a mainstream film-maker who has never shied away from commercial appeal.

In 1963 nine-year-old Ronny told a writer from *TV Guide*, "That's what I like about my father. He doesn't push me into anything I don't like." Both Rance and Jean Howard often let their son know that he could hang up his acting career whenever he chose. But for the young boy it continued to be a glorious game. No wonder that, while on hiatus from *The Andy Griffith Show*, he played major roles in three movies before he turned ten.

The first was an unlikely choice for the cautious Howards. *Five Minutes to Live*, released in 1961, was a low-budget black-and-white crime drama. In 1966, it was reissued by the famously crass American International Pictures under the new title of *Door-to-Door Maniac*, with the addition of a rape scene. The film starred country singer Johnny Cash as Johnny Cabot, a small-time crook with a twisted psyche. Cabot schemes to extort a huge payoff from a bank executive by holding his wife for ransom. Ronny is featured as the banker's young son, Bobby, who inadvertently gets caught up in the mayhem.

The movie tries for social commentary through depicting a middle-class household in an affluent suburb. A visiting thug quips early on that "people here live the kind of lives that magazine ads talk about." The viewer, however, soon discovers something quite different. Ronny plays a member of an intact nuclear family, but his film parents bear no comparison to the wholesome Cunninghams of *Happy Days*. Bobby's mother is a self-obsessed social climber; his father has a mistress. And he himself is exactly the kind of precocious, wisecracking brat that Rance decried. At the breakfast table, for instance, Mom accuses Dad of being hung over again. Bobby is puzzled: "What's hung over?" Dad quickly replies, "Sick." Bobby then asks knowingly, "Had too much to drink, Pop?"

At the film's climax, Bobby is caught in a shootout between Cabot and the police. He fakes his own death, fooling Cabot long enough for the cops to catch him, and then explains nonchalantly that "it was easy. Just like on TV." While most Ronny Howard movies exalt such positive social values as honesty and compassion, *Five Minutes to Live* seems no more than a sordid thriller, with the parents' sentimental reconciliation tacked on at the end. No wonder the Howards never discuss the film.

A far more positive movie venture was *The Music Man* (1962), a big-budget MGM adaptation of the Broadway musical hit. Ronny was cast in the key role of Winthrop Paroo after a national search. To play the part, he learned to lisp convincingly, but could never quite master the requisite dance steps. (Fans who scrutinize his brief "Gary, Indiana" soft-shoe will notice that the camera shows him only from the knees up.) And his singing is more charming than melodious. In this he took after his father, who once yearned to be a singing cowboy like Gene Autry, only to realize he couldn't carry a tune.

The Music Man, set in the early 1900s in a small Iowa town, was wholesome Americana at its best. The folks back in Oklahoma, who had eagerly been keeping tabs on Ronny's career, could not have been more delighted. In the summer of 1962, when the film opened at Duncan's historic Palace Theatre, newspaper ads contained an eye-catching, though misspelled, addendum: "You will thrill to see the outstanding performance of DUNCAN'S OWN . . . RONNIE HOWARD." Though *The Music Man* is exuberant and sunny, Ronny's part is essentially serious. He plays a fatherless boy, painfully shy, who is transformed by Professor Harold Hill into a budding cornet player. For Ronny this was a prototypical role: a lonely child who finally dares to break out of his self-imposed isolation. Several of his youthful television appearances cover similar terrain. In the "Little Boy Lost" episode of *I Spy* (1966), life in a joyless household prompts Ronny's character to take a bold risk. The stakes are huge, but he ends by trading his solitude for the pleasures of community.

Something comparable occurs in MGM's 1963 romantic comedy, *The Courtship of Eddie's Father*. Producer Joe Pasternak, who helped cast the film's leading roles, confirmed that despite Ronny's ability to portray troubled youngsters, he was remarkably well adjusted: "He's the only child I ever worked with who's still a child. He's normal! I had interviewed hundreds of kids, but the minute he walked in I knew he was right." As Eddie, Ronny played a boy who deeply feels the pain of his mother's recent death, yet is determined to bring happiness to his father (Glenn Ford) by finding him a new mate. The premise and some of the film's dialogue can seem contrived, as when Eddie quaintly explains his theory on women: "Skinny eyes and big busts—is how you tell a bad lady from a good one." But Eddie must also show heartfelt emotion, and this Ronny convincingly accomplished.

Shirley Jones, who had played Ronny's big sister in *The Music Man*, was cast as his mother substitute in *Courtship*. She calls Ronny an "old soul," explaining that "he was probably the most perfect child actor I think I've ever worked with, and I've worked with a lot of them. Because he was really a little adult, and yet not the kind that we call little brats: he wasn't that at all. He was really a marvelous child, very bright, very funny." Jones watched Ronny's parents try to shield him from the adult world of the set by weaving their own cocoon around him. Instead of mingling casually with cast and crew, he spent downtime with Rance in his trailer; Jean would often come by and join them for lunch. Jones explains, "So many kids go out and play baseball or run around the set, or whatever, and you never saw him doing things like that." The point was not that the Howards objected to Ronny having fun, but that they had a strong sense of what was fitting and proper in a work setting. They expected their eight-year-old to approach his role with the dedication of a professional. But they also provided a safe haven from the grown-up environment all around him.

During the filming of *The Courtship of Eddie's Father*, famed director Vincente Minnelli chose to handle his young star by using Rance as an intermediary. Jones praises Rance for never going against Minnelli's wishes: "So many parents take the kid aside and say, 'Don't do that. Don't do it that way. Listen to how I tell you to do it.'" Rance, by contrast, never interjected his own ideas: "He was very, very cognizant of what the movie was, what the story was, and the director was boss." Adds Jones, "When I worked in *The Partridge Family* the first couple of years, some of those children's parents didn't quite do the same thing. They wanted the child to stand out no matter what." Rance's quiet subordination of his parental ego to the welfare of the project taught his son a valuable lesson. Ronny knew from an early age that being part of a collaborative effort was always an actor's top priority.

In *Courtship*'s early scenes, young Eddie is stoic about his mother's loss. But there's a telling moment when he bursts into hysterics over the death of a pet goldfish. Jones stresses that it was Rance who helped generate the necessary raw emotions, while also making it clear to Ronny that this was only make-believe. She remembers Rance "explaining what it was and that he was sad, and probably giving him a sad situation to think on. And [Ronny] was able to do it. But . . . he never carried it after the scene was over. He let it go, and he was a little boy again." So Ronny grew up with a clear understanding of the line between reality and the serious *let's-pretend* that moviemaking is all about.

By the time he made *Courtship*, Ronny was an old hand at talking to the press. The boy who had once charmed a reporter by explaining that, as a series costar, he did "the same as the star, but not as much" was happy now to tell interviewers how he had found jobs in the film for both Rance and Clint. At Ronny's suggestion, Rance played the small role of a camp counselor, Clint appeared as one of the kids in a birthday party scene, and Ronny confided, "I didn't take ten percent or anything like that." On a *Music Man* press junket, Ronny also made friends with Hollywood's powerful gossip columnist, Hedda Hopper, to whom he declared that Jean should return to acting as well: "She likes to act and joined a workshop; everybody flipped over her."

In her column of March 17, 1963, Hopper painted a vivid picture of Ronny Howard, who had just turned nine, jumping from star to star on the Hollywood Walk of Fame. He himself was a rising star, even if he didn't know it. In his immediate future lay more movies—including an eccentric 1965 sci-fi film, *Village of the Giants*—as well as five more years of playing Opie Taylor. In 1966 he would graduate from Stevenson Elementary School and move on to new challenges at Burbank's Jordan Junior High. By 1967 Clint was the star-in-the-making, acting opposite a bear on *Gentle Ben*. The series, which ran for two years, led to a temporary splitting of the Howard household. Rance, who also played a recurring role, accompanied Clint to the Florida location, while Ronny and his mother stayed home.

As the redheaded tot became a teenager, there were new adjustments to be made, both personally and professionally. In the spring of 1968, Ronny's sojourn in Mayberry finally ended. Though the series had more devoted fans than ever, Griffith and the producers had made the decision to go out on top. Ronny found it hard to say goodbye to so many old friends: "It was very embarrassing to be fourteen years old and crying at the wrap party." But the parting was not entirely sad. The time was ripe for the young bird to spread its wings.

CHAPTER 3

Leaving the Nest

(1968–1972)

*"I have great sympathy for actors, because I
learned at a young age what it's like to go
from being a well-known actor to one who's
utterly unemployable."*

—RON HOWARD

IN 1963 WHEN *THE COURTSHIP OF EDDIE'S FATHER*
opened in theatres, an MGM publicity bio revealed that nine-year-old
Ronny Howard "collects stamps, likes Westerns, and wants to study
archaeology at UCLA." Archaeology would prove to be one of his more
fleeting passions. Most of the time, Ronny made clear he was setting his
sights on a long-term show business career. At age eight, he had told one
reporter that he planned on being an actor, a writer, a director, and a producer, "because if you don't get acting jobs, you can do other things to
support your family. And I do want a family. At least six kids." Soon his
ambitions would become even more expansive: "actor, writer, producer,
director, camera man, baseball player." He was serious about baseball,
until pitchers started throwing curveballs he couldn't hit. Once America's
national pastime was ruled out as a career, his focus began to narrow.

Ronny's youthful decision to pin his hopes on directing bemused some of his older colleagues. Don Knotts, among others, felt he was a natural actor who was bound to have a bright adult career. But from an early age, Ronny was fascinated with the notion of running the whole show. He had the example of Rance, who organized an improv group in the family living room and then went on to stage his own comedy at a small professional theatre in Hollywood. On *The Andy Griffith Show* set, Ronny also became entranced with the nuts and bolts of production. He loved hobnobbing with the crew, looking through the camera, and operating the boom mike; it did not take him long to realize that "the director was the person who got to hang out and play with everyone." Because directors Bob Sweeney and Lee Phillips had both come from acting backgrounds, Ronny quickly concluded that he too might someday make the leap.

As a birthday surprise Griffith and producer Aaron Ruben chipped in to buy Ronny an 8mm movie camera, complete with small tripod, lights, and film. Suddenly, at the Howard home, it was show time. In 1963 at the age of nine, Ronny directed "The Chase," with Rance as a hobo who climbs on the roof and steals a pie. Clint, representing the forces of law and order, catches him in the act. Footage from this classic shows four-year-old Clint on his tricycle in hot pursuit of his father, who hunches over the pedals of a kid's pint-sized bike. Howard still remembers the fun of "[telling] my dad to do something and he'd actually do it."

Later Ronny would set the camera aside, except when he had an ulterior motive. Jean enjoyed recounting how one day her son got out of mowing the lawn, a chore he detested. He approached his father with a new idea for a movie: "You put on those fatigues of yours and you will be like a colonel in the army, and you're pushing that lawnmower and you're attacking that grass!" So Rance clamped on his old steel helmet and set to work. Jean concluded with a chuckle, "Amazingly, it took just as long to make the movie as it did to cut the grass."

In his early teens, Ronny would film his first Western. Now a constant moviegoer who spent many happy hours at Burbank's Magnolia Theatre, he found inspiration in the bloody excesses of Sam Peckinpah's

The Wild Bunch (1969). His answer to Peckinpah was "Cards, Cads, Guns, Gore, and Death," starring the always-willing Clint. It features a crooked poker game, followed by a grisly shootout. The young auteur came up with the notion of using bicycle pumps to push fake blood through hoses, so that it spurted dramatically for the camera. This would not be the last time he experimented with technical innovation in the service of storytelling.

As a young teenager, Ronny settled in at Burbank's David Starr Jordan Junior High School, where his classmates were the children of aerospace workers, police officers, and studio technicians. The fights that had marked his elementary school years were over, and he was no longer viewed as an interloper. Teacher Steve Campbell, who spent twenty-five years at Jordan, compares Ronny to another redheaded student two years his junior. Mitch Vogel had played Steve McQueen's son in *The Reivers* (1969) and one of Lucille Ball's children in *Yours, Mine and Ours* (1968). The week Mitch enrolled at Jordan, he was featured on the cover of *TV Guide*, in honor of his new starring role as Jamie on the popular series, *Bonanza*. (The series ran from 1959 to 1973, with Mitch's part introduced in 1970.) Campbell remembers Mitch as "a wonderful boy, straight-A student, as nice a kid as you could ever hope to meet, but the kids simply couldn't deal with it. They razzed him: he couldn't do anything right. If he dressed up, they teased him. If he dressed down, they teased him." In fact, his peers made life so miserable that by the end of the school year he applied for a transfer to shift to another part of the district and start anew.

Campbell describes Ronny Howard, like Mitch Vogel, as "very much a straight-and-narrow good guy, really nice, really polite, very strong student." But unlike Mitch, Ronny was also "just one of the guys. He had grown up with the kids, he played ball with the kids . . . so he did not face the same problems that Mitch did in any way, shape, or form." It probably helped that Rance and Jean were also well known to the children of the community. Rance often coached his sons' sports teams, and Jean served for two years as Jordan's Parent-Teacher

Association president. She and Rance spent countless hours organizing fundraising variety shows to benefit the school. On Clint's behalf they also stayed involved at Stevenson Elementary, where Jean volunteered as a room mother, made craft items to sell at carnivals, and helped Rance stage more than a dozen children's plays for the Stevenson PTA Playhouse. In 1971, Clint's last year at Stevenson, their efforts would earn them both a PTA honorary life membership award for "Outstanding Service to Youth."

Longtime Burbank resident Nancy Pierce points out that Jean's PTA ties did not stop after her boys graduated. For the remainder of her life, she kept up a close connection with Stevenson Elementary. And in 2001, when the auditorium was slated to be refurbished, Ron Howard quietly donated $5,000 toward a school he'd attended thirty-five years before.

While still at Jordan, Ronny discovered journalism, an interest that was to stay with him throughout his high school years. Some samples of his creative writing appeared in a Jordan student publication called "The Lair." As an eighth-grader he contributed a poem, revealing an awareness of the era's hippie culture. It tells of a little girl who runs away to San Francisco's legendary Haight-Ashbury District to find a more exciting life, but finally dies, apparently of boredom. His ninth-grade efforts, which show a great deal more literary flair, include a short story in the first person about a young athlete who sells his soul to the devil in exchange for success on the playing field. The ninth-grade pieces are signed "Ronn" Howard. He remained "Ronny" on the screen, for guest appearances on such shows as *Gunsmoke* (November 3, 1969), but wanted a more grown-up moniker to use in everyday life.

The end of the era of *The Andy Griffith Show* coincided with the Howard family's move to Toluca Lake. This is an upscale area—partially in Burbank, partially in the city of Los Angeles—that contains the exclusive Lakeside Country Club. Such vintage celebrities as Bob Hope make their homes in a secluded domain near the lake itself. But the Howards' new house was on a leafy residential avenue only a few blocks from Riverside Drive, a major commercial artery. This heavily traveled thoroughfare boasts a classic Bob's Big Boy restaurant (built in 1949 and now designated a historic landmark) and a tempting array of shops and services.

The house the Howards purchased in 1968 for less than $40,000 would cost well over ten times that much today. Built in 1936, it is traditional in style, with 3,400 square feet of floor space and a roomy yard complete with basketball hoop. The white shutters, dormer windows, and used brick trim all suggest order, graciousness, and middle-American values. The neighborhood features tall magnolia trees and flowering jacaranda; today the glass towers of Warner Bros. are visible in the distance. Also nearby is NBC Studios, where in 1968 the trendsetting *Rowan and Martin's Laugh-In* debuted. This weekly comedy series made a standing joke of being broadcast direct from "Beautiful Downtown Burbank," and the American public quickly adopted the phrase.

From the family's new digs it was two miles to John Burroughs, one of two public high schools in the Burbank district. Burroughs' main building is a two-story tan stucco edifice, built in 1929. A small plaque on the exterior proclaims that "the torch of knowledge lights our way." A more recent addition to the façade is lettering designating Burroughs as a California Distinguished School. Inside the hallways are the usual lockers and trophy cases, and a "Lest We Forget" display with flags and electrically lighted torch, honoring Burroughs grads who died in conflicts from World War II through Vietnam.

Burroughs made history in 1963 when President John F. Kennedy briefly visited its senior prom. In that era, and into the 1970s, the school population was chiefly middle-class and white, except for a few Latino students. The 1980s brought a huge influx of immigrant families, especially Armenians and Koreans, into the Burbank area. The school since then has become a true melting pot, with practically every nationality represented. Longtime journalism teacher Tim Brehm, who joined the faculty in Howard's era, remembers that "in the early Seventies, Burbank was looked upon as Mayberry." Proud of its high property values and civic involvement, Burbank was "its own little enclave," boasting public services that did not depend on the city of Los

Angeles. The community was highly stable, politically conservative, and supportive of its young people; it was a good time to be a student.

Entering high school at age fifteen in 1969, Ron (or Ronn) concentrated on good grades, journalism, and basketball. He was never part of the "in" crowd, and partying was not his style. Though teachers didn't considered him short on friends, Ron himself remembers high school as a time when he felt isolated: "The kids couldn't make up their minds whether it was cooler to hang out with me or to ignore me." The situation contributed, he says, to a shyness that has never left him.

Howard says he has always been "more comfortable on the set than I am anywhere else outside of my own living room." So it didn't help that at this time he was facing the first slump of his acting career. By now, *The Andy Griffith Show* was only a memory, and—although he was learning to hustle and to prep for auditions in a way he never had before—good roles were proving few and far between. His television appearances had become sporadic. The only film in which he appeared between 1968 and 1971 was Disney's made-for-television movie, *Smoke* (1970), in which he once again played a youngster mourning a lost parent. In this movie, fifteen-year-old Chris is living with the memory of having watched his father die in a fiery car accident. *Smoke* conventionally but effectively builds to a crescendo when Chris, overcome by long-delayed grief and guilt, runs away from the family farm. With the help of a tough but understanding stepfather and a stray dog, he finally reconciles himself to a home in which his dad is no longer a living presence.

After *Smoke* aired in early 1970, Ron found himself out of work. This was not an unusual state of affairs for a teen actor, because producers vastly prefer young-looking eighteen-year-olds for whom labor laws don't mandate shortened hours and on-set supervision. Famous child actors generally find fewer roles available once they reach puberty, simply because they're no longer tiny and adorable. Some youngsters who have known stardom find it difficult to cope with their new status as unemployed actors, and Hollywood lore contains many cautionary tales about those who have turned to drugs or antisocial behavior.

One of the saddest stories concerns Rusty Hamer, who from the age of six was well known for playing Danny Thomas's wisecracking son on *Make Room for Daddy* (1953–1957) and its follow-up, *The Danny Thomas Show* (1957–1964). Throughout much of this period, Rusty was the sole support of his widowed mother and two brothers. When the series finally ended, he was seventeen, and Thomas compared him to "a fish out of water." Two years later, Rusty nearly died after shooting himself in the stomach, in what police termed "a freak accident." He recovered, and was briefly featured in yet another Thomas project, *Make Room for Granddaddy* (1970–1971). Over the next twenty years, he tried various other lines of work, but succeeded at none of them. In January 1990, at the age of forty-two, he killed himself with a blast from a .357 magnum shotgun.

Ron's supportive family and wide range of outside interests better equipped him to face rejection than most former child stars. Still, the dry spell came just when the full force of puberty was making him thoroughly miserable. In his recollection of the teen years, "You've got acne, you look in the mirror and you're not happy with what you see, you're feeling angry at your parents and frustrated at the world." When these feelings are combined with the rebuffs endured by an actor, it's no wonder that Ron says, "There was a time I used to seriously contemplate jamming my head through a plate-glass window."

Fortunately, Ron found healthier outlets for his frustrations. Basketball took up more and more of his days: he got up at 4 A.M. to practice free throws; spent hours at the Verdugo Park Gym; and helped coach brother Clint's Parks and Recreation league team, known as "Howard's Hurricanes." It became Ron's goal to grow six feet tall and play college basketball. So caught up was he in this new enthusiasm that at one point he turned down a Disney movie to keep his crewcut and his rhythm. But, although the Burroughs yearbook for 1971 lists "Ronn Howard" as a standout on the school's secondary team, he finally reached the conclusion that he was not destined to be a six-footer, and that show business, not basketball, was where his future lay.

The time spent away from the entertainment world helped him sort out his priorities. Though the acting situation might look bleak at the time, he was determined to somehow stay connected to an industry he adored. In this he was buoyed by the words of screen veteran Van Heflin, speaking to his parents' acting class: "If you really love the business, you can find a way to survive in it. You may not be an actor, but you can do something." Heflin's tip motivated Ron to revive his interest in directing. Directors, for one thing, "have a little more control over their destinies." And so he pulled out the Super 8 camera, and began to experiment once again.

While he was turning his mind to directing, Ron suddenly landed an acting role. At age sixteen he was tapped to play the teenage son in *The Smith Family,* a short-lived television series about the home life of a Los Angeles police detective. The series, which debuted in January 1971, was a clumsy attempt to squeeze the social traumas of the day (such as drug use and campus rebellion) into an old-fashioned sitcom format à la *Father Knows Best.* Ron refers to this as a "terrible show" but a "great life experience" because of the actor who played his father. Henry Fonda, one of the top movie stars of his generation, was a quiet, thoroughly professional man who largely kept to himself on the set. But he had known Rance since *Mister Roberts,* and he soon became an important mentor to Rance's eager young son. Before long, Ron was showing him scripts he had written, and short films he had made. At one point, Fonda looked him in the eye and said, "If I had it to do over again, I would have been a director." Ron says, "That moment was huge."

Before *The Smith Family* ended in 1972, Fonda gave Ron a copy of *The Cinematographer's Manual* to encourage him to keep working toward his directing dream. Fonda also left some parting advice: "Every eighteen months you've got to risk your career and frighten yourself, or else you're not growing." In his adult life, Howard has heeded this mentor's words. Despite his mild manner, he has become known in Hollywood for physical as well as aesthetic risk taking, as the director of such complex film projects as *Backdraft, Apollo 13,* and *A Beautiful Mind.*

At the time, Ron had to find his challenges in acting. In 1971 he got the rare opportunity to act side by side with Clint, then age eleven, in *The Wild Country,* a Disney theatrical movie about a pioneer family from Pittsburgh and its struggles to carve out a home in the wilds of

Montana. Ron played elder son Virgil, a city boy who learns to plow, ride, and shoot, but must also discover his own manhood as he rises to his family's defense. The film's earnest focus on communal values was consistent with Ron's youthful signature roles in both theme and tone. But soon afterward he shot a pilot that would pave the way for a whole new phase of his career.

Producer Garry Marshall remembers, "Early in the seventies, we made this lovely pilot about the 1950s with nostalgia, and nobody bought it, and they said, 'Who cares?'" Eventually it aired on February 25, 1972 on a long-running ABC anthology series called *Love American Style*, which Marshall describes as "the graveyard of unsold pilots." This particular episode was dubbed "Love and the Happy Days." It featured the Cunningham family of Milwaukee, with Ronny Howard starring as a hapless high schooler named Richie. Marion Ross played his mother and Harold Gould his father, owner of the local hardware store. Anson Williams was Potsie, his girl-crazy best friend.

"Love and the Happy Days" begins with Richie explaining in voice-over that "it's pretty hard to be sixteen and growing up. Maybe it was easier when my parents were young, but now it's the 1950s and the world is really getting complicated." Richie's problems in the episode stem from his family's purchase of the first television set on the block. Suddenly he becomes the object of the affections of Arlene Nestrock, a classmate who has previously been out of his league. To Potsie, Richie confides that Arlene "is stacked . . . but not very bright." Potsie doesn't consider this a problem: "You gonna kiss her mind? Who talks when they neck?"

Of course, in true Richie Cunningham fashion, he never gets to first base with the well-endowed Arlene. First telling him "I never French kiss on the first date," she later admits to having a steady boyfriend; she's only interested in Richie because of that magic box in his living room. This was to be the first Ronny Howard role in which sexual stirrings play a part. Richie's persistent failure with the opposite sex would become a familiar comic element when "Love and the Happy Days" evolved into a hugely popular weekly series. But *Happy Days* would not make its series debut until January 15, 1974. When "Love and the

Happy Days" aired in early 1972, the viewing public didn't pay it the slightest attention.

Like Richie Cunningham, Ron at sixteen was well aware of the opposite sex. As he would tell an interviewer from *Playboy*, he had known about male and female anatomy since the age of five, when his mother was pregnant with Clint. Ronny asked the tough questions; Rance let out a deep sigh, then sat down and drew realistic diagrams to explain how babies are made.

A later *Playboy* interview elicited his memories of a tantalizing Burroughs classmate, Rene Russo, who was not yet an actress. In those days, as Ron remembered it, "she had a great biker-chick look, with white lipstick and ironed hair. She was not part of the mainstream, not cheerleader material." Russo apparently got a kick out of sitting right behind "Opie" in tenth-grade social studies class, especially since he let her cheat off his tests. According to Ron, "I had this little practice of imagining sex with one girl in each class period. Rene Russo was my fourth-period fantasy."

Teacher Steve Campbell, who became a lasting friend of both Ron and Rene, tends to doubt the details of this story. For one thing, he says, Ron was on an honors track, and Rene could barely be bothered to come to school at all, so it's unlikely they would have been in class together. But in 1992 they did spend time at their twentieth reunion comparing notes about how cruel high school students can be. While he had been razzed as "Opie," she was teased for other reasons. After being diagnosed with scoliosis at age ten, she had spent four years in a body cast; then once she had shot up to five feet, eight inches, campus wags labeled her the Jolly Green Giant. Russo quit Burroughs after the tenth grade and embarked on a successful modeling career. Campbell adds that Howard briefly considered her for the role of the sexy female alien played by Tahnee Welch in *Cocoon* (1985). Years later, in 1996, Russo starred for her former classmate as the female lead in *Ransom*.

By the start of Ron's junior year he had something better than fantasy in his life. Love, in fact, had found Ron Howard. By this time he owned his own car, a Volkswagen Beetle, but was too shy to start dating. Then a petite redhead named Cheryl Alley took the seat in front of him in English class. She too was socially awkward, to the point that she later would describe herself as "almost crippled by shyness." Because she hadn't been allowed to watch television as a child, she'd never seen *The Andy Griffith Show*. And her father, who rented apartments to actors, had given her a low opinion of the whole profession. So Ron's show business connections weren't likely to dazzle her. During their first real conversation, Cheryl recalls that "we talked about my dog for nearly an hour before he asked me out." But the date proved to be a wonderful success, and they were a twosome from that time forward. Twenty years later, Ron and Cheryl returned to the classroom where they'd first met and asked an amused Burroughs faculty member to take their picture.

From the first, Ron and Cheryl seemed to be made for one another. Their personalities meshed completely, and many friends have noted that they looked enough alike to be brother and sister. But as the romance blossomed, Rance and Jean felt the need for parental caution. They made it emphatically clear that Ron could not take Cheryl out more than twice a week. To circumvent this decree, he claimed to be joining the Burroughs cross-country team. He'd sprint off each morning, ending up at Cheryl's: "We would just go out for breakfast, or fool around a little if her father was gone." Afterwards, she'd drop him a few blocks from his house; then he'd crank into high gear and jog home panting. Presumably his folks were fooled by the subterfuge, but it has never occurred to him to ask.

Though Cheryl quickly became Ron's number-one interest, she didn't cause him to forget his career goals. In fact, she took part in a short film he made at age sixteen to enter Kodak's nationwide Teenage Filmmakers Contest. (This was to be her first of many cameos in a Howard production; since then she has appeared in every one of his films.) The short was entitled "A Deed of Daring-Do," although some later official references changed the spelling to the more correct "Derring-Do," and Ron shot it for the contest's one-reeler category. The rules called for him to start with a single cassette of film, which ran three minutes and twenty-four seconds. He was required to shoot his reel and then—without developing or editing—send it in to be judged.

Many teens who entered this category chose animation. But Ron decided to make a live-action film, a *Twilight Zone*–style effort about a boy who wanders onto a studio back lot and imagines himself a sheriff in the Old West. Naturally, Clint played the boy. Cheryl was the pretty saloon girl, and Rance was featured as a desperado who briefly menaces the hero before disappearing into thin air. Ron carefully laid out the camera moves, timed the action down to the second, rehearsed his cast, and shot his film on the first try. When the winners were announced, he discovered he'd placed second. Ron Howard had won his first filmmaking prize, with many more to come.

The prize brought a small cash award, which caused some consternation in the Howard household. It seems that the enterprising Clint, as a professional actor, had refused to work for nothing. Ron casually agreed to his brother's demand for 50 percent of the gross, and didn't think further about it. In 1999 Clint gleefully told a television interviewer what happened next: "The dough comes in, and I say, 'Hey, great, the money's here! I'll take mine!' And Ron didn't want to give it to me. And I think Dad had to step in and say, 'A deal's a deal.' And Ron had to peel me off fifty bucks!" Clint's comments provide a helpful glimpse into the relationship between two brothers who have had very different adult lives but still remain close. The playful one-upmanship that lurks beneath the surface of Clint's remarks continues to resonate to this day, as fans of his web-based "Clint Howard Variety Show" can attest.

Ron Howard and Cheryl Alley graduated from John Burroughs on the evening of June 15, 1972. The 541 graduates filed onto Burroughs' Memorial Field to the strains of "Pomp and Circumstance." They saluted the flag, sang "The Star Spangled Banner," and sat through the usual speeches. Music from Carole King's *Tapestry* album added a contemporary touch. The ceremony ended with the singing of the school's alma mater.

Both Ron and Cheryl are visible in the senior yearbook, which in keeping with the school's Native American motif is called *Akela*. Cheryl appears with a group of other girls as a pep squad "Injunette," decked out in a fringed minidress, tennis shoes, white gloves, and a headband with a single feather. (A few years later, the Injunettes would become the slightly more dignified "Indianettes," and then disappear completely. But despite some vehement protests at school board meetings, the Burroughs Indian mascot has survived to this day.) Ron—whose name in the yearbook is occasionally spelled Ronny and sometimes Ronnie, but no longer Ronn—shows up as the opinion editor of the school paper, "Smoke Signal." Ron is also prominently featured as one of twenty-six Sealbearers, students whose superior grades have earned recognition from the statewide California Scholarship Federation. The large black-and-white Sealbearer photo shows him in coat and tie, with lots of hair and a toothy grin. Ron had done well, but one honor eluded him. In 1991, he told journalist James Greenberg, "I was always pissed that I didn't get Most Likely to Succeed. I figured I had a pretty good leg up."

Howard last lived in the city of Burbank in 1973, but he continues to be regarded as a favorite son. Ten years after he moved out, the cover of the Burbank/Toluca Lake telephone directory was emblazoned with his picture. Doris Krutcher, veteran librarian at the Buena Vista branch of Burbank Public Library, located six blocks from Burroughs High, is only too happy to share her own recollections of Howard in his high school days: "He used to come here and study after school sometimes. A nice young man. He used to come in with his girlfriend who is now his wife, I understand." Like many in Burbank, Krutcher has followed Howard's adult career with great interest. When he's interviewed on television, she makes sure to watch. She wants to see him succeed, she says, because "Ron Howard had such a great personality. Even as a kid, he smiled a lot. He was just a nice, outgoing young man." After a pause, she asks, "Whatever happened to his brother?"

PART II

Fledgling Efforts

CHAPTER 4

Turning Back the Clock

(1972–1975)

*"Stars have to worry about what to do.
Non-stars can do anything."*
—RON HOWARD

IN THE SUMMER OF 1972, RON HOWARD WAS LOOKING
forward to the challenges and privileges of college life. He had been
accepted into the Cinema Division of the University of Southern
California, better known as USC. The Cinema Division, later to be
renamed the USC School of Cinema-Television, was founded in 1929
by the Academy of Motion Picture Arts and Sciences. As the world's
first academic training program for aspiring filmmakers, it has always
enjoyed close ties with the Hollywood film community, often serving as
the gateway into a mainstream directing career. Like all applicants,
Howard submitted a portfolio documenting his creative work in various fields. His acceptance letter represented his passport into the world
of serious moviemaking.

But before he became a college student, Howard spent his summer
playing a new high school graduate not wholly different from himself.
The film was *American Graffiti*, and it would prove to be a milestone
both for American cinema and for Howard as a filmmaker-to-be.

Writer-director George Lucas, not yet thirty, used the events of one summer night in a Northern California town to capture the essence of teen life in 1962, before Vietnam became the nation's predominant nightmare. Shot in Petaluma, California (standing in for Lucas's own Modesto), over twenty-eight nights, *American Graffiti* cost a mere $775,000. After its release in August 1973, it racked up $115 million in domestic ticket sales, then earned nominations for five Academy Awards, including best picture.

Auditioning for a part in *American Graffiti*, Howard was asked to improvise scenes with other actors. This was his first hint that George Lucas didn't do things the Hollywood way. Fortunately, Lucas wasn't thrown by Howard's lingering "Opie" image. Television producer Garry Marshall boosted his chances by supplying the "Love and the Happy Days" pilot to Fred Roos, Lucas's casting director. So the videotape of Ronny Howard playing Richie Cunningham helped prove he could be convincing as Steve Bolander, nice guy and big man on campus.

American Graffiti's young cast members soon discovered that Lucas expected them to continue ad libbing on the set. He shot take after take in what he called "documentary style," hoping his actors would catch him by surprise, and then cobbled his film together in the editing room. The key emotional scene when Howard and Cindy Williams, as Steve and his girlfriend, Laurie, patch up their quarrel at the end of the film was extemporized and shot in five minutes, to capture the light of dawn. (Other directors might have spent all day on a soundstage filming this pivotal moment.) Telling a story that takes place in one night, Lucas shot more or less in sequence, a choice that Howard belatedly learned to appreciate: "As the production wore on, we became more and more exhausted. By the end we all had circles under our eyes, and we looked like we'd been up all night. Well, we *had* been up all night for weeks! And it showed."

Howard was fascinated by what he came to call Lucas's "counter-culture approach to filmmaking." He found it exhilarating to see women and long-haired men on a film crew, and to be allowed so much latitude in shaping his own performance. He also noticed that Lucas paid as much attention to the costumes on the extras, the cars on the

road, and the music on the soundtrack as he did to the central characters. Howard recently explained, "This was an absolute first for me . . .
this sort of total involvement with the complete image, the total can-
vas." Lucas, who had graduated from USC film school in 1966, found
Howard a kindred spirit. He was glad to share his filmmaking tech-
niques with Howard, who roamed the set with his videocamera, documenting the work in progress. To his lasting regret, his mother later
dumped this potentially historic footage.

The main cast of *American Graffiti* was required to be on hand for
the entire shoot, leaving the young actors free in the daylight hours to
sleep, rehearse, or make mischief. Actors Harrison Ford, Paul LeMat,
and Bo Hopkins quickly became the production's chief hell-raisers,
while Howard, Richard Dreyfuss, Charles Martin Smith, and Cindy
Williams took a more conscientious approach. To Howard the experience was liberating: "Being on location. Working all night. It was the
first time I didn't have parental supervision." On weekends he tried to
visit San Francisco nightclubs, but looked so young that he always got
thrown out.

A better bet was moviegoing, which had long since become one of
Howard's passions. Three decades later, for an interview with the *New
York Times*, he would name *The Graduate* (1967) as the motion picture
that had meant the most to him in his formative years. As he put it,
"This is the movie that I went to school on." By the summer of 1972,
he had already watched it over and over, enjoying its themes of youthful rebellion and becoming increasingly aware of the director's hand at
work. Howard told the *Times* reporter how, on the set of *American
Graffiti,* he and cast mate Charles Martin Smith spent hours discussing
The Graduate. Then, fortuitously, it was booked into a local drive-in,
so they saw it a few times more. Simultaneously, they were themselves
shooting a film that future moviegoers would study, analyze, and claim
as their own.

American Graffiti had personal resonance for Howard, as well as
audiences, because it touched on motifs that were very much a part of
real life. Two central characters in the film, Steve and Curt, wrestle with
the challenge of growing up and leaving a familiar world. On the eve of

their departure for an East Coast college, Steve is only too glad to be "getting out of this turkey town," while his friend Curt agonizes over whether it makes sense "to leave home to look for a home." A teacher chaperoning the high school dance represents an object lesson: he had once earned a scholarship to Middlebury College in Vermont, but retreated back to his hometown after only a semester. By the end of the film, a mysterious DJ named The Wolfman has persuaded Curt that "there's a great big beautiful world out there." But Steve, faced with losing Laurie, ultimately opts to stay behind. The famous epilogue of the film reveals the future of these two young men: "Steve Bolander is an insurance agent in Modesto, California. Curt Henderson is a writer living in Canada." Howard has said, "The fact that I knew that Steve was going to wind up being an insurance salesman and stay there definitely informed my performance. This was not an entirely adventuresome person."

Lucas admits that he could not identify with straight-arrow Steve. Largely for this reason, he asked the young screenwriting team of Willard Huyck and Gloria Katz for help in completing his shooting script. For Lucas, leaving home is an essential part of growing up. He'd experienced this personally, and made it a central theme both in his first commercial feature, *THX 138* (1970) and in the upcoming *Star Wars* (1977). And Howard—billed here as "Ronny Howard" for the last time—was on the brink of his own coming of age. Like Steve Bolander, he had a steady girlfriend, and a warm and safe home environment. But unlike Steve, he had a dream he was determined to fulfill.

To enter film school, Howard did not need to go far. USC is three miles south of downtown Los Angeles, which makes it perhaps a half-hour drive from Burbank. (In traffic, it might take a full hour to get from USC to California State University at Northridge, where Cheryl was studying psychology.) Thanks to Howard's past earnings, he could easily afford USC's undergraduate tuition of $2,460 per semester. The price tag for a 1972 USC education may seem remarkably low by current standards, but this was a hefty sum when compared to the few hundred dollars in annual fees that students were being charged within California's public university system.

Still, despite the prestige of the USC cinema program, the corner of the 155-acre campus then allotted to film study was cramped and inadequate. Young filmmakers-to-be learned their craft in ramshackle bungalows, a far cry from the glossy facilities that have since been donated by George Lucas and other grateful alumni. As one of USC's few freshman cinema students, Howard was expected to take mostly general education classes. But he managed to talk his way into advanced courses in editing and production. Later he acknowledged, "Going to film school opened my mind to another level of thinking about movies. Nobody around the Griffith show spent a lot of time talking about metaphors and symbols."

Living first in a campus dorm and then in his own apartment not far from Burbank, Howard was in many ways a typical undergraduate. He played a lot of pinball, worried about the Vietnam War, and tried wearing love beads. Because he hated to do laundry, he developed a technique of spreading out his dirty clothes and then spraying them with Lysol. But in an era when drug use was rampant on college campuses, Ron decided not to get involved. (A few years later, as he confided to Peter Gethers of *Esquire*, he tried to acquire a taste for pot, thinking perhaps he had missed out on something important: "But I didn't like it much. It wasn't fun. I coughed a lot.") The joke is that while Howard was sticking to the straight and narrow, rumors circulated that he was the biggest dope dealer on the USC campus. He denied this, of course, but not very strenuously: "I got too big a kick out of it."

Howard never graduated from USC. By the time he was in his second year, his show business commitments had grown too pressing to allow him to continue. But he still regards himself as a loyal alumnus. On March 1, 2001, USC proudly opened the doors of its Robert Zemeckis Center for Digital Arts, named for the director of such hit movies as *Back to the Future* (1985) and *Forrest Gump* (1994). Zemeckis had given the school $5 million; other big donors to this new facility included George Lucas and Steven Spielberg (who supports USC even though it once turned down his application). Howard funded the state-of-the-art fifty-seat screening room that now bears his name, but shied away from media attention when the gift was announced. He did return on May 10, 2002, to deliver the commencement address at the School of Cinema-Television's graduation ceremony.

Not everyone respects the USC film school and its alumni. Critic and film historian Stephen Farber, writing about "The USC Connection" for the May–June 1984 issue of *Film Comment,* sniped that "most of the movies made by the USC graduates have been lacking in audacity and originality. Almost without exception they tend to be derivative genre movies and lightweight escapist capers." Farber's accusation has at least a kernel of truth: USC graduates do usually gravitate toward commercial fare, rather than the boldly avant-garde. Still, there's no question that USC film students gain a pragmatic knowledge of the industry they hope to enter. And USC became the place where Howard reached a mature understanding of a world he'd known and loved since childhood.

Once *American Graffiti* was in the can, Howard won major roles in two feature films, both coming-of-age stories with a longing for home set against the call of the open road. For the melodramatic *Happy Mother's Day, Love George* (released in 1973, and later retitled *Run Stranger, Run*) he wore a black wig to portray a young drifter in search of the parents he has never known. *The Spikes Gang*, which opened in theatres in early 1974, concerned three rural teenagers who fall under the spell of a charismatic outlaw, played by Lee Marvin. To film this well-crafted Western, Ron lucked into a trip to Spain, his first overseas travel experience since the Howard family had flown to Europe for *The Journey* back in 1958.

Neither of these ventures earned critical kudos. But in early 1974, six months after the triumphant release of *American Graffiti*, a television movie gave Howard one of the strongest roles of his career. *The Migrants*, written by playwright Lanford Wilson from a story by Tennessee Williams, is an unsparing look at a contemporary family of itinerant farm workers, rattling across America in a broken-down jalopy to pick "beans this mornin', corn this afternoon, tomatoes tomorrow." For portraying Viola Barlow, strong-willed mother of the clan, Cloris Leachman earned an Emmy nomination. Sissy Spacek played her pregnant teenaged daughter, and Howard was cast as Lyle, the eldest child and effectively the man of the household. It is a household without a house, and the Barlows' escalating debt to the crew boss ensures that they will keep rolling down dusty roads for many years to come.

Lyle is torn between the obligation to do right by his family and the dream of going out on his own in search of a more stable and productive life. When the Barlows make camp on the outskirts of a small Southern town, he decides to supplement their meager earnings by taking a night job in a packing plant. There he meets Betty (Cindy Williams), a local girl impatient to see the world. While Viola keeps Betty's angry father at bay, the two young people head for the big city, where they hope to build a brighter future. Without Lyle, the Barlows' existence will be more precarious than ever. But Viola is determined that her most promising child escape the trap into which the family has fallen.

Before leaving, Lyle vows to his mother, "I'm gonna save money and I'm gonna buy you a house so big you won't never have to pick another bean." Of course, both of them know that these words are hollow. The Barlows have no fixed address, so the two may never connect again. Just before the final fadeout, as the Barlow jalopy limps toward the next field that needs picking, the two youngest children fantasize about the house Lyle will own some day, with its porch and its many rooms. Meanwhile, Lyle and Betty are approaching Cincinnati, quietly aware that with their limited money, skills, and education, putting down roots may not be easy. In *The Migrants*, being on the road is by no means an adventure. Home is what these characters most want, but few of them will ever know the privilege of staying put.

While filming *The Migrants*, Howard was deeply impressed by the performances that director Tom Gries elicited from his actors. Not until his own directing career was underway did he recall that in the early rehearsal period Gries had offered his cast little guidance. Instead Gries preferred to watch what the actors themselves brought to their roles, then shaped his scenes accordingly. Though Howard's own first instinct as a director was to treat his actors like puppets, imposing his interpretations on them from the start, the example of Gries helped persuade him to back off. By giving space to inventive performers such as Michael Keaton (*Night Shift*), John Candy (*Splash*), and—much later—Russell Crowe (*A Beautiful Mind*), Howard would come to earn plaudits for allowing creative work to flourish.

When *The Migrants* first aired on CBS on February 3, 1974, Howard was starting to be noticed in a vastly different role on ABC. As Richie Cunningham on the revived *Happy Days* series, he had a stable home, an intact family, and only one basic problem: he was too nice a guy to wow the girls.

Happy Days was a direct beneficiary of *American Graffiti*'s success at the box office. After the film came out, audiences rattled by Vietnam and Watergate discovered they were hungry for anything connected with the innocent charms of an earlier era. And so, as a midyear replacement, ABC decided to resurrect Garry Marshall's old "Love and the Happy Days" pilot about the Cunninghams of Milwaukee, set in the days of ducktail haircuts and poodle skirts. The first episode of *Happy Days* appeared in the 8 P.M. timeslot on Tuesday, January 5, 1974. Those few viewers who had caught the original on *Love American Style* saw a new Howard Cunningham, with lovable Tom Bosley replacing Harold Gould. But Marion Ross and Howard repeated their earlier roles as mother and son. The premiere episode, titled "All the Way," covered familiar turf: high-school junior Richie makes a date with a girl who is known to be "fast." When the time comes, however, he is too nervous to do anything but teach her to play chess.

As the series grew in popularity, Howard was often asked about his real-life resemblance to Richie Cunningham. He patiently explained to the press that he himself was more motivated than Richie, more competitive, more sophisticated about human nature. Also, "I'm a lot smarter than Richie—I'd never get sucked into those dumb schemes he gets into." But he gallantly allowed that Richie was the more courageous of the two, and that he personally found it harder than Richie to stand up to people with whom he disagreed. As for their similarities, he admitted that Richie's "nervous anxiety" around the opposite sex mirrored the awkwardness of his own high school years. In terms of general outlook, he said, "I agree with Richie Cunningham about most things."

Journalists were quick to notice another area of resemblance. Both Richie and Howard are legendary for what writer Scott Eyman calls "an innate decency that could be irritating if it wasn't totally sincere." Throughout his adult career, Howard has been plagued by the apparently dismissive word "nice." In an environment where the goal is to be hip, and where "nice" is frequently a synonym for "square," friends and colleagues rush to label Howard "the nicest guy in Hollywood." Actor William Baldwin, who starred for Howard in *Backdraft*, takes it one step further: "Well, everybody knows this. Ronny's the nicest guy in the world!" This attitude is so ubiquitous that Peter Gethers, writing in 1986 for *Esquire*, took Howard to some of New York's scummier dives in the vain hope of finding some chinks in his squeaky-clean armor. The title of his findings: "A Night of Vice with Mr. Nice."

The aura of niceness that Howard gave to Richie Cunningham became a standing joke within *Happy Days*. In one episode, Richie bemoans his bland reputation: "Nice. Mr. Nice. I'll probably be voted the nicest kid in my class. I'll wind up on the all-star Nice team. Pat Boone, Kate Smith, Captain Kangaroo, and me." And in the hilarious segment that introduced Robin Williams as space alien Mork, the point of Mork's mission is to return to Planet Ork with the most humdrum human specimen he can find. Naturally, Richie is his man.

But the character's fundamental niceness didn't mean that the audience found him dull. During his seven and a half years on *Happy Days*, he provided an effective counterweight to the goofy capers unfolding all around him. Today, Internet postings reveal that the series—seen in reruns on cable—is still popular, attracting youthful viewers from places as widely scattered as Australia, Sweden, India, France, and

Hong Kong. Arianna Bianchi, a twenty-six-year-old teacher from Milan, Italy, sounds a common note: "I really love *Happy Days* and my favorite character is Richie Cunningham because he is so sweet and adorable and he is in every situation a very good boy."

Some in Hollywood, respectful of Howard's gifts as an actor, were surprised when he signed on for *Happy Days*. He was an ambitious twenty-year-old, starting to land substantial dramatic roles, and a prankish comedy series about high school in the 1950s seemed a backward step. In truth, Howard was not a huge fan of the show's slapstick brand of humor. But, as always, he was being pragmatic. For one thing, he had a low draft number and was worried about being sent to Vietnam. He harbored the vague hope that, if necessary, he could petition his draft board for a work deferment, based on the fact that the television series in which he starred provided employment for fifty people. (This turned out to be a moot point, because the draft ended soon after *Happy Days* went on the air.) More importantly, Howard sought to gain insight into the television industry, suspecting that he might be able to leverage his acting commitment into a future directing deal.

Happy Days did indeed turn out to be an important learning experience. From Jerry Paris, who directed almost every episode during the show's eleven-year run, Howard learned physical comedy. Because the show was taped, starting in its third year, before a live audience, he learned poise and how to work a crowd. And from producer Garry Marshall, another of the industry's nice guys, he learned the value of on-set collaboration. The creative team behind *The Andy Griffith Show* had welcomed the actors' input, but Marshall took this even further. Rich Correll, who worked on the *Happy Days* production team, describes Marshall as spreading the word to every single person on the set: "Look, yes, I'm Garry Marshall and it's my show, but if you have a better idea than a joke that we're pitching, come up and give it to me. . . . If you can fix it, you can tell me anything. Now you may not have the right fix, but don't be afraid to tell me." As a director, Howard would one day emulate Marshall's strategy, which encouraged each actor and writer, each set painter and bagel buyer, to feel invested in the success of the enterprise.

Some of what Howard learned was tangential to the creative process. Tom Bosley, who played his father, had solid, fatherly advice about home buying and other financial investments. Howard's parents had been unsophisticated about such matters, and Bosley's savvy guidance turned out to be highly valuable as Howard's income grew. Also, especially during contract negotiations, Howard discovered how to wield the clout he'd accrued as the star of a hit series. It became clear, he says, that show business "was a numbers game. I learned about succeeding."

At the same time, Howard had lessons of his own to teach. The *Happy Days* set on Paramount Studios' stage nineteen was known for its warmth and civility, partly because of Howard's example. Being funny week after week is hard work, and it's well known among Hollywood folk that some sitcom casts can become temperamental. During the heyday of the *Happy Days* spin-off show, *Laverne and Shirley* (1976–1983), series regulars would signal their displeasure with the quality of a given script by ostentatiously dumping it in the trash can, humiliating the writers who had labored over every page. On *Happy Days* this didn't happen, and Howard deserves much of the credit. Henry Winkler, who soared to stardom as the Fonz, admits that at one early rehearsal, unimpressed with the jokes assigned to his character, he complained loudly and pounded his fist into his script for emphasis. Next thing he knew, Howard was quietly walking him to the rear of the soundstage, reminding him how hard the writers were working to churn out gags. Shamefaced, Winkler agreed that he was right and points out, "I never punched the script again for the next eleven years." It is this type of low-key leadership that has led Marshall to say admiringly, "Ron Howard was the big brother when the cameras stopped."

Howard also led the way in welcoming newcomers to the team. At the start of the show's third season, Pat Morita was brought on to play Arnold, proprietor of the local teen hangout. Morita was then primarily a stand-up comic making a transition into acting, and the support of the *Happy Days* regulars meant the world to him. This was especially true of the season's final episode, in which Arnold gets married.

Suddenly finding himself at the center of the story, Morita was extremely nervous. On taping day, Howard was the first to come up to him with a hug and encouraging words: "Pat, don't worry about a thing. . . .This is *your* show, and you have the best supporting cast in the world."

Howard's graciousness extended to the general public too. Rich Correll once saw him cross the street at Paramount in a rainstorm to say hello to two fans who were waving at him. But as the show grew in popularity, its cast members found themselves elevated to teen idol status, and for Howard, who had never really sought the limelight, this proved to be a daunting ordeal. By the time *Happy Days* topped the ratings charts, a scheduled appearance by its stars at a shopping mall could easily attract twenty thousand enthusiasts. And a peaceful restaurant meal was out of the question. After a while, says Howard, "I really could not do anything or go anywhere anymore. When I was doing *Happy Days*, there'd be this crush of people around me all the time. It came to a point where all the attention made me a prisoner." No wonder he increasingly craved the relative anonymity of directing.

It was partly to find respite from the outside world that the *Happy Days* folk enthusiastically turned to sports. Bosco McGowan, one of the show's production assistants, describes playing against Howard in one of the frequent pickup basketball games on the Paramount lot: "He had an awesome jump shot. He effortlessly would just flick his wrist from twenty to twenty-five feet away and swish the ball through the net." To foster *esprit de corps*, Marshall proposed the formation of a *Happy Days* softball team, which played on weekends in an entertainment industry league and later was featured before Major League baseball games at such venues as New York's Shea Stadium and Chicago's Wrigley Field.

Eventually the *Happy Days* team spent hiatus periods traveling the world under USO auspices, playing exhibition games against American troops in Germany and Okinawa. Fred Fox Jr., a young staff writer who served as team manager, remembers how the U.S. soldiers were smugly dismissive of these visitors from Hollywood, until they took the field: "I'm sure they thought they'd just kick our fannies, but we beat 'em and they were stunned!" One of the stars was Howard, whose fiercely competitive spirit always came to the fore in situations like these. During one celebrity game at Dodger Stadium, he slid headfirst into home plate. He beat the throw, but his black eye had to be worked into the next week's episode.

Because Winkler was a total sports novice, Howard helped show him the ropes, and Winkler surprised himself by becoming a competent pitcher. On the *Happy Days* reunion show that aired on March 3, 1992, Winkler paid an emotional tribute to his former acting partner: "I never would have played [softball] without you. You gave me my first mitt, you were my coach, you were my mentor, you were always there, always supportive, yelling from the outfield, 'You can do it, Henry!'" Winkler went on to add, "You're my best friend, even as we sit here today." Winkler is quick to recall for interviewers that in the beginning Howard was the star, while he himself was merely a fringe character. Even in those early days, he insists, "we had instant communication. We got along like bread and butter."

Winkler's words serve as a reminder that Howard was in an increasingly awkward position. On early episodes, Winkler's junior-grade hoodlum character, Arthur Fonzarelli, had little to do. But audiences fell hard for the motorcycle-riding, leather-jacketed Fonzie, and he became the show's breakout star. As attention shifted away from Richie, Howard was publicly philosophical, acknowledging that "there was something immediately electric about Henry. . . . The show was trailing in the first season. Henry got the demographic for us." Due in large part to Winkler, more than 17 million households were now watching *Happy Days,* leading to job security and fat paychecks for the entire cast. Yet there's no denying that Howard's own morale suffered. At the start of the third season, the Fonz was brought into the Cunningham household as a boarder and surrogate son. Howard bore this change with grace, but couldn't stomach the network's later suggestion that the series be renamed *Fonzie's Happy Days.* Fortunately, Marshall agreed, and the familiar title remained.

Marshall credits Howard with learning from Andy Griffith how to swallow one's pride when another actor grabs the spotlight. Griffith's sidekick, Don Knotts, had won four Emmys for his work on *The Andy Griffith Show*, while Griffith received not a single nomination. It helped that Howard and Winkler had a genuine and enduring friendship. Once each got married, the two couples often socialized, and Henry and Stacey Winkler later served as godparents for Howard's children. And because these cast mates also respected one another's acting skills, their time together on the set remained pleasant. So, as Howard put it, "I didn't feel the pressure at work. But I felt it from the network and the studio and the media." The media, in particular, continued to quiz him about Winkler's ascendancy, at a time when his own role on the show was starting to seem less and less challenging. Before long, he was itching to make some changes in his life. At times, driving to Paramount Studios via the San Diego Freeway, he'd wonder, "What if I just keep going to Tijuana?"

Tijuana, the Mexican border town known for its wild nightlife, figured often in Howard's fantasies during the *Happy Days* era. As a young single male, financially flush, he was hardly immune to temptation, and he has sometimes hinted that he survived a few close calls. Still, he was not about to head south of the border to visit a bar or bordello. Because he'd been a public figure from such an early age, he knew there'd be a stiff price to pay for the kind of outlandish behavior that a Tijuana weekend might encourage. As someone who valued his privacy, he had no desire to fulfill the expectations of tabloid journalists who were eagerly waiting for little Opie to screw up. And even while he and his fellow *Happy Days* cast members were as famous as rock stars, his devotion to Cheryl remained absolute. This helped him to keep the inevitable groupies at arm's length. Although his creative life occasionally seemed to be on hold, he found comfort in a romantic relationship that did not hinge on his celebrity status.

On June 7, 1975, that relationship was made official. He proposed in the spring, and the wedding took place at Burbank's Magnolia Park Methodist Church. It was a traditional ceremony, with flowers, candles, and the bride radiant in a white lace gown and long veil. The groom was decked out in a powder blue tuxedo and ruffled shirt; so were his ushers, who included *Happy Days* costars Anson Williams and Donny Most. Howard's great-aunt Julia Hall, long a collector of memorabilia about her famous grandnephew, was among those who flew in from Duncan, Oklahoma, for the nuptials. Cheryl Howard later remembered that more than three hundred invited guests tried to squeeze into a sanctuary that fit two hundred. After they were pronounced man and wife, everyone applauded: "We'd never heard anybody clap at the end of a wedding, and we loved that."

When the newlyweds emerged from the church, paparazzi who had been lying in wait snapped pictures of celebrity well-wishers such as Tom Bosley, Andy Griffith, and Don Knotts. On the following day, Ron and Cheryl's wedding was front-page news in Burbank's *Daily Review*. Bride and groom were barely twenty-one, and Cheryl was only midway through college. But Howard, despite his boyish looks and high-pitched voice, had the maturity, the ambition, and the earning power of a much older man. Richie Cunningham might still be in high school, but Howard was all grown up. His marriage gave him added faith that he could put his frustrations behind him and make a go of a directing career. In his mind, his happy days were just beginning.

CHAPTER 5

Revving Up

(1975–1977)

"My goal had always been to try to direct a feature film while I was still in my teens . . . By the time I was twenty, twenty-one I was really desperate."

—RON HOWARD

AFTER THEIR 1975 WEDDING, RON AND CHERYL HOWARD settled into cozy domesticity in Studio City, a fifteen-minute hop from Rance and Jean's Toluca Lake home. Their unpretentious three-bedroom house, in a secluded cul-de-sac on the outer fringes of Hollywood's Laurel Canyon, was Early American in style, with maple furniture, lace curtains on the windows, and brownies baking in the kitchen. The young couple did the woodwork themselves, and Clint helped landscape the yard.

The Howards' taste in automobiles remained low-key, too. Though his *Happy Days* colleague Anson Williams bought a Mercedes-Benz, and Henry Winkler started tooling around town in a BMW, Howard stuck with his Volkswagen van. (He later graduated to a Volvo 760, and test drove—but did not buy—a Porsche.) For fun, he and Cheryl took in Dodgers games, or sipped hot chocolate while watching old movies on the tube. After Cheryl earned her bachelor's degree in 1977, both looked forward to starting a family, but the hectic pace of Ron's *Happy Days* schedule made them feel it was wiser to wait. For the time being, two dogs and a monkey completed their household.

In August 1977 as *Happy Days* was about to launch its fifth season, *Los Angeles Times* reporter Paul Rosenfield questioned Howard about his morale on the set. Howard spoke about job security and spectacular pay. Yet, he admitted, "I could give it up. Laziness sometimes sets in. I like anxiety." Howard was still hoping that his hit series would prove to be a springboard to a directing career. But although his *Happy Days* fame brought unique opportunities—he was, for instance, the youngest-ever Bacchus at the 1979 New Orleans Mardi Gras—his long-term goal remained out of reach. Which led him to contemplate some fairly drastic schemes for financing a directing debut.

Howard now admits that at one time he was tantalized by the $30 million racked up by the 1972 porn film, *Deep Throat*. He reasoned that if he starred in a low-budget quickie called *Opie Gets Laid*, his legitimate acting career would be over. But, because such a film would surely attract throngs of curiosity seekers, he was convinced "that would be OK. I'd take my little pot of money and go out and make independent movies." He didn't try it, of course. It was not in his nature to crawl that far out on a limb. But he also fantasized about other off-beat fund-raising methods, such as going door to door to ask for cash. Or, during a broadcast of *Happy Days*, maybe appearing in a commercial spot in which his fans were urged to send him dollar bills. (He was miffed to discover that this was against the law.)

By 1975, although he'd long been floating ideas for film projects, Howard was no closer to finding financial backing. He paid close attention when a *Happy Days* guest star, Bruce Kimmel, announced he was making his own movie. Kimmel was the writer, codirector, composer, and lyricist for an oddity called *The First Nudie Musical*. (He also managed to keep his clothes on while playing one of the central roles.) In an era when such offbeat efforts as *The Rocky Horror Picture Show* (1975) were targeting hip young-adult audiences, major studios believed money could be made by backing such modest but potentially lucrative ventures. So despite, or perhaps because of, Kimmel's raunchy comic premise—that a porn producer desperate for novelty has decided to combine musical numbers with raw sex—Paramount Pictures signed on to help with financing. This upped the initial $50,000 budget to a semihealthy $225,000. Shooting began on May 5, 1975, at Hollywood's Raleigh Studios, virtually across the street from the *Happy Days* set.

The First Nudie Musical is unique among Hollywood's film musicals in featuring sexual situations, full-frontal nudity, and a chorus line of Dancing Dildos. But the female lead is Cindy Williams, just before her *Laverne and Shirley* days, playing the producer's sweet, wholesome assistant. She and Kimmel agreed that it would be a good joke to ask Howard, her *American Graffiti* costar, to participate. Says Kimmel, "I think he was just so fascinated that I had actually gone out and gotten the money together to do this movie. I can't remember if it was Cindy or me who asked him to come and cameo, but he was there so fast to do it."

Howard's three-line role, invented on the spot, is that of a young hopeful who's waiting to audition, but is understandably baffled by a trade-paper ad calling for "tap shoes, rehearsal clothes, possible nudity, and they don't want any albinos." He took no pay and no billing, but when the video was released in 1989, his photo was prominently featured on the cassette box. Remarkably, once *The First Nudie Musical* opened in theatres in 1976, it garnered some rave reviews; Judith Crist, writing in the *New York Daily News,* said, "It's fresh. It's funny. It's funky. It's the *Star Wars* of nudie musicals." Though the merits of this audaciously tawdry production can certainly be argued, many consider it a minor cult classic, which is why Kimmel has recently issued a twenty-sixth anniversary DVD version. The DVD includes new commentary by cast and crew, but, to no one's surprise, Howard politely declined to take part. Kimmel says, "We couldn't get Ron to do anything, unfortunately, so we've made that a running gag in the documentary. We're always saying, 'Where's Ron? He's on his way, right?' but he never shows up."

Howard may now be keeping his distance from *The First Nudie Musical*, but other cameos over the years show that he has not lost his sense of humor or his fondness for appearing in eccentric roles. In 1998 he became a hero to his children by supplying the voice for a perverse, martini-swilling version of himself on Fox's animated series, *The Simpsons*. That same year, he was interviewed on camera for *Welcome to Hollywood*, a "mockumentary" that includes well-known Hollywood figures in tuxedos pontificating on the nature of stardom. He continued his string of cameo appearances in 2001 by playing himself in *The Independent*, a spoof of the low-budget film industry. In the same year he gave voice to Tom Colonic, an unlikely good guy in the Farrelly Brothers' wacky comedy about the workings of the human immune system, *Osmosis Jones*.

Howard had pitched in to support Kimmel's filmmaking dream, but his own career seemed to be stuck in a familiar rut. The networks would not give him a television movie to direct; studio heads condescendingly hinted that he should wait until he was older. Then a call came from an unexpected quarter in early 1976, and hope sprang anew.

The call was from Roger Corman, head of New World Pictures and the maverick producer of hundreds of low-budget genre movies with such titles as *Candy Stripe Nurses* and *Death Race 2000*. Corman is widely revered within the film industry for giving promising young moviemakers their start. In 1976 his recent alumni included several who were being recognized as rising young directors: Peter Bogdanovich (*The Last Picture Show*, 1971), Francis Ford Coppola (*The Godfather*, 1972), and Martin Scorsese (*Taxi Driver*, 1976). But Corman had telephoned Howard simply to offer an acting role. Howard's popularity on *Happy Days* made him an ideal candidate to play Hoover Niebold, the lead in a raucous teen car-crash comedy called *Eat My Dust!* Under normal circumstances, Howard would have turned the role down. The script was not to his taste, and a starring role in a Corman movie was not likely to enhance his prestige as an actor. Still, he knew Corman's reputation, and suspected there might be a way to parlay *Eat My Dust!* into his first directing gig.

Telling his agent to stay home, Howard approached Corman with a proposal and a script of his own. He and Rance had written a gentle comedy-drama about a USC student bumming around Hollywood during winter break. If Corman would consent to put up half the money for 'Tis the Season, and book it into theatres through his own distribution network, Howard would accept the Eat My Dust! role. Corman, a shrewd negotiator, read Howard's script and viewed his student films before making a counter offer. He had no interest in 'Tis the Season, which did not contain enough sex or violence to satisfy New World's fan base. But if Howard agreed to play Hoover Niebold, Corman would guarantee him a chance to write a story outline, on a topic of Corman's choice, for $1,500. If that outline met Corman's standards, he could turn it into a script, for which he would be paid an additional $5,000. If the script passed muster and he played the leading role, he would be hired to direct it. If none of this came to pass, Corman offered a consolation prize: a chance to direct second-unit action sequences on another New World production.

Howard considered this proposal philosophically: "It wasn't my dream project, the film that I was trying to get off the ground, but it was the closest thing to a professional directing opportunity that I'd been able to generate." And so, he quickly found himself learning to make movies Corman-style. Eat My Dust!, which cost well under $1 million, was shot over a hectic three-week period, with Howard's scenes scheduled around his Happy Days commitments.

Howard's part was a young speed demon who goes joyriding with a pretty girl in a stolen stock car, much to the fury of his father, the local sheriff. By the time he limps home, some twenty cars have been smashed to smithereens, and Hoover Niebold has been transformed from gangly delivery boy to local hero. The role was somewhat earthier than his Richie Cunningham persona—he cursed, and sexual activity was implied—but it by no means stretched his acting abilities. Nevertheless, Howard was not one to put on prima donna airs. Writer-director Chuck Griffith remembers him as a total gentleman, who "didn't push ahead in the line or take it for granted that he was going to get fed first." Griffith, the writer of such Corman favorites as Little

Shop of Horrors (1960), was directing for the first time, and Howard's consummate professionalism made his job far easier. Whatever Howard's reservations about the project, he kept them to himself. Says Griffith, "He fit the script perfectly, and he played the script. That stuff about 'My dad named me Hoover because I put him in a Depression' he did just so smoothly, and the picture got a lot of laughs."

Griffith can't say enough about Howard's good qualities: "He's just Mr. Nice Guy. He's the part that Jimmy Stewart always played." But despite Howard's mild demeanor, Griffith didn't consider him weak. He's not surprised that Howard has the backbone needed to run a movie set, and feels sure he has developed his own way of keeping other people's egos in check. No one pushes Howard around? Griffith says, "I don't think you'd want to. There are performers who might. But . . . they'd be pushing against a pillow. And he'd probably figure a very soft, quiet way to squelch them."

Griffith's high regard for Howard extends to the rest of the family. Both Rance and Clint had roles in *Eat My Dust!* Rance wore a bushy mustache to play a dim-witted deputy sheriff, and seventeen-year-old Clint was one of Hoover Niebold's rambunctious pals. During production, Rance and Jean invited Griffith and his wife over for a home-cooked meal, at which Griffith remembers that "everything was absolute American, as if Disney got together with Martha Stewart and designed the perfect scene for that dinner." Of course the Howards were gracious hosts: "They're very fine Midwestern sort of people. You would never guess that they're in show business, until they start telling stories, and talk about raising Ron. They raised him strictly, and I don't imagine they had a lot of trouble. I imagine they had some trouble with Clint." Griffith had no complaints about Clint on the set, though he noted that Clint "seemed more animated, bouncing around, and potentially not as perfectly adjusted as Ronny." What impressed Griffith most is that, within the Howard family circle, Clint never had to play second fiddle to his more famous older brother.

In the summer of 1976, the ad copy screamed: "Ron Howard pops his clutch, and tells the world to EAT MY DUST!" Young audiences flocked to see the PG-rated film, which raked in a reported $18 million at the box office. But, although Howard regards the experience fondly, he advises today's fans not to bother seeking out the finished product. He is of course only revealing his own squeamishness about starring in a low-budget genre flick. *Eat My Dust!*, though undeniably crude and sloppy in spots, shows flashes of the appealing vigor that marks Corman's better releases.

Ironically, at the same time that he signed on to play Hoover Niebold, Howard was just completing a film role that proved one of his proudest acting achievements. The picture was a major studio release, and its star was an American icon.

The Shootist, released by Paramount Pictures in 1976, was the last film made by John Wayne before his death in June 1979. The project became doubly poignant because of its subject matter: the last days of a legendary Western gunslinger, John Bernard Books, whose body is riddled with cancer. In 1963 Wayne had himself lost a lung to cancer, and his stomach would be removed in 1979. When, as Books, he says, "I'm a dying man, scared of the dark," the truth of the moment seems palpable.

The precarious state of Wayne's health complicated the shooting schedule more than once. Because this film was widely rumored to be his swan song, many old friends in the movie industry asked to take part. That's why a Western budgeted at $8 million attracted a supporting cast that included James Stewart and such movie and television stalwarts as Richard Boone, Hugh O'Brian, Harry Morgan, John Carradine, and Sheree North. The female lead was Lauren Bacall, playing an attractive widow who verbally spars with Books but later comes to care about him. Howard was entrusted with the pivotal role of her young son, Gillom.

Gillom Rogers is a fatherless young man who feels stifled by the tiny town in which he lives, and who regards the ailing desperado with an admiration bordering on reverence. Books, despite his own violent past, takes it on himself to become Gillom's moral teacher. He imposes a code of conduct in which Gillom's rebellious habits—such as cussing and sneaking cheap whiskey—have no place. Though he tutors Gillom in the art of shooting, he also makes clear that "there's more to being a man than handling a gun." The film climaxes in a dramatic saloon shootout, in which three men try to boost their reputations by bringing the famous gunslinger down. At a crucial moment, beautifully staged by director Don Siegel, Gillom must step into the fray.

The DVD commentary by screenplay author Miles Hood Swarthout and producer William Self makes clear that the film's conclusion departs radically from the original novel by Swarthout's father. In Glendon Swarthout's novel, Gillom essentially inherits Books' mantle and will go on to a violent career of his own. The film, however, allows Gillom's behavior to be both more noble and more ambiguous. The final tracking shot is of Gillom walking silently out of the saloon, past the crowds, and through the town, his eyes fixed on the horizon. His abrupt coming of age has left Gillom, it seems, with the need to choose between the safety of home and the risks of a wanderer's life.

On the set Howard learned from Siegel's dexterous use of the camera and from how he handled Wayne's monumental temper. Because Wayne had a reputation for giving young actors a hard time, Howard was nervous at first about approaching the legendary star. To his surprise, Wayne treated him cordially: "I was twenty-one years old at the time, and he always called me 'Old Twenty-one' on the set. He never ever made me feel like a kid." They played chess together, and Wayne generally won. Many critics praised Wayne's performance, although it brought him no formal honors. Howard received the film's only major acting nod, a nomination for a Golden Globe Award. This was as close as he ever came to winning an acting prize. But by taking part in John Wayne's painful final performance, he received an indelible lesson in the meaning of grace under pressure.

Once *Eat My Dust!* and *The Shootist* were in the can, Howard turned his attention to the bargain he'd made with Roger Corman. The challenge was to hit upon a film premise that piqued Corman's interest. Howard verbally pitched stories from every genre: dramas, comedies, science fiction, bleak thrillers about the snuff film world.

Corman listened attentively, praised Howard's vivid storytelling, then dismissed each concept as not what he was looking for. Finally, after *Eat My Dust!* scored at the box office, Corman decided that he wanted more of the same. He stipulated that the follow-up must be a teen action comedy called *Grand Theft Auto*. As Howard was later to put it, he and his dad "rejigged" a story that Rance had been working on, creating a suitable New World vehicle in which Ron could star. He phoned Corman with the new pitch, and Corman immediately signed on. Howard would call this "the fastest, smoothest track to a green light that I've ever experienced."

The first step, of course, was to complete a screenplay. In this, Ron and Rance worked closely with Frances Doel, Corman's longtime story editor. Her job was to make sure that the script contained all the necessary elements—young love, car chase, action, humor—and that it could be shot on a Corman-style minuscule budget. The process went smoothly, over about six weeks. From the start, Doel found the plot nicely structured and paced, and the dialogue lively, concise, and natural. She was particularly struck by how the two Howards presented a united front. So completely were they in sync about scenes and characters that it was impossible to tell which was the major creative force behind the writing. Doel's impression, though, was that Rance had a great deal to do with shaping the script into its final form. Professional father-and-son pairings are not the norm in Hollywood, and most young men enjoying their first big break would prefer to keep their dads at a distance. But Howard has never been shy about giving his father credit for his story sense, and for much more.

Over the years, Ron has many times publicly expressed his debt to Rance. He insists he has learned to avoid fame's temptations by emulating his father's approach to life: "He's relentlessly evenhanded and moral, that Midwestern hardworking, no-nonsense breed of man." Ron also sees heroism in the way Rance has quietly pursued his own career, in the shadow of his son's accomplishments. There is, says Ron with surprising bluntness, "a kind of noble quality in his passion for it, his commitment, his willingness to just dig in even though he didn't have the gifts or the luck to emerge as a big star." In 1986, when asked to compare himself to his father, he first suggested that Rance was the more conservative of the two about major career moves. Then he quickly corrected himself, recalling that his dad had boldly walked off the farm to become an actor, and then transplanted his young family across the country to further his goal. If Howard's mature life would be marked by a willingness to take a leap into the unknown, his father seems to have served as his first and best role model.

Curiously, taking the big leap is what *Grand Theft Auto* is all about. In *Eat My Dust!* a young couple steals a car to go for a joyride. At the end, the boy comes home again. He's lost the girl but gained self-confidence, as well as new respect from those around him. In *Grand Theft Auto*, Sam and Paula steal her father's vintage Rolls Royce so they can elope to Las Vegas to get married. The film quickly evolves into an elaborate chase, involving a politico, a preacher, a Mafioso, a manic DJ, some good ol' boys, and a lot of cops. Scores of cars bite the dust, especially in the huge demolition derby at the film's climax. But the upshot is that the young lovers get away. Despite all the comic carnage, they make a clean break with the past, plunging wholeheartedly into the sweet task of building a new life together.

The filming of *Grand Theft Auto* began on March 2, 1977, one day after Howard's twenty-third birthday. He had dreamed of shooting his first feature before he turned twenty-one, but now he was in the director's chair at last. It was not lost on Howard that the great Orson Welles was three years his senior when he made his own directorial debut in 1941. Of course, *Citizen Kane* had more on its mind than car crashes.

Grand Theft Auto, budgeted at $602,000, was allotted a twenty-three day shooting schedule. Speed and efficiency would be mandatory; Howard soon learned that it does not pay to be a perfectionist on a New World project. Corman, as was his custom, prepped his fledgling director with practical maxims: plan your shots; keep movement in the frame; chase the sun; wear comfortable shoes and sit down a lot. He assured Howard he'd stay out of his hair unless he fell behind schedule.

Many on the set that first day remember Howard as cool and collected. Corman, whose own memories sometimes take on mythic pro-
portions, insists that the novice was calm enough to give instructions to
his crew, then saunter off for a cup of coffee. Howard himself recalls his
first few hours as anything but calm. Despite intense preparation, he
had only managed five or six shots by lunchtime. This would be excellent by Hollywood studio standards, but in Corman terms he was
already behind, and he feared getting fired on the spot. Fortunately, by
the end of the day, he had thirty-seven shots to his credit, and Corman,
as promised, kept his distance for the rest of the shoot.

Once the film was completed, Howard proudly shared with
Variety's Joseph McBride the news that "we broke the New World
record for most setups in one day by two units working simultaneously.
The previous record was eighty-two, on *Hollywood Boulevard*, but we
did ninety-one setups in a single day." Later in his career, Howard
would not have to move at such breakneck speed. Still, he has continued to value the need to be efficient: "I think the decisiveness involved
with the quest for efficiency leads to a cleaner, more direct line to the
heart of the matter."

Howard told McBride that, while making *Grand Theft Auto*, he
was especially proud that the production team had showed him no
resistance. He had worried that veteran crew members might challenge
his decisions or refuse to do his bidding. But Emmy-winning television
director Allan Arkush, then a Corman regular, insists that Howard's
lack of experience was never an issue: "Within the context of New
World Pictures, everyone's about the same age. Everyone's about the
same place in their lives. Everyone wants to make movies. Ron certainly
was someone we all recognized, and had a TV show on the air. Plus he
was a really good guy. So I think that everyone wanted him to succeed."

Arkush, who had codirected New World's ultra-low-budget spoof,
Hollywood Boulevard (1976), was tapped by Howard to direct second
unit on *Grand Theft Auto*. Because of the short schedule, both men
were shooting simultaneously, with Howard handling all dialogue
scenes, and Arkush focusing exclusively on action. But there was no
question as to who was in charge. Arkush says now, "I was really ful-

filling Ron's blueprint of what he wanted to do." The key, as always, was advance planning. Howard called a meeting that lasted two full days, in which they worked out careful storyboards for the entire production. As Arkush explains, "Because we had so little money, and so much stuff had to be moved back and forth between first and second unit, we had to make sure everyone knew where everything was. [You] literally had one costume per character. You couldn't let the stuntman have the entire outfit. So you're like—where are the pants gonna be at four o'clock?"

The work was grueling, but also a lot of fun. At one point, Howard talked Arkush into putting on a clown suit for a sight gag in which a car sideswipes an ice cream truck. Arkush remembers, "It was really like— 'We got a camera, we got a crew, we got some actors, we got a script. Let's make a movie!'" The only downside was the pressure applied by Corman to make the film faster, cheaper, with bigger explosions. Joe Dante, who edited *Grand Theft Auto* and would later have a solid directing career of his own with *Gremlins* and *Matinee*, explains the usual New World dynamic: "It was everybody against Roger . . . as in every dysfunctional family." In the face of Corman's more unreasonable demands, Howard had the advantage of being what Dante calls "the ultimate diplomat," able to present an affable face, no matter what. He was polite, he was eager to learn, and he was unflappable—a potent combination when dealing with someone holding the reins of power.

Howard himself admits he found some Corman methods eccentric. In that era, when New World movies were shown to preview audiences, Corman made no effort to find age-appropriate focus groups. So at one test screening of Howard's slightly raunchy teen car-crash comedy, the seats were packed with what he calls "blue-haired ladies." Nonetheless, Corman would meticulously graph these unlikely viewers' reactions. He'd then cut the film ruthlessly, casually disregarding plot points and character details intended to add texture. It could all seem slightly ludicrous, but Howard discovered that "as a result of that honing and shaping, there is no question that the movie was becoming more and more enjoyable to the audiences." The experience taught him how to craft a crowd-pleasing film. Even today, though his methods are far less haphazard than Corman's, he still relies heavily on previews that test audience reactions, "because sometimes you're surprised, and certain things just are not communicating what you'd hoped, as you'd hoped."

Grand Theft Auto will always be Joe Dante's favorite Howard project, because, he says, he finds it "such a movie from the heart." Not only was it Howard's big chance, but his whole family rallied to help him complete it. Clint and Rance played featured roles, and Rance was a constant presence in the editing room. (Dante was happy to have his company, but needed to gently persuade him that the geographic accuracy of the film's road trip was not his chief concern in the editing process.) Jean became deeply involved, along with family friends. Garry Marshall agreed to appear as a comic gangster after Howard phoned, confessing that he was nervous about his directing debut, and begged Marshall to participate. Cheryl took a break from her school obligations to make a good-luck cameo appearance. She also stepped in to prevent a mutiny when the crew couldn't bear mediocre chow one second longer.

The film was shot in and around Victorville, a somewhat bleak agricultural community in Southern California's high desert, eighty-two miles northeast of Los Angeles. While most film crews are well-fed by on-set caterers, a Corman budget precluded much more than greasy burgers from the nearest fast-food outlet. As morale began to ebb, Cheryl volunteered to exercise her cooking skills. Fortunately, she had a grandmother nearby, with a kitchen that could be commandeered for the occasion. For eleven days she bought local ingredients, such as sixteen pounds of asparagus, and served sumptuous meals to some eighty-five hungry people. Arkush fondly remembers her zesty enchiladas. He can still picture the crew seated in a parking lot, savoring a meal that Cheryl had stayed up half the night to prepare. Someone came by with a tabloid newspaper whose headline divulged that the two-year-old Howard marriage was on the rocks, and this "revelation" gave everyone a hearty laugh. It is because of the extraordinary personal commitment of all the Howards that Joe Dante calls *Grand Theft Auto* "as personal as a movie can be, considering that it's about a subject they didn't care about."

Despite Cheryl's cooking, nervous tension caused Howard to lose fifteen pounds during the shoot. Which is not to say that he was unhappy. At the wrap party, he nearly wept, telling Jean, "I can't believe I love being a director more than I thought I would." When the film was screened for cast and crew, they showed their affection by playing a practical joke. Before the movie came on, Howard was surprised by vintage footage of himself as a winsome moppet belting out the "Gary, Indiana" number from *The Music Man*. He pretended to be outraged, but everyone could see he was tickled.

Howard's regard for the key members of his crew has proved genuine and long lasting. In 1981, New World cinematographer Gary Graver was invited to shoot Howard's television movie, *Through the Magic Pyramid*. Graver marvels that, even today, whenever he calls Howard's office, Howard always gets on the line. In 1989 Dante directed *The 'burbs*, the first movie made under the banner of Howard's then-new company, Imagine Films Entertainment. And Arkush, who was making a name for himself in television, was called in to direct the 1990 television pilot based on Howard's hit comedy, *Parenthood*. Arkush, who remained friendly with the entire Howard family, was also asked by Ron and Clint to share their choice seats at a Dodgers-Yankees World Series game. Those who've worked with Howard over the years all have similar stories to tell: he remembers them even years later, is delighted by any chance meeting, and helps advance their careers when he can.

Howard probably did not expect rave reviews for *Grand Theft Auto*. After the film's release in June 1977, most critics who bothered to comment dismissed it as routine Corman fare. Lawrence Van Gelder's write-up in the *New York Times* was one of the best: "Nobody who has ever wanted to see a Rolls Royce in a demolition derby is going to walk away from this movie disappointed." In fact, this sometimes clumsy but ingratiating film ended up grossing $15 million at the box office, an excellent return for a low-budget feature, and the television rights were sold to CBS for a whopping $1.1 million.

To spread the word about his accomplishment, Howard went on the talk show circuit. On June 14, 1977, soon after *Grand Theft Auto*'s release, he visited with Mike Douglas, chatting easily about his juvenile work and grinning broadly when his directorial debut was mentioned. Douglas asked the obvious question: why would a successful actor want to direct? Howard's answer was a variation on something he has often said: "It's the idea of the control, and the fact that you're really carrying the responsibility. You're not in someone else's hands quite so much." In other contexts, Howard has emphasized that the actor's life is not one that suits his nature: "I didn't choose to become an actor. It fulfills no need I have, and the attention and adulation that go along with acting have always made me feel a little bit uncomfortable. Plus, I never enjoyed the feeling you have that as an actor you're the victim of other people's mistakes."

The Howard reflected in these quotes—a person who craves control and responsibility, and shrinks from the limelight that has always defined his life—is not uncomplicated. He's far more, it seems, than his white-bread image would imply. A fellow guest on Mike Douglas's show that evening was Broadway writer/composer Stephen Sondheim, a hip New Yorker who brilliantly dissects modern neuroses in such bittersweet musical plays as *Company* and *Follies*. In the course of the conversation, Sondheim somehow got onto the topic of niceness. He flatly asserted that "anybody who's totally smooth and totally nice I don't trust. Nobody is totally smooth and totally nice, unless they've lived in a hothouse all their life." Howard, of course, is considered the nicest of men, and some feel that his Hollywood upbringing has been a sort of hothouse. But in moving from acting to directing, Howard revealed an urge to leave a safe environment, to try something braver and bolder, to take charge of himself and others.

Thanks to the open-door policies of Roger Corman, Howard found the opportunity to take a giant leap. Directing low-rent action flicks certainly wasn't his goal. But he met the challenge and gloriously succeeded in fulfilling a Corman prophecy that would one day be the stuff of legend. On the set, when Howard had dared to gripe about an unfortunate cost-cutting measure, Corman said with a smile, "If you do a good job for me on this picture, you'll never have to work for me again." After *Grand Theft Auto*, Howard never looked back.

CHAPTER 6

Flying Lessons

(1977–1981)

"I always feel like I'm flying by the seat of my pants."

—RON HOWARD

AFTER *GRAND THEFT AUTO*, RON HOWARD WAS A DIRECTOR, at least in his own mind. Others, however, needed some convincing. For industry bigwigs as well as fans, he remained a squeaky-clean teenager named Richie Cunningham. At twenty-three, Howard recognized his dilemma: "I'm likable, all right, but the important thing is to mature. I have a transition to make. In the next few years, I hope to be directing on a fulltime basis." On hiatus from *Happy Days,* Howard grew a mustache to help him look older (but had to pencil it in for public appearances). He also went through a brief period of talking tough during interviews, making sure to swear. For all his efforts, America continued to think of Howard as the boy next door. In 1979 he was given *Good Housekeeping* magazine's Style Award "for demonstrating an exemplary lifestyle to modern youth."

Though acting roles still came his way, Howard now tried to avoid being typecast as a high school kid. In 1976, however, he worked hard at persuading novelist J. D. Salinger to grant him the movie rights to the coming-of-age classic, *The Catcher in the Rye*. But Salinger, notoriously leery of Hollywood, turned him down flat. So Howard's hope of putting together a film deal that would allow him to portray the iconic troubled teen Holden Caulfield was nipped in the bud.

Despite his ambition to produce and direct, Howard's next feature film after *Grand Theft Auto* was a simple acting gig. His character was one he had introduced in 1973.

More American Graffiti (1979), a strained attempt to recapture the magic of the original, was cowritten by George Lucas, but directed by B. W. L. Norton. One of several plot strands updates the life of Steve Bolander: in 1967, five years after the events of the first film, he is married to Laurie and the father of two-year-old twins. *More American Graffiti* is the rare motion picture that views a Howard character unsympathetically, at least at the outset. In an era of Vietnam protests and the Women's Liberation Movement, nice guy Steve has evolved into a politically conservative male chauvinist who refuses to allow his wife a part-time job. When a thoroughly demoralized Laurie runs off to join her younger brother on his college campus, Steve is furious at being left behind with two mischief-prone toddlers. Over the telephone, he rants, "I am a man, do you understand that? And a man has a certain role in life. A man goes to work and he earns money for his family. And a man is a man. A man is not a housewife. . . . My mother loved being a housewife, and my mother loved being a mother, and I'm coming to pick you up right now."

Steve's perspective alters after he unwittingly gets caught up in a student riot, then shows surprising gumption in rescuing himself and Laurie from the hands of the cops. By the time the final credits roll, the Bolander household is intact, and Steve's consciousness seems to have been permanently raised: the audience learns that Laurie will go on to head a consumer group. Certainly, by film's end, Steve has come closer to resembling Howard, who tends to have a liberal political bent and who takes extraordinary pains to include his wife in his accomplishments.

To an outside observer, Cheryl Howard may look like a traditional spouse, for whom domesticity is a natural reflex. Although during her college years she worked in geriatric facilities and tried student teaching at Howard's old alma mater, Stevenson Elementary, she has consistently put her husband's movie projects (and, later, the rearing of their children) ahead of her personal career goals. Still she has her own artistic ambitions. Early in their marriage she was a screenwriting fellow at the American Film Institute; more recently, she spent seven years researching and writing an adventure novel. Tentatively titled *In the Face of Jinn*, it deals with an American woman's quest to locate a sister who has vanished in India. Howard proudly describes Cheryl as his secret weapon when it comes to character and story. He also values her input throughout the creative process, declaring that she's "a strong, creative woman, highly opinionated, and I wouldn't change a thing."

Like *More American Graffiti*, Howard's other acting gigs in this era tackled social issues, with varying degrees of success. In early 1981 he starred with Art Carney in a television movie called *Bitter Harvest*. Based on a true story, *Bitter Harvest* details a young farmer's discovery that local cows have ingested tainted feed, and that the poisons in their systems are spreading to the people who drink their milk. Howard played a husband and father, serious and capable, who must take matters into his own hands to protect his home, his family, and his livelihood. A production executive who was often on the set emphasizes that Howard never once tried to override director Roger Young. But by keeping his videocamera always close at hand, Howard showed that he still dreamed of being the guy who called the shots. "It was clear," says the executive, "that his heart had crossed that particular divide."

Meanwhile, on Tuesday nights at 8 P.M., Howard continued as Richie Cunningham, who had finally entered college and begun a serious romance. Howard tried persistently to make a directing deal with his network, but ABC turned a deaf ear. Rival network NBC, however, proved more receptive. In September 1977 as he was beginning his fifth season on *Happy Days*, Howard joined with his father and brother to form a small company, Major H Productions, with Ron as president, Rance as vice president, and Clint as secretary. The first creative project initiated by Major H was a lighthearted television movie set in high school. Howard directed *Cotton Candy* in the spring of 1978, to air on NBC in October of that year.

In *Cotton Candy*, a Battle of the Bands forms the backdrop for the story of a loser who finds love. George Smalley, played by Charles Martin Smith, is a high school senior who has flopped at football and everything else he's tried. Egged on by best friend Corky (Clint Howard), he forms a rock band, and finds a kindred spirit in the band's female drummer, Brenda (Leslie E. King). The only problem involves their post-graduation plans: he has given no thought to moving beyond his Texas suburb, while she has accepted a scholarship to study chemistry at her father's alma mater, the Massachusetts Institute of Technology.

The film's ending parallels the original *American Graffiti*. Faced with the prospect of losing George, Brenda decides to give up her MIT scholarship and stay home. In *American Graffiti*, Steve Bolander's similar decision was seen as a sign of cowardice. But *Cotton Candy* hints that Brenda is brave in turning down an opportunity that was more her father's idea than her own. Meanwhile, George, though not a high achiever, comes off well for having the spunk to turn his garage band into a going concern. George and Brenda's long-range prospects are not really discussed, nor does *Cotton Candy* stand up under any sort of weighty analysis. It is strictly a feel-good film, marked by the amiable performances of its leads. Howard's direction, awkward at times in big crowd scenes, shines when he's exploring the budding romantic relationship.

In casting Charles Martin Smith in the central role, Howard was using an actor with whom he had worked in *American Graffiti* (as the klutzy Terry the Toad) and *The Spikes Gang*. They had become friends, but Howard's transformation into a cool and capable director took Smith by surprise. As he told Lois Armstrong, who covered the shoot for *People* magazine, "Ron can't make a decision about where to go for dinner, but he had an answer for everybody on the set. It was amazing. He was totally in control." The one thing Howard could not control, it seems, was the unbridled enthusiasm of his fans. When, during a *Happy Days* hiatus, he showed up with his film crew at Lake Highlands High School in Dallas, six thousand requests poured in for his autograph. And after a lunch in a local cafeteria, one admirer begged for his gnawed chicken bones. This bizarre request was for Howard one more reminder of why he preferred the relative anonymity of a director to the fishbowl existence of a star.

Cotton Candy teaches the rewards of teamwork, so it's fitting that Howard's personal team was again so much a part of this production. Each family member played a featured role, with Rance as the school vice principal, Jean as a teacher, and Clint strutting his stuff as the band's feisty manager-to-be. Cheryl had an amusing cameo, with several lines, as Clint's disgruntled prom date. The family also contributed behind the scenes: Rance was credited as coproducer; Clint cowrote the script with his brother; Cheryl served as production accountant; and Jean shouldered the duties of a talent coordinator, not for the last time on a Howard production. Part of the reason the Howards took on multiple jobs was purely economic. *Cotton Candy* was budgeted at $1.1 million, with any overage to come out of the filmmaker's own pocket. As Jean quipped to the reporter from *People*, "It's hard to undercut our price."

Though not the kind of film that wins awards, *Cotton Candy* has attracted its own set of devotees. In October 2001 a videotaped copy sold on eBay, after lively bidding, for over $500.

Though deeply involved with such Howard projects as *Cotton Candy*, Clint also had his own career to think of. As a child actor he never had the name recognition his brother experienced. Still, some of his roles comprise footnotes in the annals of American popular culture. Notably, he guest starred in a classic episode of *Star Trek* called "The Corbomite Maneuver," which first aired on November 10, 1966. In this episode, which borrows plot elements from *The Wizard of Oz*, William Shatner as Commander Kirk receives threatening messages from Balok, apparently a fierce, vengeful alien bent on destroying the Enterprise and its crew. When Kirk calls Balok's bluff, he turns out to be none other than seven-year-old Clint, with waxy makeup and someone else's deep voice. Kirk is stunned to discover that the tiny alien, all alone in his huge spacecraft, has issued these fearsome threats simply because he's lonesome and wants somebody to talk to.

Clint came closest to stardom when, after appearing in a 1967 movie called *Gentle Giant*, he spent two years heading the human cast of the television version, *Gentle Ben*. Though the series was moderately successful, Clint found himself in an eccentric acting situation, playing many of his scenes opposite a 650-pound American black bear. It was, in Clint's words, "like working with a bad actor. I was always taught that you look your fellow actor in the eye. Now, the bear is not going to look back. What the bear wants is its next meal." When *Gentle Ben* went off the air in 1969, Clint costarred with other animals. He acted with a young horse (and Henry Fonda and Maureen O'Hara) in *The Red Pony,* a 1973 television movie based on John Steinbeck's famous short novel, and with a sea lion in *Salty* (1974).

By the time he graduated from Burroughs High School in 1977, Clint was seeking more adult challenges. Partly because of his diminutive stature and unusual snaggle-toothed looks, he found himself being cast in offbeat roles in outrageous low-budget films. A prime example is *Rock 'n' Roll High School* (1979), a midnight-movie favorite from Roger Corman's New World Pictures. Director Allan Arkush, who had become friendly with Clint while making *Grand Theft Auto*, cast him as a maniacal young wheeler-dealer named Eaglebauer, who operates out of a smoky school lavatory. Arkush was more than pleased with Clint's work: "He sold that character really well. He knew what the joke was." From *Rock 'n' Roll High School*, Clint went on to star as a demon-possessed cadet in something called *Evilspeak* (1981). Soon he was achieving cult status by playing nerds, sickos, and serial killers in a long line of exploitation flicks. One Internet fan site praises him this way: "Clint's sort of the [Laurence] Olivier of those *Man at Bar with Stuffed Weasel* roles."

While alternating between mainstream Howard projects and weird, wacky genre fare, Clint became increasingly caught up in a self-destructive lifestyle. This behavior was not entirely new: even during his high school years, though active in journalism and other campus activities, he was experimenting with drugs and alcohol in a way his brother never had. An aspiring filmmaker named Whitney Bain, who got to know Clint at the time of *Cotton Candy*, recalls spotting him at parties, "doing blow in the bathroom" and generally running amok. Though Rance and Jean Howard had reared their boys within the entertainment industry, they had tried hard to provide a home environment that kept Hollywood's excesses at bay. With Ron they were wholly successful. Clint's problems, which came to a head in 1990, showed that even the best-intentioned parents can't protect some kids from spinning out of control.

In the spring of 1979, Howard's second television movie went before the cameras. Once again, he was directing for NBC, under the Major H banner. The new project was a family movie, written by Rance and partner Herbert Wright as a pilot for a series that never materialized. Its working title was *Tut and Tuttle*, but by the time the film finally aired in two parts in December 1981, it was called *Through the Magic Pyramid*.

This time-travel story involves Bobby Tuttle, a suburban preteen who plays football to please his father, but is far more interested in magic tricks and the occult. After a humiliating game in which he carries the ball across the wrong goal line, he retreats to his room, strokes a crystal pyramid—and suddenly finds himself in ancient Egypt. There, golden-haired Bobby, who is first mistaken for a visiting god, befriends pretty little Princess Baket and the very young future king Tutankhamen. But he also becomes embroiled in palace intrigue spearheaded by a wily general who is out to topple the emotionally weak King Akhenaten. Ultimately, Bobby must use his twentieth-century smarts to save Tut's life and help place him on the throne of Egypt. Mission accomplished, he returns to his own time, newly hopeful about his future.

Through the Magic Pyramid is by far the clumsiest of Howard's television movies, partly because of a weak script. Dialogue proves particularly stiff among the Egyptians, who spout lines such as "Our living god is dead?" The story swings between lame attempts at humor and unconvincing threats of violence; the presence of the brassy and thoroughly contemporary *Laugh-In* star Joanne Worley as an Egyptian aristocrat strikes an especially discordant note. It can't be denied, though, that the film has its heart in the right place. A nice pitch is made for religious tolerance, and back at home Bobby's dad learns not to pressure his son on the playing field. And despite the contrived story line, the interplay of Bobby and his two young Egyptian chums has a certain appeal. But what's most interesting about *Through the Magic Pyramid* is that it presents a variation on a familiar Howard theme: the need to leave home to prove oneself. In *Grand Theft Auto*, as in some of Howard's later projects, the protagonist attains his dream only when he leaves his former world behind. But Bobby, having saved the day for King Tut, finds his reward in his own front yard, both in terms of renewed self-confidence and the promise of future romance (with a new neighbor who seems to be Princess Baket in modern dress).

The film was shot for about $1 million at Culver City Studios and at Havasu National Wildlife Refuge in the desert near Needles, California. The filmmakers used a kitschy Southern California tire factory built in pseudo-Assyrian style to represent an Egyptian palace. Costumes look as though they were made out of sheets and towels, and some very modern panty lines are visible through the thin fabric of the ladies' robes. Gary Graver, the *Grand Theft Auto* cinematographer who was hired by Howard to shoot this film, remembers that its chariots came from Paramount Studios—and dated back to Cecil B. DeMille's 1956 epic, *The Ten Commandments*.

Eric Greene, eleven years old when he was cast as Tutankhamen, believes Howard's own experience as a child actor gave him special insight into the handling of youngsters on the set. The role played by Greene called for wide-ranging emotions; without ever forcing Greene to imitate him, Howard was deft at suggesting the mood that he wanted conveyed. Greene remembers that before production began, "Ron gave me a lovely, huge coffee table book to try to give me a feel for what ancient Egypt was like and put me in the mindset of where I was going to be. When you're starting something new, and the director—especially a famous director—goes out of his way to do something like that, it gives you a feeling of being welcome." Greene, who evolved into a junior Egyptologist after filming was completed, treasures his book to this day.

Once again, the whole Howard family participated in Ron's new endeavor. Rance and Clint had small roles, and Cheryl played the football mom who yells to Bobby's father, "Your son is running the wrong way!" Even the Howards' Toluca Lake house got into the act, representing the porch and front steps of Bobby's home. Jean again took charge of casting and supervising the film's many extras. Miller Drake, a visual effects editor who met the Howards during *Grand Theft Auto* and later worked on several Major H films, vividly recalls Jean rounding up the extras, coating them with sunscreen, and making sure they got paid and fed. Jean's strawberry-blond hair had by then turned completely grey, which is why she remains in Drake's memory as "a little old grandmother with the white hair and the glasses, always smiling." Drake adds, "This family was always up, y'know. They were always good-natured and they were always smiling."

The Howards smiled, it seems, even when things went wrong. Because *Through the Magic Pyramid* used a nonunion film crew, members of the Teamsters Union showed up at one location and abruptly banished the production's catering truck from the set. Gloria Greene, mother of Eric, remembers that when the food suddenly disappeared, Jean sprang into action. She "went into town and got tuna sandwiches for everybody. It was like the whole family was there, the whole family was working, and the solution was met immediately." Under the circumstances, tuna sandwiches weren't such a bad lunch.

No one can accuse *Through the Magic Pyramid* of greatness, but it did receive at least modest critical recognition. In 1982 it was nominated for an Emmy for Outstanding Children's Program. Although it was the only nominee in its category (which excluded animated specials), it was not judged worthy of an Emmy statuette. So Howard, who was the film's executive producer as well as its director, lost out on his first chance for behind-the-camera glory. Years later, he was to say that *Through the Magic Pyramid* taught him "that I never wanted to do anything with children or special effects again." (It's ironic that some of his most successful films have contained both.)

In 1979, a few months after Howard shot *Through the Magic Pyramid*, his *Happy Days* contract came up for renewal. Paramount and ABC were confident that their Richie Cunningham would stay on, because they were planning to double his salary. But to the chagrin of many onlookers, the ABC brass continued to underestimate Howard's determination to direct. NBC stepped in and offered a mix of acting, directing, and producing opportunities, as long as Howard would commit to an exclusive arrangement with the network. The deal didn't offer a lot of cash, but, as Cheryl would later put it, "Ron's always been a big risk-taker." So, shortly before the start of the eighth season, Howard told the *Happy Days* gang that he would not be coming back.

The press had a field day discussing this turn of events. Many Hollywood-watchers suspected NBC's president Fred Silverman of luring Howard away from *Happy Days* to sabotage ABC's long-running hit. Garry Marshall confidently insisted that the series would survive even without Howard playing Henry Winkler's straight man. Marshall did, however, express the hope that Howard would appear on the show to wrap up the Richie Cunningham character. As Marshall told the *Los Angeles Times* on July 23, 1980, "After seven years it would be nice to exit him gracefully. Ron very much wants to do it . . . but he's under [exclusive] contract to NBC now, so it's up to them. We'll see how nervous they are. We'll see if Silverman is out to get *Happy Days*."

In fact, Howard was eventually permitted several return visits to *Happy Days*, and he remained a presence even when not on screen. In the eighth season, Richie was initially written out on the pretext that he had joined the U.S. Army and been posted to Greenland. He would marry girlfriend Lori Beth over the telephone (with his side of the conversation unheard by the audience), and in the ninth season Fonzie would act as a substitute Lamaze coach when Lori Beth gave birth to Richie's baby. In the fall of 1983, to launch the eleventh season, Richie would appear in a two-part episode, "Welcome Home," in which he visited his Milwaukee pals before leaving for Hollywood to pursue a screenwriting career. And on May 8, 1984, during the last *Happy Days* episode, he would come back for Joanie and Chachi's wedding.

Though Howard was desperate to find a life beyond *Happy Days*, leaving the show was not easy for him. Staff member Rich Correll still remembers the moment when Howard, known to be deep in final negotiations with ABC, phoned the set, asked to speak to Winkler, and broke the news. Soon after his departure, he told reporter David Alexander that "the difficult part is leaving a real comfortable home. . . . For a while there, I was really nervous and shaken by it." To others he spoke about the cast and crew as a family he would sorely miss. The emotions he felt for the *Happy Days* team are on clear display in the "Welcome Home" episodes. In a farewell scene with Fonzie, the two actors seem to be struggling to get through their lines. And the first part of "Welcome Home" ends with a tender interlude at the local hangout, where four old high school buddies harmonize on a song that has been Richie's favorite from the beginning, the nostalgic "Blueberry Hill."

Once he left *Happy Days*, Howard's life was newly precarious. He had assured reporter David Alexander that he was prepared to be out on his own: he owned a house, three cars (one a junker), and some rental property. But opportunities weren't coming fast enough to meet his needs. There were dark days when he talked about going into teaching, if all else failed. And Cheryl was ready to work as a bookkeeper, if necessary, to help keep the couple afloat. Nonetheless, Howard had one ace up his sleeve: a television movie he had shot in the summer of 1980, to air in November of that year. It was called *Skyward*, and it turned out to be—both artistically and commercially—the most successful of the television projects with which he sought to launch his directing career.

Skyward was the first of six projects made by Major H for NBC under the terms of Howard's new three-year contract. It was produced in conjunction with Howard's former *Happy Days* costar Anson Williams, who was also looking for new career options. While making a personal appearance, Williams had once chatted with a glum young man in a wheelchair, who complained, "I'm tired of looking up." From this, Williams devised a story idea about a disabled boy and an old black man who teaches him to fly an airplane. Writer Nancy Sackett transformed this bare-bones premise into a two-hour teleplay about a wheelchair-bound girl, overprotected by her well-meaning parents, who finds a new lease on life when she learns to pilot a biplane. *Skyward* was a landmark production because it was the first television drama in which a handicapped character was portrayed by an actor with a disability. For the role of sixteen-year-old Julie Ward, Howard chose Suzy Gilstrap, a plucky teenager whose spine had been crushed by a falling tree during a school outing. Howard showed courage in hiring as his leading lady a paraplegic who was also a complete acting novice. He was equally brave when casting formidable screen legend Bette Davis as the veteran stunt pilot who shows Julie how to take to the sky.

Howard has often recounted what it was like, at age twenty-six, to direct the seventy-two-year-old Davis. Then near the end of a long and distinguished career, Davis accepted this part because she had never before played an aviator. She loved the script, but was suspicious of her director's youth and inexperience. Howard admits he lost sleep over how best to handle this dragon lady. At first, she was icily polite, refusing to call him anything but "Mr. Howard," because, as she said, "I don't know whether I like you yet."

On the set, she loudly questioned his ideas—until he sweet-talked her into trying one scene his way, and she found herself pleased with the results. At the end of the shooting day, she patted him on the rump and said, "See you tomorrow, Ron." From that point forward, life on the set improved immensely.

What Howard quickly discovered was that actors—even legendary ones—respond well when they are treated as trusted collaborators. *Skyward's* screenwriter Nancy Sackett speaks of Howard too as wonderfully collaborative and always respectful of the abilities of those around him. Sackett and Howard huddled often; he offered fresh ideas and came up with ways to improve static dialogue scenes. Says Sackett, "I just remember it being a really good creative exchange. In the subsequent twenty years, I can't remember as good a one." Howard himself would later say that *Skyward* taught him both to trust his own instincts and to work in tandem with others who had strong, valid opinions. Even before it aired, he knew he had achieved something special: "This is my first serious film, the first one I feel has something positive to say. It's the first film I've directed that primarily depends on performances, not action or music or something else."

Others shared Howard's feelings for *Skyward*. Critics praised it for broaching big issues while avoiding cheap sentimentality, and it was roundly applauded by groups that advocate for the disabled. Among its honors was an award of excellence from the National Film Advisory Board; it also earned plaudits from the National Rehabilitation Association. The film's official premiere took place in Washington, D.C., in conjunction with a year-long federal focus on disability issues. In Los Angeles, Mayor Tom Bradley proclaimed "*Skyward* Day."

The response was so good that the following year Howard and Anson Williams joined forces to produce a sequel, *Skyward Christmas*, with the intention of launching a series. Unfortunately, Bette Davis and acerbic costar Howard Hesseman played no part in this new project. Nor was Howard its director, though he took an executive producer credit. And critics who had been charmed by Suzy Gilstrap in the original decided that her acting skills were limited. A fascinating side note is that once Gilstrap gave up acting, she found a niche within Howard's production empire. She has risen through the ranks at Imagine Entertainment, and in 2002, now Suzy Barbieri, she is vice president in charge of motion pictures.

Skyward was filmed at a small airstrip outside Dallas in 110-degree heat that proved daunting for cast and crew. But both Howards remember the summer of 1980 fondly, because Cheryl became pregnant during the shoot. When their redheaded daughter, Bryce Dallas, was born on March 2, 1981, her middle name was chosen to honor the city of her conception. Among Howard's old friends at New World Pictures, word circulated that the expectant father, a filmmaker to the core, had videotaped the birth. Meanwhile, newspaper accounts such as the one that appeared in the *Los Angeles Herald-Examiner* had fun dispelling the rumor that the Fonz had zipped into the delivery room on a motorcycle. *People* Magazine revealed, in an item entitled "Pappy Days," that because both Howard and Winkler were now new parents, they spent their get-togethers debating the relative merits of Pampers and Huggies.

Nancy Sackett, who was expecting her second child during the filming of *Skyward*, reaches for superlatives when she talks about the Howard marriage: "It's like they're this fairy tale couple. There's just this genuine sweetness and love between them, and a generosity which is very rare in Hollywood couples, in particular." A few years ago, Sackett and her husband spotted the Howards enjoying an anniversary dinner at a popular eatery near the Santa Monica pier. Ron and Cheryl promptly came over to Sackett's table, where for twenty minutes the two couples exchanged news about their now-college-aged daughters. Sackett, who has known plenty of show biz moguls, pays the ultimate compliment when she says of the Howards, "You never feel with either of them that there's any agenda."

Sackett has her own theory about how Howard has managed to succeed in a business where nice guys traditionally finish last. She notes that on *Skyward*, partner Anson Williams was the "pushy one" who made things happen. Not that Williams was anything but pleasant, but he had the *chutzpah* to hustle the project past all obstacles. Sackett suggests that Howard's style is "to surround himself with others who can do the dirty work, so to speak," while he remains his affable self. Today this good cop/bad cop dynamic plays out in Howard's partnership with Brian Grazer, which has become one of Hollywood's most powerful creative forces.

Skyward reflects themes that have been central to Howard's own career since *The Andy Griffith Show*. At the end of "Opie the Birdman," a child must learn to let go of the thing he loves: the baby birds must be allowed to fly away. At the climax of *Skyward,* when Julie's parents discover that she's been secretly taking flying lessons, they adamantly oppose what she's doing. Says her father, "You can get hurt up there." But, before storming out of the house, Julie makes a poignant plea: "If you love me, you'll let me go." The film ends with the Wards watching in awe as Julie soars through the clouds, leaving her wheelchair far behind. They love her, and now they've learned to give her the freedom to grow into an independent and capable young woman. She has made the leap and found her reward. Similarly, Howard, having made the big leap away from *Happy Days*, was now poised to soar into the stratosphere.

On June 3, 1981, a star-shaped plaque was dedicated in Howard's honor on the Hollywood Walk of Fame. Fittingly, it sits on Hollywood

Boulevard, in front of the ornate Paramount Theatre (now the El Capitan), where *The Music Man* had premiered in 1962. At the unveiling ceremony sponsored by the Hollywood Chamber of Commerce, fans and friends celebrated Howard's accomplishments as a television actor. The freckle-faced youngster who had once enchanted Hedda Hopper by jumping from star to star along the boulevard now had a star of his own.

But in 1981, Howard was no longer thinking about television or movie stardom. Though he still took the occasional acting role, his mind was now fixed on other things. When he left *Happy Days*, he had assured *TV Guide* that "if I ever got so busy with directing that I wouldn't have time to act, that would be OK with me." In truth, he had come to see the downside to being an actor: "Actors are always waiting to get hired. If you're not an absolute superstar, you're sort of at everyone's beck and call." At the end of 1981, as he prepared to direct his first studio film, Howard relished the chance to control his own destiny. From this point on, he would not be simply a performer in other people's movies.

PART III

First Successes

CHAPTER 7

Getting His Feet Wet

(1981–1984)

*"Sometimes I think I should do something
really outrageous just to wake people up."*
—RON HOWARD

A 1981 COMPENDIUM CALLED *THE BOOK OF PEOPLE* provides a thumbnail sketch of Ron Howard at age twenty-seven. Author Christopher P. Andersen describes Howard as five feet ten inches tall, 145 pounds, with hazel eyes and red hair. In the Personal Habits and Traits section, the reader learns that Howard "doesn't smoke, drinks beer, [is] eager, a perfectionist, sticks close to home." His income, taking into account his *Happy Days* earnings, is estimated at $800,000 a year.

By 1980 Howard and Cheryl had moved into a bigger home. The newly built country-style house, nestled among towering eucalyptus and pine trees, was set against the foothills of Encino, an affluent community in the San Fernando Valley north of Los Angeles. It offered 4,000 square feet of living space, with an adjoining guest cottage that Howard could use as an office. Luxury features included brick fireplaces, beamed ceilings, a formal dining room, and dramatic leaded glass windows in the breakfast nook. An electric gate kept out the world at large, and kept in the Howards' growing menagerie: two beagles, a basset hound, two cats, a land turtle, and the pet monkey. Years later, Tom Hanks impishly reminisced about the days when Ron and Cheryl "dared to live on the West Coast." Tongue firmly in cheek, he compared the Howards' Encino digs to the set from *Doctor Dolittle*: "There were goats and chickens; they had a big pool in the backyard and beavers were building a dam."

Interior designer Basia Asch Frank spent a year working with Cheryl on decorator touches. The completed home boasted floral print upholstery, pillows, and drapes in shades of burnt orange and forest green. The master bedroom became a favorite spot for the Howards to eat supper and watch *Happy Days* reruns. A gourmet kitchen with hanging copper pots allowed Cheryl to whip up special dinners for company, though she told *Good Housekeeping* that "Ron will eat just about anything." She made clear that her husband was a wholehearted participant in design choices: "Ron got really involved in the decorating. If he didn't like something, I would not order it."

While Cheryl was getting their house in order, Ron was forging a relationship that would play a major role in his future. He and Brian Grazer had been briefly introduced by NBC programming executive Deanne Barkley around 1978, but didn't click. Three years later, when both had offices on the Paramount lot, Grazer spotted Howard from his window, then phoned to propose lunch. Grazer remembers, "He was Opie and I was a twerp producer." He adds that Howard was extremely shy, and didn't take kindly to lunch invitations from strangers. To make matters worse, Howard had taken one look at the hyperkinetic Grazer and decided he was probably a cocaine addict. But Grazer has never been an easy man to deter. Combining the eagerness of a puppy with the persistence of a steamroller, he has long made his way through the Hollywood system by not taking *no* for an answer.

Grazer, the eldest child of a criminal attorney and a housewife, entered the world on July 12, 1951. Though he was born and raised in Southern California, his San Fernando Valley haunts were far from the entertainment industry that Ronny Howard knew so well. Grazer grew up in what he likes to call "*Leave It to Beaver* Land," those flat, pastel suburbs where life resembled the sitcoms he watched on television. Dreaming that one day he'd be special, he read *Richie Rich* comic books and fantasized about owning golden garbage cans.

In school Grazer struggled with dyslexia, not learning to read or write until the fifth grade. Though a mediocre student at Chatsworth High, he won a swimming scholarship to USC, where he was convinced he was the only student on campus who was not rich. He put in forty hours a week flipping burgers on the late shift at a Howard Johnson's; when he had saved enough to buy a Porsche, he spread the word that it was a gift from his wealthy dad. After graduating in 1974 with a degree in psychology, Grazer entered USC law school because, as he explains, "That's what I thought I was supposed to do. I thought that to be respectable you had to have a job like medicine or law." But his goals began to change after he heard law students talking about earning easy money as summer interns in the Warner Bros. legal department. Attracted by the prospects of a cushy job, Grazer made a phone call, and was quickly hired.

At Warner Bros., he lucked into (or finagled) an office that looked as big as a handball court, next door to the chairman of the board. The day he saw the studio's incoming president, Guy McElwaine, zoom onto the lot in his new Jensen Interceptor convertible was the day he decided that a law degree was not for him. Now determined to become a movie producer, he spent his hours shmoozing with the big shots, many of whom found him an amusing fellow to have around. Before long he had a solid grasp of how the film industry was structured, and what it took to get ahead.

Once he dropped out of law school, the gig in the Warner Bros. legal department could not last forever. Besides, he rubbed some of the younger vice presidents the wrong way. Grazer doesn't blame them: "Listen, if I were them, I would have hated me." But he swiftly rebounded, first landing a job as a talent agent, and then moving into television production with veteran filmmakers Edgar J. Scherick and Daniel Blatt. By 1978 he had earned a producer credit on two top-rated television movies, *Zuma Beach* and *Thou Shalt Not Commit Adultery*. In 1980 he signed an agreement to develop and produce television movies for Paramount Pictures, but by the following year his momentum had stalled. That's when he began cultivating the friendship of Howard. He soon broached one of his favorite ideas, based on an actual news item, about two guys who operate a prostitution ring out of a New York City morgue. Grazer crows, "I was afraid to pitch an idea this racy, but he loved it."

Howard maintains that he did not take to Grazer's idea quite so enthusiastically. He did, however, immediately recognize one of its great virtues: that it was not what people would expect of him. At the time, Howard was trying to develop feature-length screenplays with Lowell Ganz and Babaloo Mandel, who had been writers on *Happy Days*. They took a stab at Grazer's concept, came up with something funny, and a deal was made. When Grazer shopped the project around town, most studio bosses warmed to its premise, but were skeptical of letting "the kid from *Happy Days*" hold the reins. Fortunately Alan Ladd Jr., who then headed the Ladd Company at Warner Bros., was willing to take a chance on the young director, possibly because George Lucas stepped in to vouch for him. Grazer has pointed out that some of the studio execs who nixed a chance to work with Howard on *Night Shift* "are still around today, except now they're all trying to kiss his ass."

At the heart of *Night Shift* (1982) is the story of two opposites who form a partnership. Chuck Lumley is a mild-mannered nebbish who left the investment world to become a morgue attendant because he wanted something quiet. Bill Blazejowski, also known as Billy Blaze, is a raucous sort who bounces from job to job because he's too restless to stay put. He announces early on, "I'm an idea man, Chuck. I get ideas all day long." It's a line that has reminded many Hollywood insiders of Grazer's own brand of manic inventiveness. Grazer does not deny the similarities, and Howard told a *New York Times* reporter in 1985 that Grazer was indeed a more sophisticated version of Billy Blaze: "He kind of explodes. He's an energy broker. He's this spark that gets the ball of fire going and he does it as well as anybody I've ever seen." Howard himself cannot be confused with the sexually repressed and generally woebegone Chuck. Still, his quiet politeness, his sense of order, and his determination to come off as a nice guy are not so far removed from Chuck's basic personality.

When *Night Shift* was filmed, Grazer and Howard were not yet officially partners. Technically, Howard came onto this project as a director for hire. But, in light of their future relationship, *Night Shift* can be seen as a movie about an odd couple, made by the oddest of couples. The methodical, contemplative Howard has been compared to Yoda, with Grazer as his rash, intuitive Luke Skywalker. Grazer puts it another way: "We live in different universes. Ron sees grey. I live in a world in which things are only black and white." Nonetheless, they have been making films together for twenty years. In that time, Grazer has progressed from a Prince Valiant pageboy haircut to gravity-defying vertical spikes; Howard has gone from floppy red hair to practically no hair. Grazer hangs out near the ocean; Howard prefers the country-side. Following a messy divorce, Grazer has remarried; Howard's home life is a model of stability. Through it all, their friendship has endured.

When it came time to cast their film, the duo went after John Belushi and Dan Aykroyd. Howard diligently wooed Belushi, but could never get him even to open the script. At last he and Grazer settled for a newcomer, Michael Keaton, to play opposite Howard's old *Happy Days* pal, Henry Winkler. The third lead, that of the perky hooker who awakens Chuck into manhood, was filled by another relative unknown, Shelley Long. Thanks to her winsome performance in *Night Shift*, Long went on to nab the part of Diane Chambers (1982–1987) in the popular television series, *Cheers*.

Night Shift gave Winkler a role that reflected his own low-key personality. By this time, Winkler had embodied Fonzie for a decade. Though he loved this outrageous hipster character, he had often told colleagues such as *Happy Days*' Rich Correll, "I wish I had a part where I could not play Fonz, [but] be more like myself." The role of Chuck Lumley gave him his wish, but had a downside. While Winkler was playing a quietly comic version of himself, Keaton walked off with the movie.

Keaton at this point was a stand-up comedian with no feature film experience. Keaton explains what playing Bill Blazejowski was like: "Not only did and do I have a lot of energy—I decided my character was somewhat hyperactive. And Ronny couldn't quite get a handle on how to discipline me at first. I think I almost got fired from the job." In fact, the studio bigwigs, unnerved by what the dailies showed them of Keaton's helter-skelter approach, soon began pressuring Howard to recast the role. But Howard was a strong believer in what he called Keaton's "improvisational genius." Convinced that the performance only required some judicious editing, he cut together a few scenes, demonstrating to the moneymen that Keaton was a good investment. Though the film was only a modest success in theatres, grossing $21 million domestically, it has had a long, lucrative afterlife on videocassette and cable.

Night Shift also earned Howard some critical respect. Reviewers were tickled by the film's rowdy humor; even the *New Yorker*'s formidable Pauline Kael wrote that "it isn't much of a movie but manages to be funny a good part of the time anyway." A piece in the *Los Angeles Herald-Examiner*, entitled "Actors Who Made Their Move to a Director's Chair," prominently featured Howard, who was quoted as saying, "I think my strength lies in bringing some humanity to what could be very silly, zany sorts of situations." After *Night Shift*, Howard was also basking in praise from his peers. Near the close of production, Winkler enthused to *Variety* columnist Army Archerd that "he's sensational. He's a good friend, the best acting partner I ever had. Now, I see him run a movie and he's so good at it. He knows exactly what he wants and how to achieve it." No wonder that when the last day of shooting was over, Grazer and Howard toasted each another with champagne and vowed always to remember how good they felt.

For Howard, making a film about the call girl industry proved a pleasant vacation from his clean-cut image. He has said that one of his favorite *Night Shift* memories is of centerfolds romping around the set semi-nude. At the time, however, his feelings were slightly more ambiguous. In 1985 he told an interviewer that auditioning undraped actresses was not as exciting as he had anticipated: "I felt bad for the women, and they felt kind of awkward. So I'm probably more interested in what a girl can bring to the scene besides just a great body." As an R-rated feature about hookers, *Night Shift* certainly has its share of casual nudity. Clint Howard plays a hot-to-trot fraternity boy who is last seen lying in a morgue drawer, making out with a topless babe. Curiously, though, despite the bawdiness of its premise, *Night Shift* is a surprisingly sweet film. It talks about sex, but it believes in love. Although Long plays a prostitute, there's a wholesomeness to her coupling with Winkler that suggests fairy tales can come true. So Howard's trademark optimism about the human condition shows itself in a most unlikely place.

Night Shift was the first motion picture that opened with these now-familiar words: A Brian Grazer Production, A Ron Howard Film. It was also the first—but certainly not the last—Grazer/Howard collaboration to shine the spotlight on someone who needs to burst out of the cocoon he's spun for himself. The character Chuck Lumley worships peace and order. He regards his glass-walled office cubicle, deep within the New York City morgue, as a personal haven, complete with neatly tended plants and photographs. But once his private space is invaded by Billy Blaze, his life will never be the same.

The viewer quickly learns that Chuck is a man who will sacrifice his own deepest desires rather than risk a fight. On the subway, he puts up with a painful serenade by a panhandling saxophone player (Ron Howard, in a hilarious cameo), even writing a check when he runs out of pocket change. At home is a demanding, weight-obsessed fiancée, who in the bedroom becomes a paranoid hysteric. Chuck has only to enter the hallway of his apartment building to be attacked by a drooling Doberman, or a gaggle of uniformed Girl Scout types who mistake him for a mugger and hit him with their boxes of cookies. (A very young Shannen Doherty is one of them.) On the streets of Manhattan, he wears earmuffs, trying in vain to shut out the world.

No wonder that Bill's boisterous entrance into Chuck's inner sanctum poses such a threat. And no wonder Chuck soon gets swept up in Bill's wild schemes. To a man who feels suffocated by other people's expectations, Billy Blaze offers a heady whiff of freedom. So when Bill proposes they become "love brokers," using the morgue as their base of operations, Chuck allows himself to be persuaded. And when the scheme gets underway, he is the capable, methodical partner who makes it work. Meanwhile, an unlikely relationship is developing between Chuck and Belinda, the amiable hooker who lives across the hall. It's symbolically apt that when she comes to his apartment to make breakfast, she finds the rooms stifling. As she adjusts to Chuck's hothouse surroundings by casually stripping down to tank top and panties, her jaunty lack of inhibitions teaches him that there's more to life than keeping things tidy.

Yet neither Belinda nor Bill could ever be a perfect role model. In fact, Billy Blaze's childish disregard for everyday reality has doomed his plan from the beginning. After a police raid reduces Chuck's orderly world to chaos, the shenanigans in the morgue come to a halt. And it takes a good deal of comic commotion (some of it involving a sex club where Bill plays towel boy in a Tarzan suit) before Chuck can bring himself to lay claim to a future of his own making. In one sense he finds his manhood slightly earlier in the film, when he has the courage to send back an incorrect take-out order. His declaration of independence is simple: "I will no longer eat a sandwich I did not order." Come what may, whether or not he finds true and everlasting love with Belinda, at least he'll finally have the strength of character to make his choices stick.

By the time the final credits roll, Chuck Lumley has shown he can stand on his own two feet. And with this directing effort, Howard revealed his confidence in his own talent. True, his film is sometimes sloppy, sometimes self-indulgent. Gags are occasionally pounded too hard. But *Night Shift* has wit and zest and promise. It also offers a glimpse of Ron and Cheryl passionately smooching: they're the red-headed couple at whom Chuck looks askance as he enters his apartment building near the beginning of the film. Who can blame them? In *Night Shift,* Howard was showing the world that he has what it takes to soar.

Grazer has always been a beach person. When he lived in the exclusive Malibu Cove Colony, he became surfing buddies with Woody Harrelson and Tom Hanks, but his passion for the ocean predates these friendships. So it's not wholly surprising that after *Night Shift*, he turned to a story about a mermaid. The idea had been in his head for years. In 1985 he told Aljean Harmetz of the *New York Times* that it came to him soon after he met his future wife: "I saw this great girl in a bathing suit running down the beach and we stayed up all night and drank champagne. For the first time in my life I realized you can have true love." This romantic encounter, he claimed, led him to wonder what it would be like to meet a mermaid and then have to give up everything to win her.

Grazer admits that he sometimes has a tendency to stretch the truth: "There was a time in my career when I exaggerated everything. I mean literally everything." So his picturesque account to Harmetz is suspect. In an earlier interview, published within months of the triumphant release of *Splash* in March 1984, he explained he had conceived the film while tooling down L.A.'s San Diego Freeway, wishing he had the Jaguar, the beach house, and the fat wallet that would enable him to meet the perfect woman.

Whatever the genesis of *Splash*, it seems clear that the kid who loved cheerful fantasies such as *Mary Poppins* was now dreaming up wish-fulfillment movies for adults. The only problem was that the studios weren't buying the dreams he had to sell. Grazer's *Splash* concept, first adapted for the screen by frequent *Playboy* contributor Bruce Jay Friedman, kicked around Hollywood for seven years. Then in 1982 Grazer asked the *Night Shift* team—director Howard and writers Ganz and Mandel—to come aboard. Howard by this time was getting offers to direct other comedies, including *Footloose* (1984) and *Mr. Mom* (1983), which could have reunited him with Michael Keaton. On the day when Howard needed to choose between *Splash* and another enticing project, he was sick with fever and nausea, which he now suspects were psychosomatic. Grazer phoned him every hour on the hour, until Howard accepted the inevitable.

One reason for Howard's hesitation was that he did not want to follow *Night Shift* with another outrageous farce. Then Ganz and Mandel contributed a new script that played down the jokey underwater scenes of Friedman's original in favor of exploring the characters on dry land, where the mermaid's tail was magically replaced by human legs. The enhancement of the love story satisfied Howard, but there were still obstacles. Just when the Ladd Company, which had previously backed *Night Shift*, was about to move forward with *Splash*, a second mermaid project appeared on the Hollywood horizon. This one, budgeted at $30 million, boasted a team of heavyweights, including producer Ray Stark (*The Way We Were*), director Herbert Ross (*The Turning Point*), writer Robert Towne (*Chinatown*), and actor Warren Beatty; actress Jessica Lange was supposedly poised to join them. In the face of this high-powered competition, Ladd got cold feet, and so did virtually every major studio in town.

At last, the ever-persistent Grazer received a nibble from Disney. Howard had mixed emotions about directing a Disney film, because "it seemed just too perfect. Little Ronny Howard grows up to make films for Walt Disney studios. That bothered me." Still, he worked hard to assure the Disney brass that he and his colleagues were young and eager, and that their mermaid film would be first out of the gate, even if he had to edit nonstop. Ironically, the $30 million project never got made. And Howard and Grazer's frugal $8 million fantasy, the first release under Disney's new and more adult Touchstone banner, took in an impressive $62 million at the domestic box office.

Both Howard and Grazer put much faith in their casting intuition. But Howard credits his longtime assistant, Louisa Velis, with suggesting that he consider Tom Hanks, whose only claim to fame at that point was a two-year stint on the cross-dressing sitcom, *Bosom Buddies* (1980–1982). At first, Hanks was up for the part of the hero's devil-may-care brother, Freddy. But both John Travolta and Michael Keaton passed on the leading role of Allen Bauer, as did comic actors Bill Murray, Chevy Chase, and Dudley Moore. Ultimately, Hanks nailed the audition and got the job. Howard says now that what he discovered in Hanks was an ability to play the film's comic rhythms, "but not sell the integrity or the honesty of the moment down the river." Hanks himself recalls that once he got the role, "literally, my life was changed forever."

It was Grazer's idea to cast Daryl Hannah, best remembered for her lethal acrobatics in *Blade Runner* (1982), as the mermaid who names herself Madison when she comes ashore in New York City. Howard was skeptical at first about Hannah's claim that as a child she had tied her feet together to pretend to be a mermaid in the backyard swimming pool. But she turned out to be a strong swimmer and also a good sport about lying still for three hours while technicians attached her thirty-five pound rubber tail. She surprised everyone, however, by announcing that despite several previous body-baring roles, she was finished with on-screen nudity. So Howard had to talk her into being discreetly undraped in several key scenes to establish the mermaid's comfort with her physical form.

Another dilemma arose during the filming of the restaurant sequence in which her character chows down on a lobster. A devout vegetarian, Hannah suddenly realized that she could not do what the script required of her. Howard respected her scruples, but cast and crew were standing by, waiting to shoot the scene. After some hasty experiments, Howard had his propmaster stuff an empty lobster shell with a concoction made of mashed potato and hearts of palm, and Hannah (though she reportedly wept between takes over the lobster's sad fate) played the part as written. Here, as elsewhere, Howard's genuine rapport with his actors helped him surmount the kind of crisis that can stop some productions in their tracks.

Critics have almost universally praised Hannah in the film for her luminous sense of innocence and wonder. In guiding her portrayal of Madison, Howard was inspired by Steven Spielberg's *E.T. the Extra-Terrestrial* (1982), which features a similarly enchanted visitor discovering the miracles of American daily life. (Howard had taken daughter Bryce to see *E.T.* when she was eighteen months old: "It was the first film she sat through all the way, completely engrossed and understanding everything. It meant a lot to me.")

For Pauline Kael of the *New Yorker*, the film's single most memorable actor is comedian John Candy. He plays Allen's skirt-chasing brother, Freddy, who in his own outlandish way comanages the family produce business and helps Allen further his love life. Kael's review called Candy "a mountainous lollipop of a man . . . preposterously lovable," and applauded Howard for having the courage to turn him loose on screen. She also described Hannah as "a beatifically sexy Nordic goddess," and noted that Hanks "has the expressiveness of a little kid who can't hide a thing." Though she found the film's plotting imperfect, coming down hard on the cartoonishness of a mad scientist subplot, she admired *Splash* for its "friendly, tantalizing magic." Kael concluded that Howard's nearly thirty years as an actor had given him "a knack for bringing sweetness out of his performers without lingering on it."

Among the supporting cast of *Splash* are several members of the Howard family. Rance plays an angry produce customer, bellowing, "Where are my cherries?" Clint has a comic bit as a wedding guest. Cheryl is in the same sequence, standing outside the church along with Howard's assistant Louisa and a tall, striking blonde who looks very much like Grazer's new wife, Corki. (Howard has fun showing Freddy, true to form, surreptitiously trying to look up their dresses.) Another familiar face is Howard Morris—who had played Ernest T. Bass and directed several *Andy Griffith Show* episodes—in the role of the kindly Dr. Zidell. When Morris came to the Disney lot to audition, he and Howard embraced and chatted about old times. After his reading, Morris returned to his car, then suddenly heard feet running and a voice yelling, "Howie, Howie, wait, wait, *wait*!" Ron had raced across the parking lot to say, "I just wanted to let you know that you got the part." Adds Morris, "That hardly ever happens. In fact it never happens. . . . That was way beyond the call of duty, to be concerned about my feelings at a time like that, when he had the big responsibility of directing a film. But there he was, and I never forgot that."

Morris gives full credit to Rance and Jean Howard for raising their son to be sensitive to the needs of others. He calls them "lovely people. There was a lot of love there. And still is." But he also wryly remembers one conversation he had with Jean after winning his *Splash* role. When Jean found out he had been cast after only one audition, she admitted that she had been called back on three separate occasions, but didn't land the part. During a 1999 television interview, Jean chuckled about her son the director: "From the time he first started with this Super 8 camera, I worked very cheap. And I even brought the food and the cookies. So I always got the jobs. Now it's harder to get a job from him, y'know, when I'm expecting him to pay me money."

Because Howard uses his family members so often, many onlookers assume that they automatically nab the roles of their choice. In reality he is a tough taskmaster who always puts his film's aesthetic requirements ahead of family feelings. In his 1986 comedy, *Gung Ho*, he decided Clint wasn't right for a key role, so he gave him a smaller part, noting that "You have to do what's best for the picture." Fortunately, Ron's parents and brother are professionals, and they understand (which doesn't stop the rambunctious Clint from lobbying for what he wants).

Splash combines some of Howard's favorite motifs. The give and take between two very different brothers will show up again in such later Howard films as *Parenthood* and especially *Backdraft*. And the moment when Madison is "outed" as a mermaid will not be Howard's last comment on the plight of the instant celebrity. The way the newshounds bombard Madison and her captors with inane questions ("I'm from *People* magazine. Is she also seeing Burt Reynolds?") anticipates his satirical handling of the mass media in his 1999 film, *EDtv*. Most important, *Splash* is a film about confinement and freedom, caution and courage. It's no accident that when Madison first comes ashore, unabashedly naked, her first stop is the Statue of Liberty. Though she immediately learns about the need to cover up, modern Manhattan is in many ways liberating for her: she discovers television, ice skating, revolving doors, and Bloomingdale's, among other wonders. But finally, after a dogged pursuit by crackpot scientists, she is imprisoned in a large fish tank, where she is poked, probed, and threatened with dissection, much as E.T. was. When the opportunity for freedom arises, she must quickly return to the sea. At that point Allen must choose whether to risk it all to remain by her side.

Allen Bauer, rather like *Night Shift*'s Chuck Lumley, begins as a man who lives inside his shell. Fascinated by the ocean since childhood, he accessorizes his home with a large aquarium, but he cannot swim. Though Madison teaches him the meaning of love, at first he's not sure of the depth of his commitment. Finally, when her life and their love both hang in the balance, he takes the plunge. The film's triumphant final image shows the two lovers swimming joyously toward an underwater world of happily-ever-after.

On *Splash*, Howard too took the plunge, in more ways than one. Though a Southern California boy, he had never much liked the ocean: "It always scared me. I never wanted to go surfing out by the breakers." But to direct underwater sequences, he had to learn to scuba dive. Along with his leading actors, he was certified to dive up to seventy-five feet, and he surprised himself by enjoying the experience thoroughly. Soon he was in the Bahamas, thirty feet down, using hand signals and body language to communicate with cast and crew.

Becoming a film director has given Howard courage in more ways than one. To further his directing career, he has learned how to spend time productively with strangers. He also confesses, "I would never have gotten started traveling if I didn't feel I had to. I wouldn't have left Burbank." In a 1984 interview with Todd McCarthy for *Film Comment*, Howard was frank about his slightly reclusive nature. Despite his many years as a public figure, "I've always been a little shy, tended to keep to myself, was never sure what people think of me, not easy to get to know." He admitted that perhaps there was a reason why his first two films with Grazer, Ganz, and Mandel had focused on mild-mannered young men who must be forced into embracing life fully: "It's probably the four of us. We're all probably a little on the timid side and would like to be a little more like Bill Blazejowski [Keaton's role in *Night Shift*] or Freddy Bauer [the rogue played by Candy in *Splash*]."

It's instructive that Howard could view the brash and cheeky Grazer as somewhat timid. But neither of them held back when it came to enjoying *Splash*'s runaway success. The night the film opened, they hired a limousine and drove with their wives from theatre to theatre, relishing the sight of long lines snaking around the block. The previous day, Howard had signed to direct *Cocoon* for 20th Century Fox, while Grazer had just gotten commitments from Dan Aykroyd and Chevy Chase to star in *Spies Like Us*, his new film for Warner Bros. So when *Splash* opened big on March 9, 1984, both of them felt that they had truly arrived. Howard was later to call this one of the greatest nights of his professional life.

Splash went on to earn major accolades, including a Golden Globe nomination for best comedy or musical. (The prize went to *Romancing the Stone*.) The film was also nominated for screenplay honors, by both the Writers Guild of America and the Academy of Motion Picture Arts and Sciences. This meant that Grazer, as the originator of the idea behind *Splash*, was up for his first Oscar, along with original screenwriter Bruce Jay Friedman and the Ganz/Mandel team. The Oscar nomination validated Grazer's stature within the industry in a powerfully public way. As a director, Howard dreamed of something similar. But although *Splash* made his reputation, it gave him no plaques for his wall and no hardware for his trophy shelf. The golden statuettes were still years away.

CHAPTER 8

Lift-Off

(1984–1986)

*"Ron is so professional that I never stopped
to consider his age."*
—DON AMECHE, ACTOR, *COCOON*

IN THE WAKE OF *SPLASH*, THIRTY-ONE-YEAR-OLD RON
Howard was becoming a prominent player on the Hollywood scene.
Steven Spielberg sent a telegram praising his work and then invited the
young director to lunch. At the time, Howard was planning to shoot
another low-budget movie for New World Pictures, a thriller about the
Greenpeace crusade to stop the killing of whales. But everything changed
when producers Richard D. Zanuck, Lili Fini Zanuck, and David Brown
ran into a snag with their upcoming film for 20th Century Fox. *Cocoon*
(1985), based on an unpublished novel by David Saperstein, concerns a
group of senior citizens who sail off in a flying saucer in hopes of living
forever. Robert Zemeckis was scheduled to direct, but he left the project
because of complications with *Romancing the Stone* (1984). Zemeckis'
departure paved the way for Howard, who inherited an $18 million
budget and a cast packed with such acting legends as Hume Cronyn,
Jessica Tandy, and Maureen Stapleton. He also inherited a great deal of
pressure: cash-strapped Fox was desperate for a hit.

The Zanucks and Brown, knowing Howard's reputation for bringing in films on time and on budget, enticed him with a director's fee of around $1 million. Profit participation was also part of the deal. Though he was not pleased with the science fiction emphasis of the original script, which struck him as disturbingly reminiscent of Spielberg's *Close Encounters of the Third Kind* (1977), the story did touch on a topic that interested him greatly. Some years before, he and Cheryl had collaborated on *Old Friends*, a script built out of insights gained through Cheryl's work at a convalescent home. *Old Friends*, which failed to get off the ground either as a television movie or a low-budget feature, explored how the elderly—with their petty insecurities and social maneuvering—are not much different from people many years their junior. After mulling over the *Cocoon* draft with Cheryl, Howard realized it lacked an in-depth focus on the hopes and needs of its aging characters. The team at Fox accepted Howard's new approach, and the project moved forward.

When *Cocoon* was shot in St. Petersburg, Florida, Rance played a detective tracking down the missing seniors. (Jean was also in the film, as an elderly woman in a green muumuu.) Arriving on the set, Rance spotted Ron high up on a Chapman crane, efficiently putting cast and crew through their paces. For the first time, he recognized the extent of his son's achievement: "My kid is a director. By God, he's made it." During a 1999 tribute to Howard on the A&E Network, Rance disclosed to interviewer Harry Smith that "even telling you the story, the hair stands up on the back of my neck."

Others in the production shared Rance's strong faith in his son's ability. Stapleton, winner of Oscar and Tony awards in a career that has spanned five decades, said of Howard, "He seems like he's been doing it for years. He has common sense, and you trust a man with common sense." Hume Cronyn remembers that the three-month production required elaborate special effects shots, along with "a lot of stunt work required of elderly people like myself. I never once saw him lose his cool." These comments would not have surprised Brian Grazer, who told the *Los Angeles Times* in 1985 that his *Splash* colleague was "the most secure person I've ever met."

Grazer might think of Howard as secure, but Howard went into *Cocoon* believing that, for the first time in his directing career, he had something to lose. The film was challenging for several reasons. It mixed such disparate genres as comedy, science fiction, and inspirational fable. It encompassed multiple plot strands and lacked a central character with whom the audience could readily identify. As director, Howard was required to cope not only with massive visual effects and logistical complexities but also with a cast of veteran actors who, "given their age, were not either my pals or people whom I could quickly make my pals." No wonder he was quietly anxious. That anxiety made its presence felt through a recurring nightmare, like the ones that had plagued him at the start of each production since he first faced Bette Davis in *Skyward*. In the dream, he says, "I'm on a set, and something is just not clicking. I'm scrambling around, trying to make it happen, but I don't really have the answers." When he offers a tentative suggestion, everyone on the set turns to him and yells, "You've got to be kidding! That's the stupidest thing we've ever heard." Then, in his dream, the red-faced Howard lurches into a desperate song-and-dance routine.

Fortunately, in his waking hours, Howard had coping strategies that did not involve soft-shoe numbers. Because *Cocoon*, with its ensemble cast and crisscrossing story lines, reminded him of *American Graffiti*, he chose to emulate George Lucas, "not worrying about camera movements or actors hitting their marks, just letting a scene flow and attempting to catch it. I'm trying to allow the actors to forget the director as much as possible." What Howard soon discovered among the senior actors in his company was that each had a different approach, which it was up to him to blend into a unified whole. Of the four cronies whose actions dominate the film, Hume Cronyn devoted much mental energy to analyzing his role, while Jack Gilford called on the skills of a trained vaudevillian. The dapper Don Ameche, whose nimble breakdancing scene is one of the film's highlights, turned out to be an old-school Hollywood film actor who begged Howard to give him precise direction. Curmudgeonly Wilford Brimley was happiest when going his own way. A prime example is the fishing scene, in which his character breaks the news to his beloved grandson that he's leaving for outer space. With Howard's blessings, Brimley discarded the scripted lines and improvised a simple but deeply moving farewell. Says Howard, "It is one of the scenes I've always been proudest of, and I had virtually nothing to do with it."

In another respect too, Howard learned by listening to his actors. Early in the story, senior citizens sneak into a neighbor's swimming pool, and become rejuvenated by its magical life force. One scene requires Brimley (age fifty-one), Cronyn (age seventy-four), and Ameche (age seventy-seven) to cavort in the pool like youngsters, doing exuberant flips and dives. Out of respect for the age of his performers, Howard hired doubles to execute these stunts, then discovered the three actors were miffed: "They wanted to do it themselves. And they did. They really taught me that you can't generalize about what people can, or cannot, do because of age." So the director who looked young and the actors who looked old proved that with talent and good will they could do just about anything.

Cocoon is perhaps the quintessential Howard film, melding themes that have continued to surface since early in his career. The fact that the story's geography encompasses both sky and ocean can't help but remind the viewer of the ideas advanced in *Skyward* and *Splash*, about the basic human urge to make a leap into the unknown. *Cocoon*, like *Splash*, is a fantasy. But its characters are seeking something even more elemental than romantic love. When they sail off to find eternal life on a distant planet, what they desperately want is a way to undo the pain and humiliation of the aging process. The film faces head-on one of the most universal human fears, and this grounds *Cocoon* in a reality that tempers its whimsy.

Bound up with the film's departure motif is the notion of choosing (or not choosing) to leave home. Mary, played by Stapleton, hesitates to forsake the earth, chiefly because of the impressionable young grandson she must leave behind. At last she opts for the journey, out of fear of death and loyalty to her husband of many years. Others, however, make a different choice. Bernie (Gilford) is one old-timer who has from the beginning strongly objected to tampering with the laws of nature. Although his beloved wife, Rose, is fading fast, he pushes aside any suggestion that he use extraterrestrial magic to save her. He tells the others, "Nature dealt us our hand of cards, and we played them. Now we're at the end of the game, and suddenly you're looking to reshuffle the deck, huh?" Bernie's argument may have some philosophical merit, but Joe (Cronyn) loudly berates Bernie's stubbornness, calling him "the most frightened man I ever knew."

For Bernie, staying within his familiar cocoon is the only conceivable option. These feelings persist even after his wife's death, when he no longer has close human ties that bind him to Planet Earth. As his friends are on the brink of boarding their spacecraft, he shows up and is greeted warmly. He's coming not to join them, however, but to say goodbye. As he simply but eloquently puts it, "This is my home. It's where I belong." Art, played by Don Ameche, holds the opposite viewpoint, and has one of the film's strongest lines: "Men should be explorers, no matter how old they are."

Cocoon, though it ends with a powerful affirmation, is enriched by a hint of ambiguity. Flying off to outer space is a great adventure, but it also represents cocooning of a sort. By protecting themselves from the pain of death and loss, the film's space travelers are cutting themselves off from those defining experiences that all the earth's people share.

Howard screened *Cocoon* for Fox's new studio boss, Barry Diller, at a dicey moment: Cheryl was about to go into labor with twins. On that morning in early 1985, fortune smiled on the young director. The two redheaded baby girls delayed their appearance for another ten days, and Diller waxed enthusiastic about a project that had been set in motion by a previous regime. In fact, he was so impressed that the opening was slated for mid-June, when studios traditionally schedule their hottest summer flicks. The gamble paid off. *Cocoon* took in $7.9 million on its opening weekend, and went on to earn $76 million domestically. The PG-13 film scored with viewers of every age group, and many critics were delighted. The more tough-minded among them, such as Pauline Kael, griped that *Cocoon* contained excessive "ecumenical niceness," but the veteran actors won almost universal praise. In the *New York Times*, Janet Maslin wrote, "The cast functions as a graceful ensemble, with a warmheartedness that seems genuine without getting out of hand." Other writers compared *Cocoon* to the morality fables of two of Howard's cinematic heroes, directors Frank Capra (*It's a Wonderful Life*) and Preston Sturges (*Sullivan's Travels*).

Howard has long viewed *Cocoon* as one of his proudest achievements. He has also described it as his "doctoral thesis" in filmmaking. Always self-critical, he noted soon after the film came out that he was still learning how to tell stories through pictures. To Scott Eyman of *Moviegoer* he explained, "I didn't catch onto the visual side of storytelling for my first films. . . . I had no idea that with compositions you could help the actors tell the story. I thought it was just a question of catching the actors, of using the camera to record." He also candidly lamented to another reporter that contemporary Hollywood films relied too much on predictably heartwarming endings: "You go to a theatre, you want to be surprised, and I'm not being surprised enough." In touting the unexpected conclusions of personal favorites like *Butch Cassidy and the Sundance Kid* (1969), he seemed to be calling into question his own invariably upbeat fadeouts.

Nonetheless, he was delighted when Fox began pushing *Cocoon* for Oscar recognition, telling one reporter that "it's a fantasy even to be working on a movie that would be considered for an Academy Award." Though he described the annual Oscar race as an "imperfect" Hollywood ritual, he made it clear that he was thrilled to be in the running. As award season advanced, *Cocoon* racked up other nominations. It was among the five nominees for a best comedy/musical Golden Globe, though it lost out to *Prizzi's Honor*. Howard was even more exhilarated to be named one of the Directors Guild of America's candidates for best director of a feature film. He lost to Steven Spielberg (for *The Color Purple*), but felt honored to be in such august company.

Traditionally, DGA nominees are prime candidates for Oscar consideration, and Howard tried to improve his chances by being ubiquitous. Although he normally disliked courting publicity, he showed up on talk shows and anywhere else he was likely to grab attention, even serving as guest host of NBC's *Friday Night Videos*. But when the nominees were named, the list consisted of Hector Babenco (*Kiss of the Spider Woman*), John Huston (*Prizzi's Honor*), Sydney Pollack (*Out of Africa*), and Peter Weir (*Witness*), along with the legendary Akira Kurosawa for his Japanese-language epic, *Ran*. In light of this apparent snub, a friend of Howard's tipped him off that perhaps all his campaigning had been counterproductive: "Akira Kurosawa does not host *Friday Night Videos*."

Howard "felt a little lousy" the day of the nominations, but was consoled by *Cocoon*'s victories in other categories. During a rare family vacation in Puerto Rico, he was cheering in front of the television set when the film's visual effects team won a statuette. He also had an unexpected chuckle when Don Ameche accepted his Oscar for best supporting actor. Ameche knew that Howard had initially offered the part to veteran actor Buddy Ebsen, who had once been featured in an episode of *The Andy Griffith Show* called "Opie's Hobo Friend." So Ameche, in his thank-yous, expressed his gratitude toward Ebsen for being unavailable. Ameche's own triumph in the role, years after his long career seemed to have wound down, is an excellent illustration of what Howard calls the heart of *Cocoon*: "the discovery that something extraordinary and unexpected can happen at any time."

For Howard the year 1985 was a time when life was truly about the extraordinary. First came the birth of the twins, whom the Howards named Jocelyn Carlyle and Paige Carlyle. (In what had become a quirky Howard tradition, the girls' middle names reflect where they were conceived, the Hotel Carlyle in New York City.) Then audiences had an overwhelming response to *Cocoon*. And in late summer, Ron and Cheryl announced they were moving to Greenwich, Connecticut.

To those who questioned the move, Howard described it as an adventure. At first he stressed that the family would simply be renting a house, to experiment with East Coast life: "When Cheryl and I were still in high school, we used to dream out loud about living back East, about experiencing things like the change of seasons. We'd always set it aside, but now, before the kids are settled into school, is the time to try." Yet other interviews from this period suggested that a concern for the children's values was uppermost in Howard's mind. As early as 1980 he told reporter David Alexander that he hoped to protect any future offspring by moving out of the L.A. area. He was particularly emphatic when speaking to Jane Hall of *People* magazine in April 1986: "I'm very happy about the way I grew up, but I want my kids to know there are people who do things beside make movies and TV shows."

The prospect of his children turning into show biz kids had clearly left Howard with mixed feelings. In 1983 when Bryce, at two and a half, was running around the set of *Splash* yelling "Action!" and "Cut, please," he told *People* magazine he'd let his daughter choose her own path when the time came. By early 1985 he said he would most likely discourage his girls from entering the business as children, "but if I saw that it was their burning desire to try this, then I would do everything I could to help them become good." In 1989 he explained to reporters that any child of his who took up acting would face comparisons with little Ronny Howard. Besides, he and Cheryl could not provide the same degree of on-set supervision that he himself had once enjoyed: "My wife is writing every day, and I am always off somewhere. It wouldn't be fair to my children."

As his youngsters moved into their teens and showed definite signs of being stage-struck, Howard's mind appeared to be firmly made up. In 1996 he told Sheryl Kahn of *McCall's* that "I wouldn't allow them to be kid actors, knowing what I know." That same year, he admitted to David Hochman of *Us* that "the question comes up about once a week. They're all mad because I won't let them go on auditions." He explains his tough stance by noting that moviemaking can sometimes be tedious, and sometimes terrifying. And frequent rejection is part and parcel of the entertainment industry: "Children, especially during adolescence, don't need more rejection in their lives." Yes, he had survived the teen slump and other hazards of a juvenile show business career, but, as he has said, "I'm one of the few child actors who got through it without a lot of anger and resentment."

So the Howards' move to Connecticut may have been partly to shield their kids from the glamorous temptations of the film industry. But there's also a sense that Ron and Cheryl were actively looking for a new hometown. While the move forced them to leave friends and family members behind, it also helped them put a healthy distance between themselves and the pervasive forces of the Hollywood dream factory. Howard said as much when he described the cross-country relocation as a way to evade "the all-encompassing influence on our lives of the motion-picture business." He explained that for him a simple breakfast at an L.A. coffee shop likely meant being approached by a hopeful with a script under his arm. And he could never spend an evening at the multiplex without bumping into an actor or a studio exec with an agenda. Life in L.A. and its suburbs was all about making movies. Connecticut, he noted, "is intrigued by show business, but I don't think they think it's very important."

Director Joe Dante applauds Howard for choosing to make the break and also for being able to do so. Dante, a New Jersey native who lives in the heart of Hollywood, stresses that "most people are in this town because they have to be. Because when you go away they forget about who you are, and you've got to be around to get that script and make that call and take that meeting. . . . Ron has now gotten to a plateau where they come to him. He does it or he doesn't do it. And that's real success."

Greenwich, Connecticut, built on land purchased from the Siwanoy Indians in 1640, was originally settled by farmers and mill workers. By the late nineteenth century, Greenwich had developed into a posh resort area for those fleeing the noise and fumes of New York City, twenty-eight miles away. The beginning of the twentieth century brought huge landed estates nestled among the woods, lakes, and rolling hills of the Greenwich "backcountry." Within its fifty square miles, Greenwich also encompasses thirty-two miles of pristine shoreline on Long Island Sound. Today Greenwich is a fifty-minute train ride from Manhattan. It is known for its palatial houses, golf courses and yacht clubs, nature preserves and equestrian trails, and the major corporations that have moved their headquarters into the vicinity. Its two common nicknames are "Gateway to New England" and "Wall Street East."

Not all of Greenwich's 58,000 inhabitants are rich, but there are pockets of enormous wealth. Realtors say that the median family income is $82,000 per year, and that in 1997 the average price of a single family home first exceeded $1 million. One resident puts it another way: housing in Greenwich "ranges from expensive to out-of-sight expensive." Although local schools are excellent, many families opt for pricey prep schools, including Greenwich Country Day (founded in 1926), which counts former President George Bush among its alumni. Many locals choose to join one of Greenwich's eighteen country clubs, which offer golf, swimming, and other recreational activities in immaculately groomed settings. Until recently, such clubs barred Jews and other minorities, and permitted membership status only to men. Now the clubs have become slightly more liberal in their admissions policies, and female guests are no longer confined to the "mixed grill" when invited for lunch. Out-of-towners, however, are still kept at arm's length: they must pay $408 in annual permits to use local beaches.

The style of Greenwich is patrician but low key. Residents report that a few years ago, the "uniform" for wives doing errands in the colder months was jeans, a polo shirt (Ralph Lauren preferred), loafers or Sperry Topsiders, and a full-length mink coat. Styles have changed, however, and now mink coats are rarely worn, and most (though not all) residents forego Rolls Royces and Ferraris in favor of SUVs. Greenwich has its eccentric billionaires and Middle Eastern princesses, along with investment bankers and Fortune 500 CEOs. Celebrities in the area include Paul Newman, Rodney Dangerfield, and Diana Ross, though most are rarely visible. Howard, however, has become a familiar part of the community. Locals often see him—wearing baseball cap, down vest, and jeans—shopping at Staples, putting his kids on the train for Manhattan, eating sushi with Cheryl, and waiting in line at the local movie house. He frequently travels to Los Angeles and to film locations, but Greenwich remains his base of operations, and he feels very much a part of the neighborhood.

The property onto which the Howards moved would not qualify as an estate, but it sits in a secluded backcountry area. The house itself is so expansive that Jean Howard has compared it to "a small Ramada Inn." Big, grey, and traditional in style, it contains seven bedrooms, a screening room in the basement, an attic for Ron's office, and a separate space for his growing collection of hats. The living room overlooks a sylvan glade; there's a backyard with plenty of room for kids' play equipment, a vegetable garden, and a pen to hold the family's outdoor pets, which have included two dogs, a sheep, two African pygmy goats, and a Vietnamese potbellied pig named Fritz. Soon after the family moved in, they could count among their indoor brood a pair of cats, a parakeet, a guinea pig, and a corn snake. This environment was a paradise for the kids, who were soon enrolled in a prestigious private school.

It might seem surprising that two graduates of the Burbank school system would bypass the chance to send their offspring to a well-regarded public elementary school. Ron's enduring celebrity, however, was surely one consideration. The children of the famous can all too easily become targets. Rosie O'Donnell, who moved into the Greenwich community shortly after wrangling with the National Rifle Association, planned to send her son to his neighborhood school accompanied by a bodyguard. (The public furor over this issue was so great that she and her family quickly moved away.)

The Howards' goal has been to shield their kids from public curiosity. For years the youngsters were never allowed to be photographed for publication; in newspaper and magazine profiles of Ron, Cheryl was sometimes included, but the children always remained unseen. This did not, of course, rule out holiday cards bearing photos of the entire brood. Actor Gedde Watanabe, who starred for Howard in *Gung Ho* (1986) still treasures a card he received from the family's first Connecticut Christmas. They're all huddled together as if for warmth, and the message reads, "Here we are, and we're freezing!"

Occasionally Howard tells reporters that his wife "ultimately twisted my arm" to move East. While longtime Howard associates insist he is no pushover when it comes to decision making, he does rely on Cheryl to provide him with a life outside the film industry. As he told

one interviewer, "This business can just devour you in so many ways."
For him it's a saving grace that Cheryl doesn't accept the Hollywood
system as gospel. Howard feels he's lucky to have a spouse who can
"very nicely say, 'Cut the crap and let's go to brunch.'"

By 1986 Howard had completed his transition from acting to directing
and from California to Connecticut. But in February, he could not resist
flying back to Hollywood to act in a two-hour television movie called,
fittingly enough, *Return to Mayberry*. There was some talk about him
directing, but he politely declined, because "I grew up on that show. I
guess I would still be a little in awe of directing Andy Griffith or Don
Knotts. I would be too worried about it." In fact, he was worried even
about showing up: "I went into it with the trepidation anyone has with
reunions. My memories are rich and special and important to me and I
hated to have them spoiled in any way." Fortunately, once on the set he
quickly discovered that "the feelings are still there." Andy Griffith
teased him about being too young to have his name on a director's chair
and seemed pleased when Howard asked for advice on his first scene.
The rest of the cast let him know they were proud of his accomplishments. And they trotted out a big cake to celebrate his thirty-second
birthday in style.

When *Return to Mayberry* aired on April 13, 1986, half the people
in the United States who owned television sets tuned in. The story
includes all the familiar characters. Andy Taylor, now married to Helen
Crump and living in Cleveland, pays a sentimental visit to Mayberry,
where his former deputy Barney Fife is running for sheriff. Howard's
character, Opie Taylor, now sports a mustache, edits Mayberry's newspaper, and is married to a young woman named Eunice, who is about
to make him a father.

The usual Mayberry high jinks occur. Barney romances Thelma
Lou; Ernest T. Bass plants a phony monster in Myers Lake; Andy gets
his old job back and delivers his grandson in the rear seat of a squad
car. Early on, Opie breaks the news to his father that he's been offered
a better newspaper job in New York State. The dilemma: should he

leave Mayberry? His hometown has given him steady work, lots of good fishing, close friends, and, as he says, "I can't imagine a better place to raise a family." When he asks, "Am I better off just stayin' put?" Andy insists this is not a decision a father can make for his grown child. Then he launches into one of his folksy stories. Reaching back to the lessons of "Opie the Birdman," he talks about raising songbirds. Even when they're no longer babies, it's tempting to keep them close to home. But one day there comes a "time to let 'em spread their wings, see how high and how far they [can] fly."

The movie's last scene is the long-delayed wedding of Barney and Thelma Lou, conducted by Rance as the local minister. After toasting the newlyweds, Andy announces that Opie and his new family will be heading for New York. His final words are directed to the entire cast: "No matter where life takes you, you always carry in your heart the memories of old times and old friends." So Opie, his heart full of memories, is flying off to find his future. Opie's impending move nicely parallels that of Howard, who had shown he could leave Hollywood to weave his own world somewhere else.

CHAPTER 9

Small World

(1985–1989)

*"At this point in my life, there are so few
things I'm sure of—that makes me a good
collaborator."*

—RON HOWARD

IN APRIL 1985, A FEW MONTHS BEFORE HIS MOVE TO
Connecticut, Ron Howard told Lisa Birnbach of *Parade* magazine that
he was a "recovering workaholic." So obsessed was he with show business that he knew he could easily lapse into sixteen-hour days. As he
explained to Birnbach, "I've only felt that I was of value to people when
I was working. That's the only time I've been useful and interesting."
Perhaps the prospect of relocating outside of Hollywood emboldened
him to think beyond this narrow self-assessment. By June 1985 he was
conceding that he had more to offer than merely his work ethic. Still,
he saw that the public's view of him had not kept pace with his own
evolution: "I am painted as a more boring guy than I am. But every time
I try to project something different, it doesn't work. I don't have the
energy to create a hipper persona."

Perhaps to upend his square, middle-of-the-road image, the thirty-
one-year-old Howard agreed to his first interview for *Playboy*. He

appeared in the men's magazine in August 1985, for a rollicking conversation that proved that nice guys don't need to be dull. A full-page color photograph seemingly designed to present a newer, hipper Howard accompanied the article. In it he's wearing jeans, a trendy mauve Hawaiian shirt, and a black fedora tipped at a rakish angle. He also sports a shaggy mustache that does not conceal an impish smirk. Howard stands facing the camera, caught in the act of dropping a fuzzy brown teddy bear into a trash can. The photo seems both offbeat and symbolic.

Since this was *Playboy*, the conversation not surprisingly turned to the topic of sex. Howard good-naturedly detailed some childhood encounters with the birds and the bees and confessed which Hollywood actresses he'd like to direct in a nude scene. (One was *Laverne and Shirley* star Penny Marshall, because "what she would go through would be hysterical.") He confessed to poor exercise habits, and admitted that he himself was not a good candidate for a nude scene: "My butt is too lumpy." Howard also set forth some earnest rules for movie folk hoping to maintain a successful marriage. He warned against extramarital affairs on the set and against undervaluing the hours dedicated to home and family. Also essential: "Never work with your wife." Citing his single script collaboration with Cheryl, he noted the end result had been quickly dismissed by studio bosses as nepotism. Even more crucial, in Howard's eyes, was the fact that having a spouse as a full-time professional partner "means you can't go home and escape the business. You don't have someone to give you real perspective on what you do."

Howard told *Playboy* that the years had taught him, above all, how to seize control of his own life. But one part of him seems to enjoy those situations in which he can safely let himself go. At sporting events, he often gets seriously rowdy when rooting for his team. In 1986 he disclosed to Debby Bull of *Us* that in the privacy of his home he has sometimes danced around naked (though only on the nannies' day off). Possibly because of the huge sums he commanded in the *Happy Days* era, he lacks his parents' cautious approach to money. He does not indulge in personal extravagances such as flashy clothes and sports cars: he may test-drive a Porsche, but his tastes run to Volvos and an

AMC 4x4. Still, interviews suggest that, to keep his household running smoothly, he spends much of what he earns. As he put it to Bull, "my directing salaries just pay for our lifestyle."

After *Cocoon*, Howard found himself in the comfortable position of no longer needing to be a director for hire. Surveys established that his name in the credits could bring audiences into theatres. Clout of this sort is priceless in Hollywood, and industry watchers began to wonder what Howard would do next.

He was sure of one thing: he did not want do Fox's proposed sequel to *Cocoon*, even though it would reunite the members of the original cast. For Howard, "*Cocoon* should stand alone on its merits—and leave the future of the characters to our imagination." So Hollywood veteran Daniel Petrie came on board to direct *Cocoon: The Return*. The new film, in which the space travelers come back to Florida to visit the loved ones they've left behind, was released in 1988, only to be dismissed by critics as a pale imitation of the original. Audiences stayed away. Howard was either smart or lucky to have given this project a pass.

But his own choice for a follow-up film was not much more fortunate. Howard, who had little interest in being hailed as an auteur, instinctively gravitated toward another comedy. Mainstream humor, he felt, suited his talents: "I'm glad some people are making esoteric pictures that only twenty people understand, but that's not for me. People have expectations from a comedy, and you have to fulfill them." *Gung Ho*, a lighthearted film about an international culture clash, was already in development when *Cocoon* hit it big. Produced through Howard's own company in conjunction with Paramount Pictures, it was released in April 1986. It would prove to be one of Howard's gravest miscalculations.

Gung Ho (1986) was inspired by a segment on *60 Minutes* covering the opening of a Nissan plant in Smyrna, Tennessee. Lowell Ganz and Babaloo Mandel, the writers behind *Splash*, concocted a story about a Japanese automaker who takes over a factory in a dying Pennsylvania industrial town and then expects the local workers to build cars the Japanese way. The film was designed to be grittier than Howard's earlier hits, dealing with such real social issues as unemployment and cross-cultural misunderstanding. In depicting a blue-collar American town, Howard called upon his memories of Burbank, where the livelihood of many family friends was bound up with the shifting fortunes of Lockheed Aircraft. But, true to Howard's optimistic nature, *Gung Ho* ends in a celebration of teamwork that transcends cultural and national boundaries.

Studio bosses were pushing for Bill Murray or Eddie Murphy as the film's leading man. When both proved unattainable, Howard was happy to go with Michael Keaton, who had been in his mind all along. Because of Keaton's breakout success in *Mr. Mom* (1983), he was now considered a bankable star. Howard wooed Keaton to play his working-class hero by saying, "I'd like to do it with you because I think we'd have a lot of laughs." Keaton's character, Hunt Stevenson, is a local with a gift for gab who is tapped to serve as a liaison between the Japanese bosses and the American workforce. His opposite in the film is Kazihiro, the very young and very conflicted Japanese manager of the plant. Gedde Watanabe won this pivotal part by convincing the audition team that he was a native of Japan for whom English was a second language. Once the role was his, he came clean, confessing to a nonplussed Howard that he had been born in Utah and his knowledge of Japan was limited.

Watanabe (who now plays a featured role on television's *ER*) has the highest regard for Howard as a director, aptly using a car metaphor to explain why Howard's actors like him so well: "You're driving a Cadillac, basically." On the set, he found Howard both responsive and remarkably patient, eliciting top-quality work from his cast and crew through the simple expectation that everyone would come through with flying colors. Says Watanabe, "I've never seen him scream or yell, but I think when he really wants something done, he just zings in. And it's done in such a way that you just do it." The term Watanabe uses to describe the atmosphere on a Howard set suggests Howard's own recollection of *The Andy Griffith Show*: "focused fun."

Gung Ho turned out to be a truly international production. The film opens by depicting Hunt Stevenson, All-American auto worker, as a fish out of water in Tokyo: Howard fondly recalls the three days in which he, Keaton, and a cameraman scooted around the Japanese capital in a minivan, inventing comic vignettes. The factory town of Hadleyville was represented onscreen by Beaver, Pennsylvania, where the local folk were so keen to be extras that 5,000 turned up, most of them willing to work until 4:30 A.M. But because American automakers would not allow *Gung Ho* to be filmed in their assembly plants, all factory scenes were shot south of the border, in Buenos Aires. The people of Argentina were cordial hosts, but Howard could sense political tensions beneath the surface.

Howard's aim all along had been to poke good-hearted fun at both cultures, ridiculing rampant American individualism along with the Japanese penchant for discipline and self-effacement. But in *Gung Ho* his balance seems off-kilter. The good guys on the Japanese team do not come into their own until they have embraced American consumerism (Hawaiian Punch, Jimmy Dean Pork Sausage Links, Green Giant Frozen Niblets) and sloppy American shortcuts on the assembly line. And although some of the American workers are little better than oafs, they remain far more amiable than the worst of the Japanese. The film has no American equivalent to Mr. Saito, the sour Japanese executive who is played by Sab Shimono with a perpetual scowl. Saito tries hard to undermine the whole cross-cultural enterprise, until the top man from the Tokyo office (after a breakfast of silver-dollar pancakes) makes an abrupt and thoroughly unconvincing about-face that saves the day.

Critic Roger Ebert of the *Chicago Sun-Times* had little affection for *Gung Ho*, which he lambasted for its lack of attention to social detail, its "fistfights in lieu of dramatic development," and its wildly shifting tone. In the *New York Times*, Vincent Canby called *Gung Ho* a very mild situation-comedy that's "more cheerful than funny, and so insistently ungrudging about Americans and Japanese alike that its satire cuts like a wet sponge." Audiences apparently agreed: *Gung Ho* took in a mediocre $36 million at the domestic box office.

True to form, Howard read no reviews for several months, finding it "just too much of a roller coaster" to contend with the critical boos and bravos. But he admits in retrospect that the film's basic plot problems were never solved. He has chalked up *Gung Ho* as a learning experience, but remains fond of its best scene, in which the beleaguered Kazihiro suffers a drunken meltdown at the local bowling alley. The scene's hilarious interplay between Watanabe and Keaton serves as a reminder of Howard's approach to life, with its easy tolerance for people of all persuasions.

After the release of *Cocoon* in March 1985, Howard would have appreciated some time off. But plans for *Gung Ho* had come together rapidly, and he shot the film starting in July, not long before the family's cross-country move. When *Gung Ho* premiered in April 1986, it marked the fourth major motion picture directed by Howard in less than five years. So he promised himself and his family a six-month break from filmmaking.

Howard candidly admitted that he hoped to spend much of his downtime working on the romantic side of his relationship with Cheryl. He confessed, "I'm looking forward to it. You get that girl revved up, and it's pretty exciting." Obviously, the spark between them was successfully rekindled. When the family flew to England in January 1987 in preparation for Howard's next film, Cheryl was once again pregnant. In April 1987 the couple's first and only son was born in a London hospital. The redheaded newcomer was dubbed Reed Cross. To those who remembered the family tradition of giving the children middle names based on the place of their conception, Howard cheerfully explained that his son bore the name of a street, because "Volvo isn't a very good middle name."

Though Howard had shifted his focus to his personal life, he did not neglect business altogether. Brian Grazer had played no part in *Cocoon* or *Gung Ho*, and he remained in Malibu while Howard moved to Connecticut. Nonetheless, the odd-couple friendship endured, and by 1986 it had evolved into serious discussion about a long-term partnership. The men planned to follow the traditional route for independent producers, first developing film and television projects, then persuading major studios to help finance them. To raise capital, they decided on a public offering. Howard made valuable contacts by taking a two-week rafting trip with a group of wealthy venture capitalists, including Herbert Allen of the investment firm Allen and Company. He also met with other potential investors, selling them on what one veteran Hollywood observer calls "the Opie vision of the world." By August 1986 he and Grazer had raised $13.3 million through sale of stock at $8 a share, and Imagine Films Entertainment was officially launched.

Grazer explains that the new company's whimsical name "came from the 'what if' premises of our movies. What if I had no job and ended up working in a morgue? What if I met a mermaid?'" Although Grazer's love of finagling made him the obvious deal maker, he has emphasized that Howard's unflappable personality was a distinct business asset from the start: "He's uniquely intelligent and he's tough. He's not an easygoing guy. He's calm, but he's not easygoing." Grazer also saw in Howard a competitive streak that rivaled his own. A great advantage of their partnership is that, in Grazer's words, "we're not competing with each other but we're competing . . . against the world."

With the help of their lawyer, Thomas P. Pollock, Howard and Grazer structured lucrative agreements with entertainment companies such as Showtime. Eventually Pollock moved on to Universal Pictures, where he rose to chairman of the motion picture group. In 1987 he worked out an arrangement through which Universal would not only distribute Imagine's films to theatres but also underwrite much of their production costs. Universal's parent corporation, MCA, committed to investing $10 million, controlling nineteen percent of Imagine's stock.

The intimate relationship between Universal Pictures and Imagine Films Entertainment was vastly different from the usual deals between Hollywood studios and independent filmmakers, in which a studio covers a film's distribution and marketing costs in exchange for a share of its box-office receipts. But Howard and Grazer's reputation for cranking out quality product seemed to promise big returns. In 1989 Pollock explained Universal's position: "Instead of setting up a situation where we have no incentive to push a picture, we have a large stake in it, and we have a large stake in the financial future of Imagine." The hope, of course, was that Imagine would make a string of hits from which Universal too could profit.

At first, profits did not come easily. The initial deal was that Howard and Grazer would each draw an annual salary of $450,000, and keep 55 percent of any producer or director fee, while plowing the rest back into their new venture. For the first few years, most of Imagine's revenue derived from the two men's earnings when they hired themselves out to other companies. A large share of the $2.2 million Howard received for directing George Lucas's 1988 movie *Willow* showed up as income on Imagine's books. Not until 1989 did audiences get a look at the first three films made under the Imagine banner.

First, however, was *Willow*. For *Gung Ho*, Howard had been a globetrotter, jetting to Japan and Argentina with his cast and crew. For *Willow* (1988) he was packing his bags once again. Principal photography for this fantasy epic took place in England, Wales, and New Zealand. But Howard also found himself traveling through misty regions that existed only in George Lucas's mind.

Lucas first conceived of *Willow* at least a decade before the film was shot. In 1983 he alerted Warwick Davis, who played tiny Wicket the Ewok in *The Return of the Jedi*, that he hoped to feature a little person as the hero of an adventure saga. But Lucas, though he had directed both *American Graffiti* (1973) and the original *Star Wars* (1977), was a shy man who did not have an easy rapport with actors. Lucas, in fact, much preferred the producer's role, and throughout his career has often delegated the director's job to someone else.

Howard had kept in contact with Lucas since his *American Graffiti* days. For *Cocoon*, he used Lucas's renowned special effects company, Industrial Light and Magic, known in the industry as ILM. In 1985 Howard visited Lucas at his Skywalker Ranch in Marin County, California, to discuss his own idea for a fantasy film. That project didn't fly, but Lucas soon approached Howard about directing *Willow*, which he would finance. Howard was at first hesitant about making someone else's movie, but the prospect of collaborating with Lucas and the ILM wizards intrigued him. He also thought back to his childhood, when his father had delighted him with made-up stories about Tiny Tim and his magic toothpick. Cheryl's pregnancy eventually tipped the balance. It reminded him that five-year-old Bryce and his toddler twins would soon be the perfect age to appreciate big-screen fantasy.

The script for *Willow* required an ongoing conversation between Lucas, Howard, and screenwriter Bob Dolman, who had first worked with Howard in 1983 on a failed *Our Gang*-style television project called *Littleshots*. Dolman's strength lay in characterization, while Lucas focused on action sequences and on the story's mythic underpinnings. He even invited Joseph Campbell, noted mythologist and author of *The Hero with a Thousand Faces* (1949), to dinner, so the collaborators could look to him for inspiration while developing the broad outlines of their plot.

At the center of that plot is the journey of Willow Ufgood from his home among the Nelwyns, a race of little people less than four feet tall. A farmer who dreams of becoming a magician, Willow suddenly finds himself entrusted with a full-sized (or "Dakini") baby. This baby is Elora Danan, whose survival spells doom for the evil Dakini queen, Bavmorda (Jean Marsh). In his travels to return the infant princess to her rightful home, Willow encounters vicious "deathdogs," frightening trolls, beautiful fairies, a sorceress trapped in the body of a rodent, and pugnacious brownies nine inches high. He also meets a scalawag Dakini warrior named Madmartigan (Val Kilmer) who becomes his friend and strong right arm along the way. They survive battles and breathless escapes aplenty before Willow uses his budding magic skills, along with his native wit, to defeat Bavmorda and restore the forces of good. With the future of the Dakini realm ensured, Willow can go proudly back to his own people, knowing that his small stature has not stopped him from becoming a true hero.

As the script for *Willow* evolved, Howard frequently functioned as the voice of reason. He demanded that the use of magic within the story be consistent and logical, given the internal rules of the world the team was creating. It was a tough role, and Howard soon came to realize the perils of trying to deliver another man's vision. Lucas had made

clear from the start that during production he would be present only
to lend technical support, allowing Howard to be fully in charge.
Steven Spielberg, who had directed all three *Indiana Jones* films for
Lucas, assured Howard that "you're going to love working with
George. Sure, he used to be a director, but he believes in directors completely, and any time he steps on your toes, it'll just be out of excitement." Still, the force of Lucas's personality remained unavoidable. On
the set, Howard would quip that he didn't always view himself as the
director of the movie: "I feel like I'm vice president in charge of cinematic affairs for Lucasfilm." He was joking, but once *Willow* was
completed, he vowed that he would never again try to convey a world
with which he couldn't personally identify.

Nonetheless, *Willow* was a remarkable learning experience. For one
thing, Howard got a full education in cutting-edge visual effects. The
film, which was nominated for an Oscar in this category, contains some
four hundred special effects shots, an enormous number for 1988
(though today's effects-heavy action films might feature as many as two
thousand). Thanks to the ingenuity of the folks at ILM, the on-camera
transformation of the good sorceress Fin Raziel from a goat to an
ostrich to a turtle to a tiger to a woman was accomplished through a
new computer process not yet called "morphing."

While discovering the power of visuals in telling a story, Howard
also gained from *Willow* a new understanding of how to stage action
sequences. The film features massive battles, one with a two-headed
dragon, and such bravura moments as a breakneck ride on a runaway
sled. The sled ride was among the dramatic sequences filmed in the
snowfields of New Zealand, a thirty-hour flight from London.
Because of the rugged terrain, cast and crew had to be shuttled to
their mountaintop location each day via helicopter, and went through
their paces in the freezing cold. Behind-the-scenes footage shows
Howard comfortably bundled into a parka and woolen cap, while his
bareheaded performers are trying to keep warm in their thin costumes. (This, Howard has pointed out, is another advantage that

directors have over actors: they can dress for the weather and never worry about how they look.)

His work with the actors in *Willow*, especially Warwick Davis in the title role, made Howard feel most at home. Davis had played various *Star Wars* creatures for Lucas, but had never had a role of this magnitude. For the first time, he would be without a mask and a creature suit, and the range of his emotions within the film would be huge. Though Davis was Lucas's clear choice, Howard exercised his director's prerogative to conduct a worldwide search for other short actors. Part of his concern was that Davis was only seventeen years old. Not only did the part of Willow call for him to interact with a baby, but his character was supposed to be a loving husband and the father of two young children. There followed an extensive audition period, which culminated in Davis reading opposite a series of actors (John Cusack among them) who hoped to play Madmartigan. Davis still recalls Val Kilmer sauntering in, scruffy and sandaled, with his face sunburned from a ride in an open-topped convertible. Once the session was over, Davis learned he had won his role.

From then on, Davis, who had never before lifted a baby, was put through an informal training course on how to care for an infant, diaper changing and all. Howard also arranged lessons in diction, sleight of hand, and horsemanship. Davis recalls that Lucas was more of a technician as a director, telling his actors where to start and stop, and leaving them free to shape their performances as they chose. Howard, he notes, devoted much rehearsal time to discussing interpretations and was skillful at suggesting (though not forcing) the emotions he wanted conveyed. For *Willow*, Howard suggested that Davis study the films of James Stewart, because Stewart's natural, down-to-earth style was what Howard sought in his leading actor.

Davis calls Howard "the most giving director" he's worked with, and says he cannot imagine anyone in his position being more supportive. Howard's patience particularly stood out when he guided the young actors who played Willow's children. They, like most of the 250 little people who were recruited from around the globe to populate the Nelwyn village, had never acted before. The two weeks spent shooting on Nelwyn-sized sets outside London proved both challenging and exhilarating. Howard has emphasized how much he relished being part of this miniature world among people much smaller than himself: "To see them interacting, performing, working hard, laughing, playing, carrying on . . . that was to me I think maybe the greatest experience in the movie."

Willow provided other experiences as well. In Wales, Howard spent four days shooting a major battle sequence in unrelenting rain and mud. In New Zealand, minor injuries occurred and an expensive camera got broken. A nicer surprise was the real-life romance that ignited between Val Kilmer and his leading lady, Joanne Whalley, who played Bavmorda's fiery warrior-daughter, Sorsha. Their blossoming relationship prompted Howard to reshoot the film's big romantic scene, to take advantage of the added heat. Through it all, Howard quietly bore up under the strain of being in charge of such a massive undertaking. Davis remembers Howard as always focused and introspective between shots. Instead of idly chatting with the others, "he would walk around, with his head down, and he would always be fiddling with something in his hand, like a twig or just some sort of object he would be moving through his fingers. . . . That's one of the images I have of him when I think back, just thinking about the next shot, and what he had got so far in the day, whether it was what he needed."

Although Howard focused intently on the work ahead, he made time to be with his family. During preproduction he wore a pager that could alert him to speed off to the hospital for Cheryl's impending delivery. It seems fitting that the story of *Willow* has a baby at its center. The film's opening shot is of the newborn Elora Danan, and throughout the hero's many adventures, the baby's plucky reactions are a highlight. (Some critics, however, have strongly disagreed on this point.) The seven-month-old charmer used for this role has a wonderful mop of curly red hair. The DVD commentary discloses that twins play the baby and the hair is a wig: it's amusing that Howard (a redhead and the father of four redheads) chose this particular shade for the little princess.

Aside from this small joke, Howard found other opportunities to involve his family. Neither Rance nor Clint had roles in *Willow*, but

Cheryl can be glimpsed as a ragged peasant in one of the New Zealand snow scenes. Midway through the film the hero meets an ethereal fairy queen whose name, Cherlindrea, represents three women of great importance to the creative team. The first was Cheryl; the second was singer Linda Ronstadt, then closely linked to Lucas; the third was Andrea Martin, the actress-wife of screenwriter Bob Dolman.

Willow itself can be seen as a testament to family ties. At the end of the film, Elora Danan has found surrogate parents in Madmartigan and Sorsha. And Willow, on the crest of his greatest triumph, yearns for the moment when he can go back home again. In a film that hasn't much time for deep emotion, the tender scene in which he reunites with his wife is surprisingly moving.

The heroes of *Splash* and *Cocoon* bravely left their familiar worlds, never to return. Willow leaves as well and is all the better for his exploits, which give him a new faith in his own abilities. But ultimately the plot shows him coming full circle, as in Howard's long-ago *Through the Magic Pyramid*. *Willow*'s final message is a time-honored one: there's no place like home.

In a 1988 promotional documentary entitled "*Willow*: The Making of an Adventure," Howard briefly pretends to be a comic huckster, urging the viewer to "step right up, and get your *Willow* tickets right now! . . . You gotta little action, you gotta little adventure, you gotta little magic, you gotta coupla chuckles. Come on, folks, and bring the whole family!" Howard's boyish enthusiasm here hints at his genuine pride in his accomplishment. Despite his basic reservations about *Willow*'s size and scope, he was vastly relieved that his characters had not been overwhelmed by the special effects that are George Lucas's stock in trade.

But Howard's humorous spiel promoting *Willow* helps suggest the film's chief problem. It tries to provide, literally, something for everybody. At base, *Willow* is an uneasy blend of life-or-death adventure, heartfelt sentiment, golly-gee wizardry, and comic riffs. The two pint-sized Brownies who wisecrack their way through the film are meant to serve as the equivalent of *Star Wars*' witty R2-D2 and C-3PO, but come off as irritating special-effects intruders on the medieval landscape. Elsewhere, humor takes the form of jokes designed to tickle insiders. The fire-breathing, two-headed dragon is named Eborsisk, after movie critics Gene Siskel and Roger Ebert, who had been known to give George Lucas films a hard time. In the same vein, the evil queen's chief battlefield officer is General Kael, a clear reference to the *New Yorker's* perilous Pauline.

The critics who were singled out within the film did not treat it kindly. Ebert chastised *Willow* for its lack of originality: "There can be no true suspense in a movie where even the characters seem to be inspired by other movies." Kael, who pointed out the reference to herself with some amusement, complained that the film's plethora of supernatural creatures makes the viewer feel "as if you'd fallen into a pile of mixed metaphors." To Kael, Howard's "gentle talent" comes through only in his handling of the appealing title character. Other reviewers were no more enthusiastic. Desson Howe of the *Washington Post* sniped that the plot "taketh forever," and Janet Maslin in the *New York Times*, while praising a few of the performances, called the film "as vast as it is secondhand."

Ebert's review had indicated that because of its hefty special effects budget, *Willow* cost "umpteen million dollars" to make. Just before the film's premiere, a reporter had tried to quiz Howard on the actual size of its budget. The reporter tossed out figures of $35 million and $40 million, but Howard stayed mum, explaining his silence with a reference to one of his favorite baseball players. Just after Pete Rose signed with the Philadelphia Phillies for $800,000, Howard went to see a game in which Rose bobbled the ball at first base. When a man in the stands started hollering about Rose's $800,000 price tag, Howard reflected that this whole line of attack was inappropriate: "You shouldn't have to think about the money at the game."

But many people couldn't help thinking about the money. *Willow* cost in the neighborhood of $50 million. The average cost of prints and advertising expenses for mainstream films then was about $10 million, which suggests that upward of $60 million was shelled out on *Willow*. This was a steep price to pay for a movie that faded after three weeks, earning $57.2 million at the domestic box office. Clearly *Willow* was a fiscal disappointment. Still, over the years it has attracted loyal fans among the fantasy crowd, with parents reporting that their children have worn out their videocassettes after repeated viewings. (Many of those children, now grown up, rushed to buy the DVD version upon its release in November 2001.)

Once *Willow* was completed, it was time for Howard to find a new directing gig. He had a good idea what he wanted: "After having done several difficult projects with which I had connected emotionally but not personally, I thought it would be great to do a film about something I felt deeply about." As it happened, he did not have far to look.

PART IV

Ups and Downs

CHAPTER 10

Keeping the Home Fires Burning

(1989–1991)

"Working with him is a writer's dream. He's also just a lot hipper than he cares for anybody to know."
—LOWELL GANZ, SCREENWRITER,
PARENTHOOD

WHEN IMAGINE ENTERTAINMENT'S FIRST FILMS BEGAN appearing on screens across America, Brian Grazer explained the formula he and Ron Howard used in selecting projects: "We try to make warm-spirited movies with some moral camouflaged within their entertainment, either about friendship or love." The three Imagine films released through Universal Studios in 1989—*The 'burbs, The Dream Team,* and *Parenthood*—were all comedies, and all had the advantage of big-name stars to help them at the box office. To a greater or lesser degree, all flirted with a realistic depiction of human behavior. But each also sought to temper realism with outrageous elements straight from sitcom land.

Two of those films brought back actors who had first gained

attention for their leading roles in Grazer/Howard films. *The 'burbs* featured Tom Hanks as an overstressed suburbanite convinced that his new neighbors are engaging in skullduggery. *The Dream Team* starred Michael Keaton as one of four mental patients taken on an outing to a ballgame, only to end up stranded in New York City. Neither film was more than marginally profitable: *The 'burbs* made $36 million, while *The Dream Team* took in less than $29 million. Although Howard did not have his name on either film, and although most of his energy went toward his own new venture, he kept tabs on both productions.

Howard devoted most of his time, however, to *Parenthood*, his first stab at concocting a story since *Grand Theft Auto* and his battle-of-the-bands television movie, *Cotton Candy*. For this personal project he looked straight to his own life, taking inspiration from a hilariously horrible plane flight to Argentina during the filming of *Gung Ho* in 1985. Bryce was four, and the twins were about seven months old. What was intended as an opportunity for family togetherness quickly turned into a near catastrophe. Howard found himself schlepping mountains of suitcases and bags, which he had to parcel out to members of the cast and crew boarding the same commercial jetliner. Forty-five minutes into the seventeen-hour flight, Bryce vomited all over him. And the twins could not both be coaxed to sleep at the same time. Once the whole episode was behind him, Howard realized that the comic, heroic, and life-changing business of being a parent deserved to find its way to the motion picture screen.

His initial idea was a zany sketch comedy along the lines of 1977's *Kentucky Fried Movie*. But a few discussions with Grazer and writers Ganz and Mandel convinced him that a deeper and more thoughtful approach was needed. All four knew something about parenting. By the time the film went into production, Grazer had two young children, Ganz had three, and Mandel had six, including triplets. The completed script contained four interlocking story lines to which each man contributed vignettes from his own family annals. Virtually everything in *Parenthood*—the birthday party at which Dad saves the day, the incriminating photos picked up at the camera shop by the wrong member of the household, the very untimely pregnancy—was drawn from life, then given a comic spin.

Parenthood encompasses multiple generations of one suburban family. Frank (Jason Robards) is a hard-drinking and cantankerous sort who's always been more successful as a businessman than as a husband and father. Eldest daughter Helen (Dianne Wiest) is a divorcée obsessing over her sixteen-year-old daughter's sex life and her own lack of one. Martha Plimpton plays Helen's daughter Julie; Keanu Reeves is Julie's feckless boyfriend; Joaquin Phoenix (then called Leaf Phoenix) portrays Julie's thirteen-year-old brother, who is keeping secrets of his own. Frank's elder son is Gil (Steve Martin), a dedicated dad who agonizes over his fatherly obligations, to the point of jeopardizing his corporate career. Meanwhile, Gil's younger sister Susan (Harley Jane Kozak) is married to Nathan (Rick Moranis), who has taken it as his mission to turn their picture-perfect tot into a genius. The film also contains the surprise return of Frank's youngest child, Larry (Tom Hulce), a flamboyant ne'er-do-well with a half-black offspring in tow. Finally, Grandma (Helen Shaw) is the last surviving remnant of an older generation. She seems to inhabit a world of her own, but as Gil's entire family life teeters in the balance, it is Grandma who steps in with the story of a long-ago roller-coaster ride, which she found both frightening and thrilling. Some people, she notes, prefer the merry-go-round. But that goes nowhere. She declares, "I like the roller coaster. You get more out of it."

The message, of course, is that becoming a parent is like climbing aboard a roller coaster. Raising children means surviving both highs and lows. There's no way even the most attentive dad or mom can remain in full control, so the best option is to hang on and try to enjoy the ride. Though the ending of *Parenthood* captures the blissful, impossible happiness of a fairytale, the film also acknowledges the dark corners that exist within family relationships. Cowriter Ganz credits Howard with a clear grasp of the fact that life and Mayberry are not identical, that Mayberry is "a lovely fiction" quite distinct from the way human nature works. Ganz sees *Parenthood* as illustrating

Howard's mature outlook on the world: "He is a person who worries. He lives an examined life."

For *Parenthood*, Howard molded a large group of established screen personalities into an acting ensemble, much as he had done in *Cocoon*. During the casting process, he chose actors who could physically look like a family unit. But Gil is the movie's focal point, and the hiring of Steve Martin was the first order of business. Martin, who signed on for $5 million, was then at the peak of superstardom, and Howard confessed to being nervous about guiding his performance. Happily, Martin proved to be a team player, and the whole experience seemed blessed with good fortune. As Howard remembers, "the creative process was a joy, shooting was great, editing just wonderful, and when it got reviewed it was a hit."

Which is not to say that it came easily. The two dozen child actors featured in the cast posed a special challenge. In staging birthday parties and Little League scenes, Howard occasionally felt like a camp counselor; despite all his empathy for young performers, he often wished he could discuss their roles with them on a conceptual level. Instead, with moppets such as three-year-old Zachary Lavoy, who played Steve Martin's youngest child, Howard had to resort to parental tricks. Because little Zachary got cranky during multiple takes of the same scene, Howard would sometimes hold him upside down to keep his excitement level high. This ploy ended up becoming the central image on the *Parenthood* poster, which shows Martin cheerfully dangling his two youngest screen children by their ankles. As always, Howard brought his family with him to the film's Orlando, Florida, locations, where it was not rare to find him directing scenes of familial chaos while balancing one of his own kids on his hip.

Given *Parenthood*'s subject matter, Howard sometimes felt that each morning he "was leaving one chaotic household to go to another." Though he has "a pretty high tolerance level for kids," he normally relishes working in an adult environment where he can be firmly in charge. Distinguishing between his workday and the private time he spends with family, he admits that being on the set is easier, because there his place in the hierarchy is never questioned. He quips that at work, as the director, he's the absolute boss, but at home he ranks no higher than a prop man.

It's clear, however, that he's a doting dad. In fact, in typically self-effacing fashion, he has told interviewers that show business and parenting are the only things he's any good at. He readily ticks off his failings: he's not an expert on cars; he isn't Mr. Fixit around the house; his kitchen repertoire is pretty much limited to scrambled eggs and oatmeal. As the children have grown older, filmmaking has sometimes taken him away from home for extended periods during the school year. But when he returns he is almost obsessively conscientious about checking in with their teachers and guidance counselors, making sure he is keeping abreast of any possible problems.

Cheryl agrees that her husband is a wonderful father. She adds, "He spends much more time second-guessing himself than I do. I'm a little bit more self-assured, whether I should be or not." The implicit dynamic between a dad given to self-reproach and a quietly confident mom seems a close parallel to the relationship in *Parenthood* between Gil and his wife, Karen. Steve Martin's Gil worries so intently about his eldest son's adolescent growing pains that while coaching a Little League game he fantasizes about two possible future scenarios. In one, a grown-up Kevin is graduating from an ivy-covered college. Hailed by the dean (played by Rance Howard) as class valedictorian, he mounts the podium and launches into a heartfelt tribute to his father, who has made him "the happiest, most confident, most well-adjusted person in this world." Gil's second fantasy also takes place on a college campus: Kevin has barricaded himself in the bell tower with a rifle, and he's spraying bullets at everything that moves. He says it's all because of his father, who "made me play second base."

In contrast to Gil, who sees himself as personally responsible for every second of unhappiness his son endures, Karen (Mary Steenburgen) takes a more relaxed approach. A woman of great warmth and spirit, Karen is also wise enough to laugh at disaster, as when the three-year-old wanders into his sister's school play and brings the sets crashing down. Unlike her worrywart husband, she's enjoying every moment of the roller-coaster ride.

By the time he made *Parenthood,* admittedly his most personal film to date, Howard was thirty-five years old and a father of four. It's not surprising that he felt a new compassion for the sort of man who stands his ground to protect home and family. Although Gil's obsession with his son's social adjustment is neurotic, his determination to put Kevin ahead of everything, including his own safety, is nothing short of heroic. This is best seen in the film's backyard birthday party sequence. When a gaggle of young guests is dismayed at the nonappearance of Cowboy Dan, the Gunfighting Balloon Man, Gil steps into the breach. Wearing a makeshift cowboy suit, he puts on a wild impromptu performance that culminates in a near fall off the roof and a mad gallop into the sunset on a runaway pony. His reward comes at bedtime, when Kevin asks, "Dad, when I grow up, can I work where you work? That way we can still see each other every day."

Tom Hulce's Larry, in contrast to his older brother, has grown up with the conviction that he's something special. He careens fearlessly through life, plunging into get-rich-quick schemes, staying one step ahead of bookies and thugs. For him a "crappy office job" has no allure; as he puts it, "I am better than that. I am not Gil." Frank clearly loves his younger son's roguish spirit and his willingness to live on the edge, which reflect the brazen side of Frank's own personality. Inevitably, however, Larry's gambling debts catch up with him, and loan sharks threaten his life. Resisting his son's attempt to hustle him out of his retirement nest egg, Frank offers to teach him the plumbing supply business. But Larry opts instead to light out for South America, leaving behind the small boy named Cool, a by-product of a casual Las Vegas liaison with a chorus girl as irresponsible as he is. Larry's leap into the unknown comes off here as less bold than cowardly. It is Gil, overprotective though he may be, who is *Parenthood*'s symbol of frazzled but genuine valor.

Audiences and critics alike embraced *Parenthood.* Its domestic take was just under $100 million, making it the first Imagine film to move into blockbuster territory. Honors included two Academy Award nominations, for Randy Newman's original song and for Dianne Wiest's hilariously angst-ridden performance. Even *Rolling Stone*, not known for its family orientation, was impressed, noting that "*Parenthood*, heartfelt and howlingly comic, also comes spiced with risk and mischief." In the academic world the film also got attention. Wes D. Gehring's scholarly book on *Populism and the Capra Legend* focused on *Parenthood* in a chapter tracing how Howard was following in Frank Capra's footsteps as a cinematic champion of the common man. Gehring wrote, "The exciting development about *Parenthood* was Ron Howard's growing ability to take the most fundamental of populist stories (the celebration of the family) and push it to updated extremes."

Yes, the film can fairly be accused of oversimplifying its subject. Its maternity ward finale, with babies being born, the adults happily coupled, and all the children thriving, might seem to tie far too neat a bow on the whole messy business of parenting. There's no question that Howard prefers tidy, happy endings. But most viewers remember this film for the breadth of the experience it covers, and respect it for treating an important part of life with honesty, humor, and affection.

Parenthood makes clear that adults who are raising children also remain the children of their own aging parents. This certainly applies to Howard. Throughout his life he had looked to Rance and Jean as role models, both for their personal values and for their common-sense approach to show business. In the late 1980s Rance continued to work steadily as an actor, especially on television. And Jean was beginning to land roles in projects her son did not direct. In 1987 she appeared on the detective series, *Matlock*, starring old friend Andy Griffith. Her snow-white hair and cheery disposition made her a natural to play Mrs. Claus in Bill Murray's 1988 feature film, *Scrooged*. In the next decade, she had featured roles in a number of leading sitcoms, notably as a leapfrogging nudist in a 1995 episode of *Roseanne*.

But as her renewed career blossomed, Jean's health began a slow decline. In 1989, at age sixty-two, she underwent heart bypass surgery. A few years later, she endured a second heart operation. Seeing his mother in pain, Howard discovered a new side of her. During his formative years, she had deferred to Rance, whose natural strength overshadowed her own. Ron admits, "It was very moving for me when I saw her face these things with the kind of courage and commitment to life that I didn't know she had."

While Jean was quietly teaching her son about hope and dignity in the face of the unknown, she also found the energy to be a devoted (though long-distance) grandmother. In 1985, when asked which of Ron's achievements made her proudest, she had promptly answered, "My grandchildren." For Jean, sewing her grandchildren's clothing and creating wardrobes for their dolls was a supreme pleasure. Her friend Phyllis Cohen remembers that she made "the most gorgeous dolls' clothes. You can't imagine the intricacy of these dresses."

Neither career commitments nor illness stopped her from enjoying Ron and Cheryl's brood. And clearly she was relieved that they were not destined to be show biz kids like Ron and Clint. Cohen had a delightfully cute granddaughter, but Jean discouraged her from seeking an agent for the child. Jean advised her friend in no uncertain terms that the rejection inherent in Hollywood was very hard on most youngsters, especially girls.

Jean was among those basking in the glow on March 23, 1990, when Ron was honored at the fifth annual Moving Picture Ball. This black-tie gala raised $350,000 to benefit the American Cinematheque, which was building a state-of-the-art film complex in Hollywood. The guests included 1,200 entertainment industry big shots; Grazer cochaired the benefit committee and Henry Winkler served as executive producer and genial host.

The Cinematheque's board of directors, comprised of such top filmmakers as Martin Scorsese and Francis Coppola, annually honors a rising young cinematic talent. Previous recipients had included Eddie Murphy, Robin Williams, and Steven Spielberg, so Howard was entering impressive company. Traditionally, the evening is an opportunity for roasts as well as toasts. George Lucas, a board member and the evening's honorary chairman, targeted Howard's reputation for blandness: "I couldn't think of anything to remember about Ron. In fact, I could hardly remember what he looked like." Lucas then humorously groused that even though he had written a letter to the USC film school on Howard's behalf, Howard soon dropped out because he thought he knew it all. Lucas also claimed to have advised Howard, "Never do a movie in or on water, stay away from special effects, and don't start your own company." Lucas concluded with a grin: "I'm proud of the effect I seem to have had on his career."

Among the actors who sang Howard's praises were Steve Martin, Mary Steenburgen, Daryl Hannah, and Jessica Tandy. Marion Ross, who played Richie's mom for 255 episodes of *Happy Days*, thanked Jean for doing such a good job as a parent, then announced, "It's been a pleasure to be your mother, Ron, even if it's just on TV." Jean and Clint spoke, as did Cheryl, who emotionally told her spouse that she looked forward "to spending my life with you, no matter how much hair you lose."

The evening's surprises included a baseball (inscribed "Opie's come a long way") from Howard's childhood hero, Sandy Koufax. The USC Marching Band made a rousing appearance, playing "Seventy-Six Trombones" from *The Music Man*. Howard's own remarks included heartfelt thanks to his parents and early mentors Andy Griffith and Roger Corman. Howard admitted he felt awkward about looking back at his achievements when his goal was to keep moving ahead. He told reporters that the giant surprise-party atmosphere "runs a little counter to my personality," then quickly added that it was nice to honored in midstride.

In the summer of 1989, while discussing *Parenthood* with Susan Royal of *American Premiere*, Howard compared parents to firemen. He noted that a household might be running smoothly, but then "suddenly there's a fire and the alarm goes off and parents must go to the rescue." Less than two years later, in May 1991, *Backdraft* appeared in theatres.

Backdraft began as a concept by Gregory Widen, a graduate of the

UCLA screenwriting program who had earlier written the action fantasy *Highlander* (1986). Before entering film school, Widen had spent
three years as a Southern California fireman. In the line of duty, he saw
a buddy blown across a six-lane highway and impaled on a metal post
by the deadly explosion known as a backdraft. Widen's goal was to
write a tense thriller built around the working lives of firefighters and
their heroic dance with danger.

When Howard came on as director, he saw the possibility of making a film with more bite than his previous efforts. It was he who prod-
ded Widen into playing up the complex rivalry between two brothers
from a Chicago firefighting family. Stephen (Kurt Russell) and younger
brother Brian (William Baldwin) are both still reeling from the death of
their fireman father many years before. Stephen has grown up with a
personal vendetta against fire. As a leading member of a firefighting
unit known for its toughness, he's the first to rush into any precarious
situation, and he refuses to wear a safety mask. In contrast, Brian has
tried in vain to stay away from the family profession. Returning to the
force, he's both enthralled and intimidated by his elder brother's brash
heroics. He also sees in Stephen's crumbling marriage a reminder of the
price some firemen pay for their obsessive insistence on grabbing every
fire by the throat.

The brothers' story is bound up with a tangled plot that encompasses a shady politician and a mysterious arsonist. The whodunit
strand is unconvincing; so is an attempt at a sexy scene between Brian
and his romantic interest (Jennifer Jason Leigh) atop a fire truck, just
before a major blaze. (In one of the film's silliest moments, her black
lace brassiere ends up dangling from an unspooling firehose.) Where
Backdraft works best is in its depiction of fire itself. Howard discovered
that firefighters see fire as a living creature with a will of its own. His
research taught him that "it has its own thought patterns, it behaves in
odd ways, it slithers and it laughs and hisses and giggles." Through
state-of-the-art visual effects by ILM, and the gutsy willingness of cast
and crew to move close to actual flames, *Backdraft* conveys the elemental power of fire as no previous film had ever done.

The *Backdraft* team chose to focus on the Chicago Fire Department

In 1961 Ronny Howard poses for a publicity shot at age seven.

Eight-year-old Ronny Howard, arriving in Mason City, Iowa, for the June 1962 world premiere of *The Music Man*, receives the key to the city from a young local resident. Behind them stand (from left to right) the film's director, Morton DaCosta, and its stars, Robert Preston and Shirley Jones.

Ronny Howard, as Opie Taylor, makes friends with a telephone lineman played by Karl Swenson. This episode, entitled "Mr. McBeevee," first aired on October 1, 1962, kicking off the third season of *The Andy Griffith Show.*

Don Knotts and Andy Griffith, close friends even before their years together on *The Andy Griffith Show,* laugh it up while taping a television program on October 20, 1967.

Rance Howard arrives with sons Ron (19) and Clint (14) for the February 1974 premiere of *Where the Lilies Bloom*. Rance played a featured role in this family film set in the backwoods of Appalachia.

Ron Howard was listed as "Ronny" for this senior class photo, which appeared in the 1972 yearbook (*Akela*) for John Burroughs High School in Burbank, California.

Senior class photo for Cheryl Alley, future wife of Ron Howard, in the 1972 John Burroughs High School yearbook.

Ron Howard is shown in his office on October 2, 1980. On the wall behind him are mementos of his first directorial efforts, *Grand Theft Auto* (1977) and the television movie *Cotton Candy* (1980).

Director Ron Howard checks out a camera during the filming of *Gung Ho* in August 1985. In the center of the photo, father Rance wears a suit to play the mayor of a small Pennsylvania town.

Director Ron Howard, wearing his lucky cap, signs autographs outside New York City's Paramount Theatre on the occasion of the opening of *Willow* (May 21, 1988).

Ron Howard, who considers himself bicoastal, arrives at Los Angeles International Airport on April 26, 1993. Howard makes his home in Greenwich, Connecticut, but his company, Imagine Entertainment, is headquartered in Beverly Hills, California.

Ron Howard greets the Grinch at the November 2001 release party for the DVD version of *How the Grinch Stole Christmas.* The film had been the highest-grossing theatrical release of the year 2000; video and DVD sales broke additional records.

Ron and Cheryl Howard attend the premiere of the 1997
Imagine Entertainment comedy, *Liar Liar.*

Brian Grazer and wife Gigi Levangie Grazer attend the post-Oscar party hosted by *Vanity Fair*, 1999.

Clint Howard, along with wife Melanie, at the 1998 MTV Awards ceremony. Clint was honored with the MTV Movie Lifetime Achievement Award. (Previous recipients have included the Three Stooges, Jackie Chan, and Chewbacca of *Star Wars* fame.)

The irrepressible Clint Howard, wearing a "Grinch" T-shirt, at the July 2000 premiere of Imagine Entertainment's *Nutty Professor II: The Klumps*.

Ron Howard greets his *Happy Days* mom, Marion Ross, at the premiere of his 1999 romantic comedy, *EDtv*.

Ron Howard helps daughter Jocelyn (9) get a better look at astronauts approaching the launchpad for an April 1994 space shuttle flight. Howard was visiting Florida's Kennedy Space Center as part of his research for *Apollo 13*.

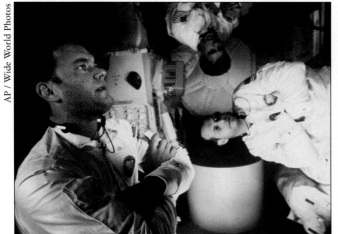

Actors Tom Hanks, Kevin Bacon, and Bill Paxton in a scene from *Apollo 13* (1995) that illustrates how director Ron Howard met the challenge of depicting astronauts under weightless conditions.

Ron Howard shows off his hands after pressing them into wet cement at Hollywood's Grauman's Chinese Theatre on March 23, 1999. Behind him are his mother, Jean (partially obscured), and wife, Cheryl.

Director Ron Howard joins producer Brian Grazer and star Russell Crowe at the December 2001 premiere of *A Beautiful Mind*.

Producers Ron Howard and Brian Grazer pose with their Oscars backstage after their film *A Beautiful Mind* was named Best Picture of 2001. Howard won a second Oscar as the year's best director.

Rance Howard congratulates his Oscar-winning son at the Governor's Ball following the 74th Annual Academy Awards ceremony on March 24, 2002.

because of its long-standing reputation as the most stubbornly macho in the country. Chicago firemen traditionally disdain those who stay on the perimeter of a burning building, shooting water from hoses in what they call a "surround and drown." Their own preferred method is to rush inside and tackle the blaze, thus exposing themselves to the possibility of great personal harm. In shooting *Backdraft,* Howard and his crew followed much the same pattern. Though camera operators were encased in fire suits and though the leaps of the flames were carefully choreographed, danger was always present. By the time shooting ended, the cast and crew had faced more than one close call. When Howard chose the wrong moment to cue a mortar shell, he nearly incinerated Russell. An actual fireman playing a minor role had his eyebrows singed off, his first accident after twelve years on the force. The moment production wrapped, Howard nearly wept with relief. Soon afterwards, he insisted that if movies, like Olympics events, were judged on a degree-of-difficulty scale, "this would be a nine and a half. I was constantly riding this line, trying to maximize the excitement and be safe at the same time." No wonder he's never considered a sequel.

Backdraft's actors, who also included Scott Glenn and Robert De Niro, enjoyed the sheer physicality of their roles. Russell got so caught up in the fireman's world that he had to be stopped by Howard and Grazer from spending his off hours riding to fires with a Chicago ladder company. The Chicago Fire Department willingly cooperated throughout the project. It helped train the actors, provided equipment, and recruited 600 men in dress blues to march in the solemn funeral procession that ends the film. Since *Backdraft*'s release, firefighters throughout the nation have treated Howard as a hero. His heightened awareness of the hazards faced by firemen has led him to appear on Capitol Hill, lobbying for federal funds to improve their training. (But he still appreciates Universal Studio's *Backdraft* theme-park ride, in which visitors experience an actual chemical blaze. Far from finding this attraction crassly commercial, he respects its entertainment value, admitting with delight that it managed to scare him.)

Despite the difficulty of the shoot, cast and crew came away from *Backdraft* with high regard for their director. He wasn't an intimidating figure: on one of the few quiet days, the production team played a raunchy joke on him, substituting Cheryl in a wig and huge false breasts for the firehouse moll who was set to make an appearance, topless, at a second floor window. He didn't notice at first, then blushed beet red. (The entire episode ultimately wound up on the cutting-room floor.) Although Howard liked being treated as one of the guys, *Backdraft* star Russell warns against underestimating him: "Ronny is a *nice* person, yes. But maybe it's just one of the things that's in his bag of tricks."

That bag of tricks by now included a growing understanding of the uses of film music. Though he plays no instruments beyond a few chords on the guitar, film composers as eminent as John Williams have praised his innate musicality. Hans Zimmer was hired for *Backdraft* because Howard admired his eerie synthesizer score for the 1989 police thriller *Black Rain*. Zimmer found himself working with Howard on almost a cue by cue basis, discussing the logic of his musical choices. The result is a dignified score, heavy on percussion and brass, that captures the blue-collar nobility of Chicago's largely Irish-American fire department. On the scoring stage where a full orchestra recorded Zimmer's work, Howard became a frequent visitor. Says Zimmer, "Growing up as a child actor did something wonderful for Ron. It made him a true pro. There's no ego, just an unbelievable stamina. Ron doesn't stop caring and goes after the music until it's right."

The results of all this effort paid off, at least at the box office. *Backdraft* took in over $77 million domestically, making it one of 1991's top-grossing films. When the year's Oscar list was revealed, *Backdraft* had been honored for its technical achievements—with nominations for sound, visual effects, and sound effects editing—but had received no acknowledgment in such prestige categories as best actor, picture, or director. Critics generally ridiculed the film's plot and its bombastic dialogue. (An example is Robert De Niro's tribute to fire: "It's a living thing. It breathes. It eats. The only way to beat it is to think like it. You gotta love it a little.") Desson Howe of the *Washington Post* called *Backdraft* "a conflagration of hyped-up movie clichés." His *Post* colleague, Rita Kempley, caustically wrote, "Howard, who brings so much empathy to his domestic comedies, approached this barn-burner with all the restraint of an incontinent spaniel who has just spied a hydrant."

Backdraft may be less than an artistic triumph, but is a good example of Howard stretching his talents, trying something that for him is stylistically new. Though *Backdraft* ends, like most Howard films, with a celebration of the human spirit, its tone is much more somber than his previous efforts: the final affirmation comes on the heels of pain and loss. Thematically, however, *Backdraft* sets up familiar polarities, between bravery and caution, between the willingness to risk all and the recognition that it's wise to know one's limits. The failure of Stephen's marriage can be traced directly to his wife's resolve to protect herself and their son from the pain of his reckless behavior. She tells Stephen at one point, "The chances that you take—you scare me now." Firefighters, however, by the very nature of their jobs must be willing to put their lives on the line, so self-protection can never be their absolute goal.

Backdraft is also notable for its return to the two-brothers motif. *Splash* was the first Howard film to introduce a pair of brothers, one reckless and one responsible, bound together by family history and mutual affection. The tenuous bond between brothers had played a secondary role in *Parenthood*, but *Backdraft* is Howard's fullest exploration of the topic. Although Stephen's brash, angry streak is foreign to his own nature, Howard drew on personal experience to help shape the character of the big brother who is professionally more successful and more sure of himself than his younger sibling. Howard admitted to the Encore Channel's Robert J. Emery that he had always wanted to look closely at a brother relationship on film: "I've got a very close relationship with my brother Clint, who's five years younger, and particularly at [the time of the making of *Backdraft*] the relationship was a pretty complicated one."

In 1990, when *Backdraft* was filmed, one Howard brother was a big name and one was not. Ron, following years of television stardom, was becoming increasingly respected as a film director. Clint, while continuing to work regularly, found his best non-Ron parts in low-budget schlockfests such as 1990's *Silent Night Deadly Night 4*. For a change of pace, Clint continued to play small but choice roles in his brother's films. In *Parenthood*, he was an obnoxious Little League dad heckling Gil about son Kevin's athletic ineptitude. In *Backdraft*, he shared a scene with De Niro as a lab pathologist nonchalant about corpses.

Though Clint claimed to be satisfied with his offbeat career, in 1990 his personal life was in shambles. This news would have surprised those who read a brief, cheerful profile of Clint in the February 6, 1989, issue of *Us* magazine. In it he disclosed that he had recently taken time off from film work to enjoy his new marriage to a ceramicist named Annie. He told *Us* readers that "I crave normalcy. Show business is my job, not my life." Though this interview made Clint, then close to his thirtieth birthday, sound happy and well adjusted, the opposite was in fact true. Since the early 1980s, he had been caught in a downward spiral of alcohol and drug dependency. When it was clear he was not going to clean up his act, Rance, Jean, and Ron joined Al-Anon and studied the group's "tough love" credo, which teaches that the substance abuser must take responsibility for his own actions. The roles Ron gave his brother during this period were, as he later told *People* magazine, partly an attempt to keep Clint's face before the public and also to remind Clint of the value of his own talent.

Clint hit bottom just after the 1991 Gulf War. His marriage had long since ended and watching the war coverage on television had become a favorite form of recreation: "When it was over, there I was, sitting with a pint of vodka in my hand with no war to watch." That's when he finally tried Alcoholics Anonymous, quickly becoming a dedicated member. A year later, he found happiness with a Pacific Bell salesperson named Melanie Sorich; as Clint put it, "Funny how that works when you're sober." They married in 1995.

Clint has never blamed his problems on show business, his parents, or his famous brother. But actress Shirley Jones, who has known the entire Howard family since *The Music Man* and *The Courtship of Eddie's Father*, has a hunch that Clint's difficulties were almost inevitable: "When you have a successful brother like Ron, it's awfully hard to take, really. When you see, as a little kid, all the praise going that

way. I'm sure his parents tried to dissuade that, but it's impossible. . . .
Oh, I know it well." In the late 1970s, Jones' own youngest son Ryan
Cassidy fell into the same trap, at least partly because two older siblings,
brother Shaun and half-brother David, had become pop idols with huge
teen followings. At an early age, Ryan succumbed to the lure of drugs,
and had to be sent away from his family to recover. Jones adds that of
her children, "He's the only one that went through that whole thing, and
the reason was obvious. His self-esteem was just nil at that point, and I
imagine Clint went through the same thing."

Clint's years as a child actor did give him a steady diet of rejection,
along with opportunities that most kids his age didn't have. When faced
with temptation, Clint's tendency was to dive right in. What's fascinating is how two brothers, the offspring of the same loving parents, could
have followed such different paths. Howard would surely see this as
one more proof "that each human being is an absolute individual." It
was a truth he had discovered when his twins were born: "My daughters have been different people from day one; their cries were different
as they entered the world . . . they reacted differently to stimuli." So
parenthood has taught him that "you can't mold people. You can help,
but they are who they are." In Clint's case, risk-taking was an ingrained
form of behavior. He never developed, until the age of thirty-one, the
self-preservation instincts that have served his brother so well.

CHAPTER 11

Near and Far

(1991–1994)

*"I like that he lives in a protected environ-
ment. We are a good counterpoint to each
other."*

—BRIAN GRAZER

THE EARLY 1990S BECAME A PERIOD OF TRANSITION FOR
Ron Howard and his circle. In 1991 Clint finally beat the bottle. That
same year, a few months before Brian Grazer's fortieth birthday, his
wife, Corki, filed for divorce. Grazer moved out of their beachfront
home and by the end of 1992 had purchased a 5,000-square-foot house
on a three-acre knoll in L.A.'s Pacific Palisades, not far from Tom
Hanks, comic actor Garry Shandling, and producer Norman Lear.

Thanks to Grazer's thoroughly Hollywood lifestyle, with its endless
shmoozefests at L.A. glamour spots, Howard could live in Connecticut
while still maintaining what one writer has called "a window on the
main event." As the decade moved forward, the two men continued to
function as unlikely friends and colleagues. In May 1990 Howard was
ranked thirty-first in *Premiere* magazine's influential listing of the hundred most powerful players in Hollywood; rumors immediately circulated that Grazer had lobbied to appear on the list as well. He first

made the grade in 1992 and by 2002 had moved up to twenty-third, six places ahead of his partner. By 1992 Grazer was enjoying recognition of other sorts. At its ShoWest convention, the National Association of Theatre Owners named him Producer of the Year, and *Esquire* published a wacky but endearing profile that focused on his passion for surfing. (*Esquire* writer Michael Angeli said of Grazer, "If the pace of this man's talk is any indication, he pisses adrenaline.")

Meanwhile, Howard was slowly getting used to being feted. In 1991 he bought his first tuxedo; two years later he wore it when he and Grazer were honored at an all-star March of Dimes gala chaired by Beverly Sills. On the dais, Howard drew laughs when he quipped that the Imagine duo had just bought Paramount Pictures for $60,000. Grazer added that they'd raised the dough by cashing in Howard's home video library: "He has tapes of all the *Andy Griffith* and *Happy Days* episodes."

By this time, several Imagine films were making serious money. After *Parenthood*, *Kindergarten Cop* raked in $91.5 million in 1990. The following year saw the release of *My Girl*, an endearing PG-rated film that capitalized on the skyrocketing popularity of *Home Alone*'s Macaulay Culkin. *My Girl* earned a respectable $55.2 in domestic grosses and considerably more in overseas sales and rentals. Grazer produced both *My Girl* and *Kindergarten Cop*, and his name would be on such comedy blockbusters as *The Nutty Professor* (1996) and *Liar Liar* (1997). Imagine also dared to get behind some smaller, riskier movies, including an earnest chamber drama called *Closet Land* (1991) and John Waters' typically outrageous *Cry-Baby* (1990). These less commercial ventures failed to attract audiences, but won the young company some healthy critical respect.

After *Parenthood*, Howard explored several creative options. In late 1991 the scuttlebutt was that he would direct Nicole Kidman in something called *Parole Officer*, but the project never came to fruition. The next year, Howard gathered family members and some of the old *Happy Days* gang for a read-through of Lowell Ganz and Babaloo Mandel's latest screenplay. This comedy about a family's schemes to get at its patriarch's money eventually became *Greedy*, starring Michael J.

Fox and Kirk Douglas. Imagine produced it, but Howard—who was becoming increasingly choosy about his commitments—played no further role in what turned out to be an artistic and fiscal flop.

Although both Howard and Imagine were best known for comedy, the box-office success of *Backdraft* was an inducement to expand further into dramatic territory. In 1993 there was a fierce bidding war for John Grisham's then-unpublished legal thriller, *The Chamber*. Universal Pictures bought it for a record $3.75 million as a potential directing vehicle for Howard, who claimed he had long wanted to make a film about the death penalty. Though Oscar-winning screenwriter William Goldman came aboard, Howard turned skittish about both script and casting and ultimately passed. When Imagine finally brought *The Chamber* to the screen in 1996, under the direction of James Foley, its returns did not justify its $50 million price tag.

Howard also sidestepped the chance to direct Tom Hanks in *The Postman*, the apocalyptic drama that would later prove a fiasco for Kevin Costner. Under the circumstances, it's tempting to see Howard as prescient. But friends also accuse him of exasperating indecisiveness. Ganz deadpanned in 1996 that Ron can be maddeningly slow in committing to projects: "He's still trying to decide if he'll direct *Parenthood*."

For his next film after *Backdraft*, Howard finally chose something that had been in his head—and his heart—for a long time. When *Far and Away* opened in May 1992, he told the press that it had been nine years in the making. In reality, the seeds of this movie took root decades earlier, in 1958, when he and his parents flew to Europe to make *The Journey*. It was his first flight, and crossing the dark Atlantic in a prop jet was a frightening ordeal for a four-year-old boy. When the sun rose on the beautiful green fields of western Ireland, he was vastly relieved. Once the plane finally set down at Shannon Airport for a refueling stop, little Ronny got out to stretch his legs on the tarmac, and a workman ruffled his red hair in friendly fashion. "You look like you belong here," he said. "Maybe you should stay behind."

Like many Americans, Howard could trace his ancestry to many lands. Though he also knew he came from Dutch, English, German, and Cherokee Indian stock, he took special pride in his Irish heritage and believed that a story of Irish immigration was an apt way to get at the core of the American melting-pot experience. One other aspect of his family history intrigued him. At age six he had listened with wonder as Rance's elderly grandmother spun the tale of three family members who had ridden in the 1893 Oklahoma Land Race. She even produced a faded newspaper photograph that, according to family legend, captured a blurry glimpse of Ron's great-grandfather, Ralph Tomlin. He was on horseback, racing pell-mell toward some of the precious free acreage offered by the U.S. government to whomever was fast enough to claim it.

Though Howard treasured both his American pioneer forebears and his Irish roots, the idea for a film combining the two did not occur to him until the early 1980s. At a concert by the Chieftains, a group specializing in traditional Irish music, he found himself transported by a simple ballad in which two lovers say farewell before one of them sails for America. From this Howard began concocting a romantic saga inspired by his great-grandfather and great-grandmother. It was far from an accurate version of how they met, but was, he explained, "the story I wish I could tell."

Years before they worked together on *Willow*, screenwriter Bob Dolman embraced Howard's concept, and the two men found themselves shaping what they called "the Irish story" even on the set during *Willow*'s production lulls. Cheryl listened to their ideas, made suggestions, and became an enthusiastic advocate. Once *Willow* was completed, they needed to bring Grazer on board. In 1988, Howard and Dolman took Grazer to Ireland, hoping their enthusiasm would prove contagious: they downed a lot of Guinness, and had a rollicking good time. Back home again, Grazer reminded Howard that neither of them could predict how the film would do commercially. But he added, "If you don't go ahead and make it now while you've got the shot, you're going to kick yourself forever."

Howard was savvy enough to know that Grazer didn't care for the project. Though the two share a fondness for upbeat romantic stories, Grazer dislikes films that meander, as well as those that rely heavily on accents and period dress. He is also more resistant than Howard to florid sentimentality. In this case, however, he let his partner pursue his dream. Universal Pictures made a commitment, and the production process began.

Perhaps Howard should have been forewarned by the film's rapidly widening scope. What he had envisioned as a sexy romp along the lines of Frank Capra's *It Happened One Night* (1934) was quickly expanding into a big-budget epic. To some extent, this had to do with his casting choices. First he pursued Nicole Kidman for the female lead, on the strength of her work in such Australian films as *Dead Calm* (1989). He was not aware until Tom Cruise expressed interest in the project that he and Kidman had become an item while shooting *Days of Thunder* (1990). Once Hollywood superstar Cruise had signed on to play Joseph Donnelly opposite Kidman's Shannon Christie, *Far and Away* automatically became a major event.

Then, because the film's climax takes place in the big sky country of the American West, cinematographer Mikael Salomon began lobbying to shoot in a wide-screen format. He explained to Howard that a larger negative would allow for superior definition and clarity, and that the cumbersome cameras of the past had become far more user-friendly. Howard, always interested in technological advances, was ultimately persuaded. As a result, *Far and Away* became the first film since David Lean's *Ryan's Daughter* (1970) to be shot in 70mm, instead of the usual 35mm. Upon its release, Howard spoke delightedly of having made a true "movie movie" on a heroic scale, augmented by John Williams' lush symphonic score. Only later did he realize that viewers were anticipating a *Doctor Zhivago*-style extravaganza instead of the intimate romantic comedy he had intended to make.

Location shooting in Ireland involved a few mishaps. Some were funny, as when Howard got his comeuppance from the donkey that would carry Cruise at the start of the film: Howard decided to go for a jaunt, but quickly landed in the dirt. Far more serious was a helicopter crash off the rocky coast of Dingle, County Kerry, that briefly endangered the lives of two crewmen. But the greatest production challenge was the filming of the Cherokee Strip Land Race. On July 8, 1991, the plains of northwestern Oklahoma were represented by a ranch outside Billings, Montana, where Howard assembled 800 expert riders and 200 horse-and-wagon teams. He readied nine cameras—one in a helicopter, and several others buried in the ground—to record the race from multiple angles. All the action had been carefully storyboarded, after a close study of famous muscle-epics from *Cimarron* (1931) to *The Road Warrior* (1981), by way of *Ben-Hur* (1959).

Amid the flurry of preparation, Rance came to his son with a request. Rance was playing a horse dealer named Tomlin, patterned after his own ancestor, in several key scenes leading up the race. Now he sought permission to ride in the race itself. Only trained stuntmen were scheduled to ride, and Ron explained it would be irresponsible to let his father participate. If sixty-three-year-old Rance fell off his horse and were injured, the entire production would suffer. But Rance, usually a model of professionalism, would not be dissuaded. Both father and son knew that Rance was an excellent rider. And Rance underscored his own family history: both his grandfathers had taken part in this race, one on a racehorse, the other driving a buggy. Rance conceded, "I know it's your call. I'm not overriding you; you're the boss." Still, he desperately yearned to follow the path of his forebears. Finally, Ron could hold out no longer. "Dad," he said, "go get your horse."

During five takes, Howard felt he was reliving his childhood dream of owning a time machine. So convincing was the re-creation of pioneer life that he was nearly too emotional to say, "Roll the cameras." But the cameras rolled, Rance stayed on his mount, and the result was six taut minutes that critics agree were the film's most riveting. Not that everything went smoothly: four people broke bones, one horse died, and some disgruntled locals threatened personal injury lawsuits. But Howard, who early in his directing career had doubted his own ability to choreograph large masses of people, showed himself able to stage a truly breathtaking action sequence.

As befits a project so close to Howard's heart, *Far and Away* contains one of his favorite motifs: leaving home to find a home. Joseph is a dirt-poor Irish tenant farmer who at first wants only to work the soil, though it does not belong to him. But his father's sudden, violent death spurs him to head for the manor house of the Christie family with revenge on his mind. What he quickly learns is that the wellborn are hardly content with their lot in life. The landlord, Daniel Christie, drunkenly confides that he craves adventure: "If I had wings I'd fly to the stars." And Christie's daughter, Shannon, whom Joseph meets under tumultuous circumstances, is bent on fleeing her gilded cage to find freedom in America. Through a far-fetched chain of events, Shannon ends up rescuing Joseph from a duel he can't win and whisking him off to America as her reluctant servant. But their relationship is upended when thieves steal her nest egg. For a time they share squalid quarters among the Boston Irish, but are unable to admit their passion for one another. It surfaces only in a fairy tale–like winter scene in which they break into a vacant mansion and pretend to be its lord and lady, cozily sheltered from the storm outside.

When their romantic dreams are dashed, Joseph gallantly returns Shannon to her parents, who had moved to America after a peasant mob burnt down their ancestral manor. Shannon seems destined to wed haughty Stephen, the tax collector who had once terrorized the peasants back home. But Shannon and Joseph reunite out West, where both compete in the land run. Shannon's crafty father has figured out how to grab a piece of land without riding for it, while Joseph must not only ride like the wind but also take on the nefarious Stephen. The film ends in a near death, followed by a joyous resurrection, as Joseph and Shannon claim their land and one another.

Howard's personal attachment to this story stems from his admiration for anyone who can boldly embrace uncertainty. He's fascinated by people with the courage to make spur-of-the-moment decisions that change their lives. Howard adds, tellingly, "I'm not inclined to do things like that. But I did ask my wife to marry me on the ramp of a freeway." And this film celebrates those who plunge into the void and emerge triumphant.

The making of *Far and Away* was a happy experience for the major participants. Newlyweds Cruise and Kidman referred to the film as "the honeymoon picture." Kidman, looking forward to starting a family of her own, was especially buoyed by the presence of Howard's four "really really good kids" on the set. The filming of the land rush sequence coincided with the children's summer vacation, and allowed all the Howards to be together. Kidman came to regard Ron and Cheryl as role models, demonstrating how to raise healthy youngsters within the film industry.

But though Howard and his family have fond memories of the production period, life took an unpleasant turn once the film was released. Critics across the nation came down hard on what they called *Far and Away*'s romantic excesses, silly pratfalls, and swollen plot. Kenneth Turan of the *Los Angeles Times* spoke for many when he carped, "It's almost as if director Howard, who literally grew up on sets and on location, cannot tell movie reality from the real thing and doesn't know dialogue that rings naturally when he hears it."

Cheryl has reasoned that perhaps *Far and Away* was a victim of bad timing, that its release strategy failed to help it capture its natural audience. She insists, however, "I love that film, and I don't love all of Ron's films." Howard himself departed from his usual gentlemanly style to blame journalists for a poor audience turnout. According to him, *Far and Away* had been doing well in test screenings, until "all of a sudden it was rejected by the press—the general media to some extent, the critics to a large extent—and it undermined the movie." A few years down the road, he was ready to concede that perhaps the film was "really a girl's movie." At any rate, a project budgeted at about $60 million before the addition of marketing costs only recouped $58 million in domestic grosses, and about $130 million worldwide. So, while *Far and Away* was by no means a disaster for Imagine and Universal, sky-high expectations made it feel like an embarrassment.

Howard responded to the first major failure of his directing career by retreating into the bosom of his family. He spent the summer of 1992 reading, watching movies, and poring over the journals he'd kept since his *Grand Theft Auto* days. In the meantime, a tempest was brewing on another front.

Though Howard loves the creative process, he prides himself on keeping up with the business side of show business. When one reporter tried likening him to actor James Stewart, he accepted the comparison by pointing out that Stewart, for all his aw-shucks affability, also knew how to read a balance sheet. Howard says, "I don't think I'm a gifted businessman. But I'm solid and I understand the fundamentals, so I don't hurt myself." A former close associate agrees that Howard, although he'd rather focus on artistic questions, has a methodical mind that can absorb financial details: "It's not like he's Van Gogh, who doesn't even know where the decimal points go."

Since 1986 Howard and Grazer's Imagine Films Entertainment had been a publicly held company whose film projects were backed by Universal Studios. By 1989, thanks to *Parenthood* and other hits, some significant revenue was starting to come in. Though Imagine was still far from showing a profit, the partners began a joint venture with MGM to produce television programming and acquired an ownership interest in Chicago's famed Second City comedy troupe. This diversification made sense from a business standpoint, but distracted Howard and Grazer from what they saw as their true mission: telling stories on film. In 1990, amid much fanfare, Imagine launched a television series based on Howard's hit movie, *Parenthood*. It starred Ed Begley Jr., with Leonardo DiCaprio in the role of the secretive teenager Joaquin Phoenix had played on the big screen. But Howard and Grazer, though totally supportive of this foray into television, could not supervise the series closely, because of their involvement with *Backdraft* and other films. Without a strong hand at the helm, the show quickly foundered, and Imagine's television division was temporarily dismantled.

This and other disappointments led Imagine's founders to rethink their situation. Besides feeling pressure to produce a steady stream of blockbusters, they were weary of plowing their own fees back into Imagine's coffers to satisfy shareholders. Other Hollywood filmmakers of their stature were earning $2 million to $8 million per project, and receiving a percentage of the gross. Howard's directing fee was now close to $5 million per film, while Grazer made about $2.2 million when he produced pictures for Universal, or $1.25 million for outside projects. These sums, however, were automatically reinvested in Imagine. In compensation each man reportedly netted an annual salary of $1.3 million plus a percentage of Imagine's overall revenues. Such incomes may seem handsome, but the two were beginning to feel underpaid with respect to their peers. By December 1991 rumors were circulating that, when their contract expired the following November, Howard and Grazer might leave Imagine behind.

In May 1992 under the new HG Productions banner, the duo negotiated a six-year pact with Universal Pictures, signaling their readiness to do business as a small privately held entity separate from Imagine. At the same time, they made it known that they were willing to buy back outstanding Imagine stock for $9 a share. They already owned 54 percent of the company's stock, with Universal controlling another 24 percent. It became their goal to consolidate the decision-making power at Imagine entirely within their own hands.

Investors immediately cried foul. Pointing out that Imagine had amassed revenues of $1.2 billion worldwide, they argued that the stock many of them had purchased in 1986 for $8 a share was now worth far more than the price being offered, perhaps as much as $12 a share. They accused Howard and Grazer of trying to acquire Imagine on the cheap, though Wall Street experts pointed out that entertainment company stocks are notoriously volatile, partly because those in charge tend to put filmmaking ahead of business considerations. (As one insider phrased it, "Creatives shouldn't run companies.") The first shareholder lawsuit was filed in May 1992, just before the release of *Far and Away*, and others soon followed. One investor poignantly told reporters that he had used his life savings to buy 30,000 shares of Imagine at $10 a share, because "I had complete faith in Ron Howard as an honest person."

By the beginning of 1993, it became clear that Howard and Grazer were going to have their way. The majority of the Imagine board of directors voted on January 13 to accept the founders' $9-a-share buyout offer. Universal Pictures chipped in with a $14 million loan to help cover the total $23.5 million price tag, receiving in exchange the rights to Imagine's film library as well as full involvement in most future Imagine movie projects. By February 1993 with the buyout in process, the company drastically cut overhead by shuttering its New York office and trimming its staff from forty-two to seventeen. At the same time,

Imagine was quietly making moves toward settling the disgruntled shareholders' lawsuits.

With Imagine Entertainment reemerging as a scaled-back private company, Grazer and Howard aired their revamped goals. Grazer indicated that they wanted "to make the same amount of movies (four to five a year) in a smaller family environment—and of course we hope to make more money." Howard was clearly relieved that he could now let go of the blockbuster mentality that had helped turn *Far and Away* into an overblown epic. When asked what he would do next, he said he was on the lookout for a simple, straightforward script that that did not need special effects to make it fly.

During the tense period when Imagine's future was uncertain, Steven Spielberg introduced Howard to David Koepp. Koepp, author of the screenplay for *Jurassic Park* (1993), would later write *Mission: Impossible*, and two major 2002 films, *Panic Room* and *Spider-Man*. When they first met in 1992, Koepp told Howard that he and his brother Stephen had used *Parenthood* as the model for a new script on which they were collaborating, one that combined multiple story lines with an essentially comic perspective. Stephen Koepp is a veteran journalist, a former Milwaukee news reporter who had become a senior editor at *Time* magazine. The brothers' work-in-progress was a shrewd but affectionate look at twenty-four hours in the life of a New York tabloid newspaper.

Howard had long had a soft spot for journalism as a profession. He had been active on his high school newspaper, and later mused that if film school didn't work out, the life of a reporter might be a good alternative. Richie of *Happy Days* was keen on journalism too, and in *Return to Mayberry*, Opie had grown up to become the editor of the local newspaper. So Howard was delighted by the premise of the Koepps' script. A week after reading their final draft, he signed on to direct.

Because *The Paper* (1994) is set entirely in Manhattan, Howard enjoyed staying close to home. He spent months doing research at the *New York Daily News* and the *New York Post*, jotting down jargon and newsroom idiosyncrasies in his own reporter's notebook. He also was able to place an old favorite, Michael Keaton, at the head of a well-tuned acting ensemble that included Robert Duvall, Marisa Tomei, Randy Quaid, Jason Robards, and Jason Alexander. Clint had a featured role as a frazzled rewrite man ("Hey, Henry, you got another word for *mangled?*"), and Cheryl could be spotted tending bar during a tense scene at a reporters' watering hole. *The Paper* also gave Howard an opportunity to cast one of his favorite actresses, Glenn Close, in a typically gutsy role. Her part, that of a tough-as-nails managing editor, was originally written for a man. It was Howard's brainstorm to change the gender, giving an attractive female face to a character that everyone in the newsroom loves to hate.

Howard also was attracted to this project because of the light it shed on his own domestic situation. To some extent, *The Paper* can be seen as the flip side of *Parenthood*, where Steve Martin played a dedicated father who struggles to keep his career from intruding on the time he spends at home. In *The Paper*, Henry Hackett, played by Michael Keaton, finds impending fatherhood an intrusion on his round-the-clock devotion to a job he adores. Howard fully understands the push and pull between career and home life, admitting, "I love the business. I love my family. . . . There are periods when I'm not seeing them much and it gets a little uncomfortable."

Howard can sympathize with Henry's workaholic bent. So, in a way, can Henry's very pregnant wife, Martha, played by Tomei. A former ace reporter, she misses the excitement of the newsroom and dreads putting her professional life on hold to rear a child. During *The Paper*'s carefully plotted twenty-four hours, she steps back into her husband's domain, using her razor-sharp news instincts and contacts to grab the big scoop. Only when the paper has finally gone to press does the script allow her to deliver her baby.

The film starts at 7 A.M., when Henry Hackett, metro editor at the *New York Sun,* awakens on top of his bed, fully clothed from a marathon stint at the office the night before. He mumbles a few words to Martha, slugs down a Coca-Cola, and drags himself off to his job.

At the *Sun,* closely modeled on the muckraking *New York Post,* foreign crises matter only if New Yorkers are involved. The staff is a motley bunch of eccentrics, presided over by a bone-weary editor in chief (Duvall) and a managing editor with dollar signs in her eyes (Close). The air conditioning is out of whack in midsummer, which accentuates the hothouse atmosphere of the *Sun*'s newsroom. Henry thrives on the place's manic energy But Paul Bladen (Spalding Gray), top man at the prestigious *New York Sentinel*, offers Henry the post of assistant managing editor, hinting at future advancement.

The *Sentinel*, an obvious stand-in for the *New York Times*, sees itself as a beacon of journalistic integrity. Henry, however, views the job offer as an act of condescension by someone who has just called the *Sun* "a cute little paper." He can't resist stealing an important news tip off Bladen's desk and passing it on to his reporters at the *Sun*. The outraged Bladen quickly rescinds his offer, sniping, "You just blew your chance to cover the world." In part, Henry's fierce loyalty to the *Sun* is a populist gesture against the snootiness of the uptown paper. But the film hints that Henry fears entering a bigger, more complicated world, much as he is shying away from the responsibilities that go with parenthood.

The Paper ends on an upbeat note. Exactly twenty-four hours after the story starts, the morning light shines on Henry's small, hectic universe. All the fallout of the previous evening has caused no lasting damage; Martha has given birth to a healthy baby; the *Sun* has hit the street with a lead story that scoops the competition. Even Close's character has learned her lesson, and has done the right thing before the final fadeout. It is a wrap-up that is pure Howard: clever, tidy, and a bit false. Perhaps this is one reason that, despite its raucous energy and its all-star cast, the movie was not a box-office smash. Mindful of *Far and Away*'s budgetary bloat, Howard had finished production $1.5 million under budget and eight days ahead of schedule, bringing in *The Paper* at a relatively lean $31 million. But its $36.7 million in domestic box-office revenue was hardly a triumph. Howard's past successes notwithstanding, the formula for hit movies seemed to be eluding him.

Howard later confessed he had dreaded journalists' reaction to *The Paper*, figuring he was "walking into a propeller with this one," because "there was no way that we could get it 100 percent right." In fact, it was partly to court the press that he shrewdly handed out cameos to New York media stars such as Bob Costas, E. Graydon Carter, and the *Post*'s former editor, Pete Hamill. He needn't have worried. Most reviewers, even those who criticized *The Paper* for being glib, have declared their affection for the film. They like it because they see themselves in it. Roger Ebert began his review in the *Chicago Sun-Times* by calling *The Paper* an accurate rendering of how the job of a newspaperman "screws up your personal life. You get cocooned in a tight little crowd of hyperactive competitors, and eventually your view of normality begins to blur." *The Paper* further reminded Ebert of "how good it feels to work at the top of your form, on a story you believe in, on deadline."

Though the plot of *The Paper* touches on questions of racial profiling and the power of the media to expose injustice, Howard admitted at the time that he had yet to delve deeply into social issues: "I don't think I've pushed any boundaries yet as a director. I may be a little braver in the future." His next film would by no means prove controversial, either in terms of its themes or its aesthetic approach. Still, *Apollo 13* would require all the bravery he could muster.

CHAPTER 12

A Giant Leap

(1994–1996)

*"I'd be lying if I said I didn't dream of some-
day winning an Oscar."*
—RON HOWARD

ON MARCH 1, 1994, THE FORMER CHILD STAR TURNED
forty. The following evening, Brian Grazer hosted a birthday party at
Periyali, a smartly casual Greek restaurant in the hip Lower Manhattan
neighborhood known as the Flatiron District. Howard cronies Michael
Keaton, Tom Hanks, Steve Martin, and William Baldwin were on hand
to celebrate.

As an adult, Howard has enjoyed an ever-widening circle of pals.
Several of them, including Winkler, Grazer, and brother Clint, have publicly called him their best friend. Yet many who are fond of Howard
agree that he always remains somewhat unknowable. In 1991 Grazer
said of his partner, "He's warm to a certain, exact point. It's a little
impersonal and detached. I've known him ten years, and he doesn't
reveal everything." Howard has been keeping his peers at arm's length
ever since high school, when his celebrity status made him wonder if the
friendship of his classmates could be trusted. Today he maintains social
relationships with many actors and with such fellow directors as Steven

Spielberg, George Lucas, and Robert Zemeckis. But because of the extraordinarily competitive nature of the film business, he is cautious about showing any hint of weakness or insecurity. In Hollywood, says Howard, "people are guarded. They're funny, friendly, great to have lunch with, but you have to choose very carefully who you're [going to] bare your soul to." He locks himself up tight, as a form of self-protection. That's why such longtime colleagues as writer Bob Dolman are still trying to figure out what Howard is truly like behind the affable facade.

Howard's fortieth birthday brought a swarm of journalists, all asking him to wax philosophical about his long career. Characteristically, he focused less on his past accomplishments than on his potential for future growth. He was fully convinced that his best work still lay ahead of him, between the ages of fifty and sixty-five, when he could use all he had learned "to really push the limits a little more." Howard's director heroes include Billy Wilder, who shot his last film at seventy-five, and John Huston, who completed a major work (*The Dead,* 1987) just before his death at eighty-one. Howard too hopes to be what he calls "an old man director." It is his goal to emulate Huston, "out there at eighty-one or eighty-two, wheezing in a wheelchair."

Howard also wants a career that is meaningful. As he entered his fifth decade, he confessed he aspired to move beyond lighthearted commercial fare and into *Schindler's List* territory. He noted, however, that Steven Spielberg had Thomas Keneally's book on his shelf for ten years before he knew how to bring Oskar Schindler's story triumphantly to the screen. *Schindler's List* (1993) has been revered in many quarters as both an artistic accomplishment and a social milestone. Certainly, its powerful source material gave this film a sense of purpose that helped it transcend the realm of entertainment. But Howard in 1994 was not yet ready to take a chance on important but risky subject matter. Nor was he eager to tailor his projects to the tastes of others, in hopes of coming up with a prestige film. He frankly declared that "I'm also not stumbling over myself to search for that particular quality. I'm not looking for the Oscar movie."

He may not have been specifically looking for an Oscar-worthy subject, but his next film after *The Paper* was to be one of his most widely honored. In telling the story of an abortive trip to the moon, Howard made a giant leap in his career.

Howard had never planned to make a movie about astronauts. Like many Americans, he was proud of his country's space program, but generally gave it little thought. When the USSR launched Sputnik in 1957, and when the Soviets' Yuri Gagarin became the first man in space in 1961, Howard was too young to register the implications of these historic events. But as a ten-year-old in 1964, his imagination was briefly captured by the space walk performed by American astronaut Ed White. At school he read *Weekly Reader* articles about the future and imagined, "we'd all be flying in our own spacecraft soon like in *The Jetsons*. Back then it seemed so possible. I was all set."

When White and his two fellow Apollo 1 astronauts were killed in January 1967 in a launchpad fire that nearly aborted the U.S. manned space program, Howard was twelve and preoccupied with *The Andy Griffith Show*. He has a clearer memory of July 1969's landmark Apollo 11 mission, which occurred while he was shooting a television movie, *Smoke*. On the evening of July 20, director Vince McEveety threw a party where everyone crowded around the television set to watch blurry black-and-white images of Neil Armstrong taking his first steps on the moon. During the seemingly doomed flight of Apollo 13 in April 1970, Howard was out in the Utah desert, filming an episode of the popular television Western, *Gunsmoke*. He recalls the production crew listening to transistor radios, trying to keep abreast of the crisis. When the three astronauts safely splashed down in the Pacific Ocean, he shared in the world's jubilation. But, like so many others, he was baffled by the chain of events that had led to the very real prospect of the men being stranded in space.

Just before beginning production on *The Paper* in 1993, Howard received an after-hours phone call from Grazer in California. It seemed that James Lovell, commander of the ill-fated Apollo 13, was writing a first-hand account of the mission. His memoir, to be titled *Lost Moon*, was no more than a ten-page outline, but had quickly inspired a bidding war among Hollywood studios and production companies. Imagine Entertainment's vice president Michael Bostick, whose father, Jerry, had served for years on NASA's Mission Control team, was especially persuasive about the dramatic merits of the Apollo 13 story.

On Howard's behalf, Bostick quickly sketched the plot elements. Astronauts Lovell, Fred Haise, and last-minute replacement Jack Swigert were on an apparently routine trip to the moon when— 205,000 miles from earth—an exploding oxygen tank crippled their main spacecraft. With no other choice, the three men crawled into the tiny attached module that had been designed to touch down on the lunar surface. This fragile craft, which had been built to accommodate two men for forty-eight hours, was now their home for four tense days and nights. Power sources and oxygen supply grew dangerously low. But the astronauts were saved by sheer grit in the face of disaster, supplemented by radio contact with mission controllers working feverishly to plot a course of action. Thus a potential tragedy turned into a rousing true-life story of survival against all odds.

Forced, for once, into making a snap decision, Howard decided he wanted to be involved with this project. After four hours of tough late-night negotiations, Imagine won the movie rights to *Lost Moon*. The film was budgeted at $52 million, not a luxurious sum because of the technical demands involved. It would take a year of preparation, four months of shooting, and another six months of shaping, editing, and special effects work before *Apollo 13* blasted into theatres in June 1995.

Howard was attracted to the *Apollo 13* material partly because it would not need "Hollywoodizing." The story was so compelling that there was no reason to pump it up for dramatic impact. In his first long meeting with Lovell, Howard became enthralled with the idea of depicting astronauts on screen. Once he had worked closely with several former astronauts, he did not change his first impression of them as uniquely gifted individuals. He says, "They are honestly the first people I've ever met who could wear me down in a meeting. They seem to have no fatigue level. They apply themselves intellectually like nobody I've ever met." At the same time, the astronauts struck him as wholly accessible human beings, not simply robotic paragons. It became part of Howard's task to convey their normality along with the qualities that make them special.

But *Apollo 13* posed far more complicated challenges. Howard knew he had to find a way to tell his story from multiple perspectives without losing its central thread. He also had to figure out how to maintain suspense, because most viewers would be well aware of the mission's happy ending. Finally there was the question of accuracy. His own instinctive wish was to keep as close to the truth as possible. This goal was reinforced by NASA's hope for a factual record of a mission that could be seen as a victory of American brainpower against tremendous odds, although it hadn't achieved its original goal. Astronaut Dave Scott, who served as one of the film's technical advisors, made the compelling case that human beings would probably not return to the moon for a hundred years. Given that the existing documentary footage of the Apollo 13 mission was far from complete, Scott argued that Howard's film must preserve for future generations an important episode in the history of manned space flight. So Howard took on the burden of historic correctness.

This passionate quest for authenticity meant that spacecraft sets were designed to the precise dimensions of the originals, and that every knob and toggle was carefully scrutinized. The film's art department replicated NASA's Houston command center on a soundstage at Universal Studios in California, down to slide rules on the consoles and vintage matchbooks in the ashtrays. Howard also enlisted James Cameron's special effects house, Digital Domain, to apply computer wizardry toward simulating outer space phenomena.

Because Howard wanted his movie to sound as well as look accurate, he strove to incorporate genuine NASA jargon, while staying mindful that too much technical talk could leave audiences baffled. The actors playing mission controllers were encouraged to huddle with their real-life counterparts and studied transcripts of the mission to help them ad-lib appropriate background conversation. When directing the all-important scenes within the space capsule, Howard had a secret weapon in his leading man. Tom Hanks, who had progressed from the light comedy of *Splash* to Oscar-winning dramatic roles in *Philadelphia* (1993) and *Forrest Gump* (1994), earned a reported $12.5 million to play Lovell. Knowing that Hanks had been a huge fan of the space program since childhood, Howard gave him the extra task of immersing himself in the specifics of the flight, to ensure that the astronauts' words and gestures were on target.

In casting the other Apollo 13 astronauts, Howard turned to Hollywood veterans Kevin Bacon and Bill Paxton. The important role of Ken Mattingly, who was bumped from the flight crew because of his exposure to German measles, went to Gary Sinise. Gene Kranz, the unflappable NASA flight director who becomes the focal point of the Mission Control scenes, was portrayed by Ed Harris. Harris had played astronaut John Glenn in another major film about U.S. manned space flight, Philip Kaufman's *The Right Stuff*. That iconoclastic 1983 film, based on Tom Wolfe's book, viewed the training of the original seven Mercury astronauts with a jaundiced eye. Though nominated for several Oscars, including best picture, *The Right Stuff* fared only moderately well at the box office, one reason that Howard shied away from predicting commercial success for his own venture.

For some of *Apollo 13*'s featured roles, Howard chose people with whom he had a personal connection. Early in the film, savvy moviegoers can catch a glimpse of Roger Corman, who had earned Howard's undying gratitude by starting him on his directing career. Corman alumni have frequently invited their former mentor to make cameo appearances in their movies, beginning with Francis Coppola's *The Godfather: Part II* in 1974. In the years following *Grand Theft Auto*, Howard had sidestepped this tradition, because he considered Corman a poor actor. But director Jonathan Demme, who used his old boss to good effect in both *The Silence of the Lambs* (1991) and *Philadelphia* (1993), persuaded Howard that Corman's acting skills had improved. Howard relished the joke of having Corman play a visiting congressman who questions the high cost of the space program. The part was a perfect fit for a man notorious in the film community for his penny-pinching ways.

Clint, himself a space buff, lobbied his brother to be part of the Mission Control team. He turned in a solid performance in the meaty role of a life-support systems expert modeled on NASA's Sy Liebergot, nicely underplaying a few strong dramatic moments in the heat of the crisis. Earlier, in a more lighthearted sequence, Clint ad-libbed a quip about a tardy income tax return that Ron points out with some amusement in his DVD commentary on the film. (In the spirit of brotherly one-upmanship, Ron lets it be known that Clint has endured his own troubles with the Internal Revenue Service.) Also on the DVD, Ron reveals that his father's brief appearance as a minister standing by to comfort the Lovell family is all that's left of a much better scene. He ruefully describes an awkward telephone conversation: "Dad, you did a good job, but it's on the cutting room floor."

Of all the Howards, Jean won the best role in *Apollo 13*. When writer-director John Sayles (*Lone Star*) was brought in to polish the original script by William Broyles Jr. and Al Reinert, he added the real-life character of Blanch Lovell, elderly mother of the spacecraft commander. As the crisis unfolds, Blanch's unwavering faith in her son forms a vivid counterpoint to the tension rising around her. Jean campaigned to win this plum role, with Rance pressuring Ron to give his mother a chance. He put her through three auditions, but worried that—despite her snow-white hair—she didn't look old enough. "Because," explained Jean later, "of course he still thought I looked like I did when he was in high school. And I said, 'Ron, I'll take my teeth out.' And that got the job." In the finished film, Jean's best line never fails to win over the audience. To Lovell's frightened daughter she says, with true motherly conviction, "Don't you worry, honey. If they could get a washing machine to fly, my Jimmy could land it." At test screenings, when Jean's character elicited laughs and cheers, her son felt justifiably proud.

Howard's oldest daughter, Bryce, asked for and got a walk-on part in the film. Nearly fourteen at the time, she was clearly not shy about expressing her opinions. Howard credits her with suggesting a tricky but dramatic special effects shot, which starts in the space capsule and travels out into space. He also asked Bryce for help in improving a brief character scene between Lovell's wife, Marilyn, and his teenaged daughter, Barbara. The resulting exchange, in which mother and daughter clash over Barbara's clothing choice, has led Howard to chuckle, "This is pretty much the way my house is all the time!" His willingness to turn to his daughter for script advice confirms his colleagues' view of him as a director who solicits suggestions from every quarter. And it's no surprise that Bryce's glimpse of the inner working of a film project strengthened her resolve to have her own show business career someday.

Though Howard's younger children were less intimately involved with *Apollo 13*, they were welcome on the set. Aerial cinematographer David Nowell happened to be on the soundstage at Universal Studios one day when Howard was rehearsing in the mockup of the spacecraft. Howard was lying on his back, planning out his shots, when Cheryl arrived with Reed, then about seven. In Nowell's words, Reed "sees his dad inside of what looks like this great playhouse. He goes, 'Hey Dad, whatcha doing?' And of course you hear that great laugh that Ron has. He says, 'I'm just in here playin'!'"

When *Apollo 13* went into production, Howard was not yet certain how to handle its greatest technical conundrum: the simulation of weightlessness inside the space capsule. Because the computer imaging technology of the day could not meet the demands of this story, he had vague notions of shooting underwater, or maybe suspending his actors from wires. From the first he had warned those hoping to be cast as astronauts that "you're going to be miserable." Fortunately, none of them flinched at the idea of physical discomfort for the sake of the project.

His friend and fellow director, Steven Spielberg, first mentioned the possibility of trying out weightlessness in NASA's zero-gravity simulator, known as the KC-135. This is a specially outfitted Boeing 707, first used in the space program's early days for the training of astronauts. When the KC-135 reaches an altitude of 36,000 feet, an expert pilot guides it into a series of parabolic arcs. At the height of each parabola the plane's occupants can float weightlessly for twenty-three seconds, before slamming to the floor when gravity hits them with double its usual force.

Though NASA had never allowed a film crew to board the KC-135, the space agency's good will toward this production encouraged Howard to push hard for permission. Howard, Hanks, Paxton, Bacon, Sinise, and second-unit director Todd Hallowell made the first flight. All six submitted to a battery of written and physical tests, including a stint in a pressure deprivation chamber, and then spent two weeks at NASA's space camp in Huntsville, Alabama. The original notion was that they'd simply experience weightlessness, so that the actors could effectively mime it on a soundstage. Quickly, however, after all had enjoyed the thrill of breaststroking buoyantly in midair over some fifty dives, they arrived at the idea of shooting footage in the KC-135's hollowed-out rear compartment.

Filming aboard the KC-135 meant building special sets that were both easy to assemble within the body of the plane and flexible enough to allow maximum coverage by a small camera crew operating in tight spaces. It also meant coping with fatigue and even fear. Bacon never was totally comfortable aloft, and Grazer admitted that he found the whole enterprise disturbingly risky: "They're gonna be up in this jet, doing a thousand parabolas. It seems ridiculous. Seems like something will break." The film folk also encountered bouts of airsickness, not surprising in a plane the astronauts had nicknamed "the Vomit Comet."

Howard worried at first about setting a good example: "If I'm the first one to hurl, are they going to lose all respect for me or what?" But he rapidly became an enthusiast, comparing the KC-135 to a roller-coaster ride: "Once you're not afraid of it and you're not nauseous, it's wonderful." For him, the experience was ultimately one of the best of his life, second only to witnessing the birth of his children.

David Nowell, the chief cameraman during the filming of the airborne sequences, explains that meticulous planning made it possible to maximize each twenty-three seconds of weightlessness. The filmmakers concentrated on moments that would be enhanced by the actors' weightless state: Paxton as Haise squirting globules of orange drink into his mouth, Bacon as Swigert spinning exuberantly in midair, a cassette recorder bobbing between the men as they work at basic tasks. For a later scene, when loss of power has reduced the capsule's temperature to near freezing, Nowell himself suggested that Bacon—desperately doing calculations—temporarily let his pen and pad float beside him while he blew on his fingers for warmth. (In the editing room these medium and long shots would be carefully spliced together with close-ups filmed more conventionally on a sound stage.) While the two cameras rolled, Howard was stationed just outside the walls of the spacecraft set, floating in front of the monitors that displayed their feedback. Because no dialogue was being recorded, he was free to shout directions to his actors through a megaphone. Nowell still remembers the excitement shared by cast and crew: "This was one of the greatest toys that we were ever going to be able to play with."

NASA veterans had at first been skeptical about the stamina of men they considered, in Howard's term, "Hollywood wusses." But they swiftly changed their tune when the *Apollo 13* team showed it could handle more than ninety parabolas a day, with each day consisting of two flights of three hours each, in grueling three-day stretches. (The astronauts themselves never trained on the KC-135 for more than two days in a row.) Nowell calculates that by the end of the shoot he and the others had survived 564 parabolic dives, giving them almost as much time logged under zero-gravity conditions as astronaut John Glenn in his three orbits around the earth. The dives were filmed over two distinct periods. In October 1994, once the first few days of aerial filming were completed, the KC-135 went down for emergency repairs. Howard approached Universal Studios with his zero-gravity footage, persuasively arguing that it was worth spending an additional $450,000 to return to the plane in January with more elaborate sets, rather than trying to simulate weightlessness through costly special effects. It became a source of great pride to him that this film, unlike any previous Hollywood space epic, had truly taken the audience outside the earth's gravitational field.

Howard also conveyed the astronauts' experience through other ingenious means. Some close-up shots of the men bobbing weightlessly were filmed at Universal Studios, using teeter-totter devices, wire rigs, and camera tricks. The climactic sequence in which the three try to stave off panic while enduring near arctic conditions was a hardship for the crew as well as the cast: Howard had the entire 170,000-cubic-foot soundstage chilled to thirty-four degrees Fahrenheit. The atmosphere was so cold and damp that signs were posted warning of the dangers of hypothermia and frostbite. While crew members went about their tasks wearing wool gloves, fur hats, and parkas, the actors drank hot liquids between shots so that their breath would visibly condense for the camera. Doubtless, they were relieved when their ordeal was over, but Howard was having the time of his life. He admitted to feeling depressed when the production ended and announced a new personal goal: to be "the first director to shoot a movie on the moon."

Apollo 13 aims to be far more than a simple adventure story. As a historical representation, it captures the spirit of an era marked by the optimistic belief that man's capacities are limitless. The film also has much to say about the crucial bond between an individual and a group. The astronauts of that day, many of them former test pilots, were accustomed to relying on their own well-honed skills for self-preservation. Once they were zipped into their pressurized spacesuits at Cape Canaveral, they were figuratively and literally cut off from the rest of humanity. But in a time of crisis, these rugged individualists learned how much they were dependent on others.

Some scenes set aboard the capsule hint at the tension arising from the prelaunch replacement of Mattingly, long a trusted part of the Apollo 13 team, by newcomer Swigert. The three astronauts not only needed to learn to work together as a unit, but also faced the urgent necessity of getting help from an earthbound source. The film makes clear that when the crew's survival was at stake, the mental heroics at Mission Control were as essential as the physical exertions of the men in space. The value of collaborative effort is shown in many Howard films, including *Gung Ho* and *Backdraft*, which portray men at work. His temperament makes it fitting that he be drawn to projects that celebrate collective endeavor as well as individual achievement.

Howard speaks about *Apollo 13* as both a survival story and the tale of a lost dream. He was thrilled to learn that one of his idols, director Billy Wilder, had praised the film for its focus on Lovell as "a man who didn't make it to the moon." Lovell, a crew member on Apollo 8, had been one of the first three men to orbit the moon. It was not surprising that he dreamed of following the lead of his colleague Neil Armstrong in taking a "giant leap" onto the lunar surface. The title of his memoir, *Lost Moon*, underscores the depth of his disappointment when the explosion aboard Apollo 13 made a lunar landing impossible.

Apollo 13 is artfully structured so that its turning point comes as the astronauts, circling the moon, approach where their landing site would have been. As familiar spots on the lunar landscape come into view, Lovell at first doesn't choose to look. When the others point out the peak he had previously named Mt. Marilyn in his wife's honor, he keeps his head averted, glumly noting, "I've seen it." Soon after, in an effective fantasy moment, he imagines himself triumphantly stepping onto lunar soil. Then, returning to reality, he shows that his priorities have shifted, saying to his fellow crew members, "Gentlemen, what are your intentions? I'd like to go home. . . . Let's go home."

Home is where Marilyn Lovell, poignantly played by Kathleen Quinlan, bravely awaits her husband's return. Through quiet scenes such as the one in which Marilyn is drawn to her husband's videotaped image on her television screen, *Apollo 13* becomes their love story, a tale of a husband and wife yearning for each other across the void of outer space.

Howard has noted that "the Lovell marriage is one of the few to actually survive the space program." Having spent extensive time with both of the Lovells, he credits their marital success to the fact that Marilyn, though highly respectful of her husband's accomplishments, "seems to always have a healthy dose of reality ready for him." Howard's language here approaches how he speaks about Cheryl, who supports his dreams but does not allow them to get out of hand. It's apt that *Apollo 13*'s central character lets go of his dream of faraway glory with the knowledge that life on earth, his home planet, has its own rewards.

Apollo 13 was an immediate box-office hit, riding the crest of the summer movie season and continuing to pull in audiences later in the year. The figure of $100 million serves as Hollywood's informal dividing line between blockbusters and also-rans, and this film's final domestic revenues were in the range of $172 million. It also proved popular overseas. Many critics raved: veteran film historian Leonard Maltin spoke of *Apollo 13* as "exhilarating," adding that it represents the "rare instance where special effects actually serve the story and help make it completely credible." True, some reviewers found flaws in the film, even seeming to begrudge Howard his moment of glory. Kenneth Turan of the *Los Angeles Times* complained that *Apollo 13* is badly marred by instances of apparent dramatic phoniness, such as Marilyn Lovell losing her wedding ring in the shower just before the flight. Turan was right in noting that the shower scene comes off as excessively portentous (although it actually happened), but calling Howard "the master of Opie-vision" seemed curmudgeonly. Turan's thesis—that *Apollo 13* is the epitome of "sentimental, middle-of-the-road filmmaking"— implicitly suggests that Howard's talents are limited to technical craftsmanship. This attitude may perhaps help explain what happened when awards season rolled around.

In broad terms, *Apollo 13* received its share of honors. These included Golden Globe nominations for best dramatic picture, for the supporting performances of Quinlan and Harris, and for Howard as director. (Mel Gibson ended up winning the best director trophy for *Braveheart*.) The *Apollo 13* team went home from the January 1996 Golden Globes dinner empty-handed, but there was great joy when the Academy Award nominees were announced the following month. *Apollo 13*'s nine Oscar nominations—for best picture, best adapted screenplay, best supporting actor and actress, and a host of technical awards—made it an Oscar frontrunner. But Howard was not on the list of best director nominees. The rules are that Academy members with expertise in various categories choose the nominees for the individual achievement awards, but everyone votes to nominate the best picture. Though the Academy had judged Howard's film one of the year's five best, his peers in the Academy's directing branch had overlooked his contributions as director.

The snub wounded Howard deeply. Cheryl wept, knowing how much the honor would have meant to her husband. Grazer reveals that Howard let his children know about his hurt feelings, so they realized that not everything came easily to him and that facing up to disappointment was an important part of life. The situation was made all the more awkward because, when the nominations were announced, Howard was directing Mel Gibson in *Ransom*. Gibson was a double nominee that year, as producer and director of the historical epic, *Braveheart*. On the set of *Ransom*, the two men handled their mutual discomfort about the slight to Howard through playful banter, with Howard asking plaintively if Gibson would still take direction from him, and Gibson replying, "It depends on the direction." Gibson also joked that it was not *Apollo 13* but *Braveheart* that had the best moon shot, in a scene where Scottish soldiers bare their bottoms to their English foes.

On March 2, however, Howard received the Directors Guild of America's plaque for his achievement on *Apollo 13*. The directors who vote on the DGA Award tend to be younger and more actively involved in the profession than those who select Oscar nominees; many work exclusively in television. Though the DGA Award is less prestigious than an Oscar, all but five DGA winners have gone on to win that year's best director Oscar. Howard was delighted to accept his directing colleagues' recognition of his work. He remembers, "I wasn't expecting to win. I told my wife when we were driving home after I won the DGA Award that it was almost like being weightless again." On the night of March 25, Grazer (who as *Apollo 13*'s producer was hoping to accept his own golden statuette) flew Howard out from the East Coast to attend the Oscar ceremony and related festivities, saying, "He's my partner. He should be there." Mel Gibson was the evening's big winner: *Braveheart* nabbed five awards, and two of them belonged to him. *Apollo 13* won Oscars only for editing and sound.

Howard's exclusion from the list of *Apollo 13*'s Oscar nominees continued to rankle. In November 1996 he confided to David Hochman of *Us* magazine that he "felt like an ass" for anticipating something that didn't happen. He noted that throughout all his years on *The Andy Griffith Show* and *Happy Days*, he had never been nominated for an acting Emmy. Despite his belief in the value of collaborative work, he was not above wanting personal glory. But perhaps it wasn't in the cards. As he put it, "I just don't seem to be an award-winning kind of guy."

PART V

Soaring

CHAPTER 13

"Fame on You"

(1996–1999)

"I wouldn't trade off my career for privacy."
—RON HOWARD

BY FOLLOWING *APOLLO 13* (1995) WITH *RANSOM* (1996), Howard was moving from a film that celebrates mankind at its best to one that explores human behavior at its worst. The dark mood of *Ransom*, which revolves around the kidnapping of a child, took many Howard-watchers by surprise. But he has always considered it a director's prerogative to try out a wide range of tones, themes, and genres, free from the typecasting that plagued him as a young actor. True, Howard remains fond of films that affirm human potential. But as far back as 1983, while completing the lighthearted *Splash*, he admitted, "just once I'd really like to make a bleak, depressing movie."

By 1996, the year he turned forty-two, Howard was wise enough to know that life sometimes takes ugly turns. While he has always considered himself upbeat by nature, he says, "You get older, and sometimes it's a chore to hang on to your optimism." Grazer notes, "Ron seems to be a cheerful, easygoing guy. But inside is a very complex, very competitive person who has darkness and pain. He just doesn't show it to people." Grazer believes that Howard chose *Ransom* to come to terms with his darker emotions. By tackling the sort of topic he had sidestepped since the *Splash* era, Howard could satisfy his need to "get everything out of [himself] that's locked inside."

Although he had long toyed with the idea of shooting a crime drama, *Ransom* didn't start out as a Howard project. When Howard and Grazer first heard about this well-crafted script by Richard Price and Alexander Ignon, it was in the hands of executives at Disney's Touchstone Pictures. To get on board, Grazer won a short-term release from the pact through which Universal Studios backed and distributed Imagine Entertainment's films. Although Grazer committed early on to produce *Ransom*, Howard's participation was never a sure thing, even though he took time away from *Apollo 13* to work with screenwriter Price (*The Color of Money*) on sharpening the film's multiple twists and turns. Not until superstar Mel Gibson accepted the leading role of Tom Mullen (for a deal that could reportedly net him $20 million) did Howard agree to take the helm.

Though a film buff, Howard was slow to realize that *Ransom* was an updated version of an obscure 1956 thriller starring Glenn Ford. His version of *Ransom* pumps up the psychological gamesmanship between the chief kidnapper and the distraught father played by Gibson; it also develops the kidnappers' side of the story far more than the original. Howard believes that as a director he must truly connect with all the main characters in a film, no matter how he might judge them on moral grounds. Whether they are good guys or bad, he says, "it is important that, as a human being, you really understand them—at least to the extent that you understand the choices that they're making. I'm looking for the logic in the characters, an emotional logic."

The disappearance of a child is, of course, every parent's nightmare. In making *Ransom*, Howard hoped to tap into the common perception that children today are less safe than in years gone by. He found himself incorporating his private anxieties, as well as the terrifying memory of briefly losing one of his daughters in a crowd. Howard admits he tends to be what he calls a "catastrophic thinker." He notes that when something goes wrong, he's "one of those people who spins it out to its darkest place." In Mullen he saw a possible reflection of himself: "I relate to the character's high-visibility career, his ambition, love of family and trying to find the middle ground there, which is almost always impossible because at any given moment something always seems out of balance."

Howard and Gibson pushed the writers to expose Mullen's shortcomings. Gibson, who then had six children of his own, was adamant that his character be more than simply a paragon of fatherly devotion. Although today many stars demand rewrites that play up their on-screen nobility, Gibson was eager to get inside the skin of a sometimes ruthless entrepreneur who gambles on a hugely risky ploy to save his son's life. In Howard's view, the Tom Mullen who emerges in this film is "a winning character, but flawed." He found it invigorating to explore how Mullen handles a crisis that strikes at the core of his being. The result is a film that is less a celebration than an acknowledgment of the brute instinct for survival.

With *Ransom*, Howard was determined to break away from the style and tone of his previous films. He studied Alfred Hitchcock thrillers and *In Cold Blood*, the semidocumentary crime drama directed by Richard Brooks in 1967, based on Truman Capote's book of the same title. As his cinematographer, he chose Piotr Sobocinski, well known on the art-house circuit for shooting *Red* (1994) and other provocative works by fellow Pole Krzysztof Kieslowski. The result is a *film noir*–style effort molded out of shadows, odd angles, and unusual perspectives. New York City, which had looked sunny and inviting in *The Paper*, appears ominous here, and the disparity between the Mullens' sumptuous penthouse and the kidnappers' rundown lair becomes significant.

Howard's work with the actors on this film belies his public reputation as simply a nice guy. His goal was to show Mullen and wife Kate (played by Howard's former Burroughs classmate, Rene Russo) making an emotional descent into hell. He filmed their scenes from the time of their son's abduction through the movie's slam-bang finale in sequence, so that the intensity of the material would gradually take its toll on the two actors. Howard feels especially proud of one moment near the end of what he himself calls a "fairly slick and urgent and fast-paced thriller." Mullen and Kate, convinced by an ominous phone call that their boy is dead, let go of all restraint in pouring out their grief. Russo describes Howard relentlessly pushing her, until her nerves felt raw. At the time, she worried about lapsing into melodrama, but she now believes that the intensity of her performance thoroughly vindicates Howard's approach: "This piece needed the pure essence of pain and fear. He got me to a very pure place."

But some of Gibson's haggardness in the film's later scenes has nothing to do with Howard's direction. Midway through production, he underwent an emergency appendectomy that removed him from the set for several weeks. His absence, combined with the worst New York blizzard in many years, prolonged the shooting schedule, delaying the movie's release date from summer to mid-November 1996. Despite missing the summer popcorn-movie season, *Ransom* scored at the box office, raking in $35 million in its opening weekend. This was the second biggest opening for a Disney movie (after *The Lion King*), as well as the biggest debut yet for both Gibson and Howard. The public's enthusiasm for the film never flagged, and it earned $136.5 million in domestic grosses. On the heels of *Apollo 13*, Howard had his second blockbuster in two years.

This movie also sparked popular discussion. Audiences flocked to *Ransom* for its suspense, but they also debated the merits of Gibson's character, whose grandstanding determination to go it alone in time of crisis arguably heightens the jeopardy faced by the son he loves. Naturally, Howard was delighted by the fierce reactions his film was provoking in theatres across the country. Critics too felt strongly about *Ransom*. Peter Travers in *Rolling Stone* praised it as an exciting departure from Howard's usual approach, promising that this thriller "will shake your head and rattle your brain, and not just because Ron Howard, the Mr. *Happy Days* director of *Splash*, *Parenthood*, and *Apollo 13*, is dealing with child torture, gratuitous gore, and people who call each other 'motherfucker.' The surprise is how well he pumps out the pulp." But others, both reviewers and casual moviegoers, harshly questioned an ending that seems to move into *Death Wish* territory, with Mullen taking the law into his own hands by gunning for his nemesis.

At the time of the film's release, Howard explained this shoot-'em-up ending—one of several that had been considered—as a way of showing Mullen's moral culpability in the events surrounding the kidnapping. From its opening moments, the film portrays Mullen as an outsized figure, a colorful maverick on the order of Ted Turner or Donald Trump. As the plot unfolds, the audience learns that his son has been singled out as a kidnapping target because of his own past ethical lapses, widely publicized in the media. Howard eloquently made his case to journalists: he did not want the protagonist to walk away untainted from a fiasco for which he deserved some blame. But many who have seen the film believe that its blood-soaked final scene puts a stamp of approval on Mullen's shift into vigilante mode. Howard may have wanted a morally ambiguous conclusion, but *Ransom* ends by turning its complex leading man into someone akin to a conventional action hero, for whom might makes right. Because the film's crowd-pleasing finale undercuts what has gone before it, Howard's quest to bring to the screen a human being in all his complexity is as flawed as Tom Mullen himself.

As a parent, Howard did not find it easy to show a ten-year-old boy being threatened with bodily harm. He admits that some colleagues suggested he refrain from showing the child's treatment at the hands of his captors. Howard, however, decided that such scenes were dramatically essential, and so "I shot . . . what I thought I could stand." His willingness to push the limits of his personal comfort level demonstrates how ready he was to take a risk on behalf of this project. Aptly, *Ransom* is a story peopled with risk-takers, including the bitter, capricious chief kidnapper as well as the frantic father.

By the same token, *Ransom* is a far cry from *Apollo 13*, in which the uncharted realm reserved for those who make the leap is weighed against the safety of home. *Ransom*'s startling lesson is that home may not always be a safe haven. Young Sean is snatched away from his parents in a friendly, familiar setting, during a youth science fair organized by his mother in Central Park. Near the end of the film, the most sinister of the kidnappers walks directly into the Mullen family's private domain atop a swank Manhattan residential tower. He easily penetrates the cocoon woven by the Mullens to keep the outside world at bay. Part of his mission is to taunt Tom with the realization that Sean will never live free from fear: "I got to him once. I'll get him again."

The concept of home is under assault, but not just by the kidnappers. From the start, Mullen and his family are bombarded by media attention. In the first scene, a probing reporter invades a social gathering in the Mullen penthouse; later, after word of the kidnapping breaks, print journalists and television news teams tirelessly clamor to get the inside scoop. This journalistic feeding frenzy hampers Mullen in his desperate race to save his son, but in the past he has shrewdly manipulated the media for his own ends. *Ransom* opens with the screening of a television commercial that capitalizes on Mullen's larger-than-life public image to promote a small airline he has founded. Midway through the film, when he concocts his bold scheme to turn the tables on the kidnappers, he uses the facilities of a local television station to broadcast his threat against the "human garbage" who are out to destroy him through Sean. His faith in the potency of mass media is so strong that he stakes Sean's life on the notion that the public will help him flush out the bad guys in return for the $2 million bounty he displays for the TV cameras.

Ransom is not the first Howard film to examine the power of the press, for good and for ill. *Splash* showed a raucous gang of reporters hungry for a story about a mermaid in Manhattan. *The Paper*, Howard's most affectionate look at the news media, portrayed tabloid journalists as men and women who are capable of being heroes despite themselves. In *Apollo 13*, by contrast, the astronauts' wives view reporters as ghoulish intruders, who take little interest in the mission when all is going smoothly, but are ready to camp on Marilyn Lovell's front lawn when they smell a tragedy in the making. After *Ransom* Howard's next film, *EDtv*, would confront head-on the way the mass media repackage private lives for public consumption.

But first Howard took a breather from the business of making movies. *EDtv* did not appear until the spring of 1999, a full two-and-a-half years after the premiere of *Ransom*. During this period, however, he wasn't out of the public eye.

The year 1997 saw the release of *Passions & Achievements*, a compact disk billed as "A Twenty-Year Retrospective of Soundtracks from Films of Director Ron Howard." This lovingly produced tribute on the Milan label contains within its accompanying booklet perceptive comments by Howard on the role of music within his movies. In addition, leading film composers James Horner, Randy Newman, John Williams, and Hans Zimmer offer detailed reminiscences about the scores they've contributed to Howard films.

In 1997 Howard hosted a television documentary entitled *Frank Capra's American Dream*, honoring the legendary filmmaker, who had died in 1991. Capra's films (which include *Mr. Smith Goes to Washington* and *It's a Wonderful Life*) were some of Howard's favorites. In high school, he had read Capra's best-selling autobiography, *The Name above the Title* (1971), and this lively work helped fuel his own creative dreams. On one of Howard's early directing projects, the aging filmmaker agreed to serve as producer, but the deal fell through because of Capra's ill health.

In *Frank Capra's American Dream*, the words Howard speaks on camera reflect the bond he feels with this Italian-born immigrant who melded whimsy with social realism to convey the complexity of American life. At one point, Howard observes that Capra's films and their maker are "filled with darkness as well as light." This description could also suit Howard and his movies. Though their career trajectories have not been similar, Howard knows something of the self-doubt that wracked Capra's later years. He surely identifies with Capra's way of turning to his family to find "solace and relief from the anxieties and depressions" the film industry can so easily foster.

Meanwhile, as cochairman of Imagine Entertainment, Howard was involved in launching several film and television projects. He took a producer credit on a 1997 film comedy, *Inventing the Abbotts*, and on a short-lived sitcom, *Hiller and Diller* (1999). As executive producer (a title that implies a certain detachment from the day-to-day effort), he was involved with several additional series, the most successful of which was *Felicity* (1998–2002). His proudest television moment came as a producer of the twelve-part miniseries, *From the Earth to the Moon*, which followed *Apollo 13* with an in-depth look at the entire Apollo manned space program. When this impressive blend of dramatization and archival footage won an Emmy award for best miniseries of 1998, Howard was among those jubilantly collecting statuettes.

This was also when he appeared as a guest voice on the Fox network's satiric animated series, *The Simpsons*. His first episode, "When You Dish Upon a Star" (November 8, 1998), shows family patriarch Homer Simpson fawning over Hollywood celebrities who relocate to Springfield. Howard, complete with red hair, freckles, and baseball cap, is portrayed as a sadistic and uncouth lout who favors odd alcoholic concoctions and has chosen Springfield as his new home because, as he says, "it's the only town in America that'll let me fish with dynamite." At episode's end, Howard has sold a Fox studio executive on *The Terminizor*, a wacky new film concept he has unceremoniously swiped from Homer.

By playing himself in this episode, as well as in the "Hello Gutter, Hello Fadder" episode that aired on November 14, 1999, Howard showed once again that he could laugh at his own public persona. His appearances on *The Simpsons* also suggest how much he remains an American icon, long after the end of his acting career. It's rare indeed for a director or producer to be as instantly recognizable as most Hollywood stars.

In "When You Dish Upon a Star," the Fox executive who buys Howard's concept for two large sacks of money is voiced by Grazer, who was now coming into his own as a celebrity. On March 20, 1997, flanked by Howard and Mel Gibson, Grazer witnessed the unveiling of his own star on the Hollywood Walk of Fame. Grazer's star, in front of the venerable Hollywood Roosevelt Hotel, sits next to that of Eddie Murphy, who played the title role in Imagine's 1996 blockbuster, *The Nutty Professor*.

Romance also was in the air for Grazer. In early 1995 over dinner at the renowned Chasen's restaurant, he proposed marriage to his longtime love interest, the feisty and attractive Gigi Levangie. She is a screenwriter whose major credit—*Stepmom* (1998)—was inspired by her evolving relationship with Brian's children. The two were married on September 20, 1997, and Howard, Lowell Ganz, Babaloo Mandel, Tom Hanks, and comedian Don Rickles were among those toasting the bride and groom. Following the hilltop ceremony, the Grazers honeymooned in the south of France. Two years later, their son, Thomas, was born.

With Hollywood developing new respect for the spiky-haired guy who has launched so many hit films, Grazer found himself pondering several offers to run a major studio. Though intrigued by the thought of expanding his talents into new realms, he has made no move to budge from his position at Imagine. Apparently, the stratospheric salaries earned by studio heads do not tempt him. Grazer claims he once told a very wealthy man, "I'll never have a couple of hundred million in the bank. It is just not a goal." True, his 1998 income was estimated at $26 million by *Forbes Magazine,* which ranked him among its fifty highest-earning celebrities. But he insists that becoming rich is by no means his obsession: "I am driven more by pride. I want my children to be proud of me."

In 1998 just before shooting *EDtv,* Howard cited one key reason for the success of his relationship with Grazer: "I bow to many of his instincts and decisions. Then when I'm directing, he lets me make my movies the way I want to make them." Grazer's forte is initiating new projects. As preproduction gets underway he has a major say in financial matters and has been known to fight hard on behalf of his casting hunches. But once filming starts, he retreats into the background, so that the creative choices are Howard's. After the movie is completed, Grazer returns to spearhead the marketing campaign.

EDtv (1999) is a typical Imagine venture because it began with Grazer. An agent sent him the videotape of an obscure 1994 French-Canadian comedy, *Louis 19, le roi des ondes,* also known as *Louis 19, King of the Airwaves.* Grazer watched half the film—in which a contest winner is followed by television cameras for three months—then decided to buy the remake rights. Ganz and Mandel, the screenwriting duo behind *Splash* and *Parenthood*, seemed the obvious choice to craft an extensive rewrite. After reading a one-paragraph description of the Canadian film, the normally cautious Howard immediately joined the team. Following the the bleakness of *Ransom*, he was eager to return to more cheerful fare: "I couldn't wait to get back and do a comedy. It's great to laugh at dailies again." And he could closely identify with *EDtv*'s focus on the price of fame.

Howard calls the yearning for celebrity status "the ultimate American dream, even more so than wealth." Most Americans, he feels, crave the fifteen minutes of fame promised by Andy Warhol and would gladly sacrifice their privacy to attain it. Howard views celebrity from the vantage point of a former child star who first learned to write his name to sign autographs. Those close to Howard feel that he's by no means addicted to public attention. Says one longtime colleague, "If all that went away forever, he'd be completely fine." Still, there's no question that his notoriety has shaped his life. Howard explains, "As a kid, I had to learn to deal with fame or go nuts. My character in *EDtv* thinks he can deal with it, until he almost goes nuts."

The story of *EDtv* illustrates what it feels like to wake up and find yourself a media star. The unlikely celebrity is Ed Pekurny (Matthew McConaughey), a thirty-one-year old San Francisco video store clerk whose happy-go-lucky nature has captured the fancy of the folks at True TV. To bolster sagging ratings, cable television exec Cynthia Topping (Ellen DeGeneres) proposes the ultimate in reality programming: her network will devote itself to capturing every moment of Ed's existence. As Ed moves through his days with a camera crew in tow, the focus inevitably widens to embrace the people who share his life. They include his self-promoting brother (Woody Harrelson), mismatched parents (Sally Kirkland and Martin Landau), and the spunky UPS worker (Jenna Elfman) who starts out as his brother's long-suffering girlfriend, then falls for Ed as millions cheer them on.

Once she and Ed become an item, Shari must contend with a constant media presence. With Ed swiftly turning into America's newest fad, she faces advice from total strangers, as well a *USA Today* poll that has readers passing judgment on her sex appeal. When during her delivery rounds she tries to fend off an autograph seeker, she is blasted with a snide remark: "Uh-huh. On television a minute, and already you got an attitude." Although Ed remains blithely unperturbed, all this public exposure is not conducive to romance.

While Ed's relationship with Shari begins to self-destruct, the True TV execs are only too ready to meddle. Happily improving upon reality, they maneuver sexy Jill (Elizabeth Hurley) into becoming Ed's latest romantic interest, much to the delight of viewers nationwide. (During his DVD commentary, Howard has fun pointing out Cheryl as "the redhead with the lascivious grin" in one of the film's many cutaways to Ed's voyeuristic TV audience.) Meanwhile, the Ed phenomenon has grown so all-pervasive that he becomes the target of Jay Leno's jokes, while George Plimpton, Arianna Huffington, Harry Shearer, and Merrill Markoe ponder his social significance with scathing wit.

In showing what happens when private lives become fodder for public debate, Howard is revealing one of the downsides of celebrity. As Howard ruefully notes, "once you're on television, there seems to be another set of rules." All of which suggests that Howard's own nice-guy persona is partly a defense mechanism born out of the hope of avoiding public rebuke.

EDtv explores a truth that Howard has long known: members of the viewing public feel entitled to claim any personality who enters their homes via the television screen. As a celebrity, Ed cannot ignore the fact that he belongs to his fans. Once he and Shari are certain of their commitment to one another, the challenge is to find a way of escaping back into anonymity. With a clever ploy and help from an unexpected source, Ed vaults away from his media bosses. After they pull the plug on his show, he relies on the fickle public to turn its attention to the Next Big Thing, while he and Shari return to a private life that Howard surely sometimes envies.

When casting *EDtv*, Howard deliberately chose actors who had survived the full force of media attention. Matthew McConaughey brought to his role the memory of the first time he saw himself on a magazine cover. In 1996 just before the release of his first major film, *A Time to Kill*, a *Vanity Fair* spread literally helped make McConaughey famous overnight. Elizabeth Hurley, who in 1995 became part of a media furor when then-boyfriend Hugh Grant was arrested for soliciting sex from a prostitute, is not a stranger to public scandal. And DeGeneres made headlines in 1997 when she came out as a lesbian while starring in a popular sitcom. Filming occurred at the height of the controversial romance between DeGeneres and Anne Heche, when reporters were hounding them daily. Gedde Watanabe, who had starred for Howard in *Gung Ho* and returned to play one of the junior media executives in *EDtv,* found it refreshing to see the two women together on the set: "It was just very accepted and very nice; it was like no problem."

About his leading character, Howard has said, "As you get to know [Ed] you realize there's no such thing as a simple, straightforward person—when you take a good close look, people have so many shadings, ideas, feelings, and tastes, so it's wrong to categorize anyone." The same, of course, holds true for the members of Ed's family. One way *EDtv* differs from the Canadian original is in its inclusion of the hero's tangled family life. Clearly, part of what keeps the Ed-watchers glued to their sets is the interplay of Ed's quirky relatives, who can easily be labeled dysfunctional. But Howard resists judging them, saying, "Nobody's family could hold up under that kind of scrutiny."

Howard's gift for tolerance helps explain his appreciation for brother Clint, whom he apparently never takes to task for deviating from his own personal standards. In 1995, the year of his second marriage, Clint gloated to a *Los Angeles Times* reporter about how much he enjoys starring in cheesy horror flicks such as *Ice Cream Man*: "Cutting the heads off two policemen and placing them on ice cream scoops and doing a puppet show for the neighborhood kids—how much better does it get?" Clint contends that his brother envies him his offbeat career, and his argument may have some merit. Certainly, Ron can grow wistful when discussing the joys of low-budget filmmaking: "You're working on raw energy and idealism, and when you do something that's really good—or even just kind of good—it's exhilarating."

That's why Clint suspects his brother would like to sneak off and make a little movie one day.

Despite their personality differences and their separate lives on opposite coasts, the two siblings keep in close touch. Says Ron, "When I have a lousy day, I phone Clint on the drive home." For his part, Clint claims not to mind being in his brother's shadow: "Ron is . . . you know, actually a really cool shadow to be in." Though he can poke fun at Ron's image as well as his own, he also readily describes his brother as protective and supportive. In 1998 Clint was chosen for a typically eccentric honor, the MTV Movie Lifetime Achievement Award. (Previous winners have included the Three Stooges, Jackie Chan, and *Star Wars* character Chewbacca.) Ron asked to be invited to the always-raucous MTV event, and later he confided it was a relief to attend an awards ceremony without having to worry about being up for a prize.

In this period Clint won featured parts in some big-budget comedy hits, including *The Waterboy* (1998) and two *Austin Powers* movies (1997, 1999). But to the dismay of his loyal devotees, he had no role in *Ransom*. When *EDtv* went into production, Clint surprised Ron by asking for the peripheral part of Ken, the nerdy director of Ed's cable show. Clint relished the irony of playing a director in one of his brother's films. He also saw untapped potential in the role: Ken's job, overseeing all the output from the cameras trained on Ed, allowed Clint to act as an offbeat Greek chorus, adding humorous asides. While Ed lovingly clips his toenails in a giant close-up, Ken deadpans, "If this guy collects his toe cheese, I'm outta here." Howard interjects on the DVD commentary, "For the Clint Howard fans out there, I'm sure you'll recognize that as an ad lib."

Both brothers seem amused by the hairplugs Clint wears in the film. Clint, who has the Howard men's trademark bald pate, had suggested that his character be fitted with a hairpiece. Ron suspected that Clint hoped to walk away from the production with an expensive toupee. Instead, Ron settled on a simulated "bad plug job," with the result, he points out, that Clint "didn't get the fancy hairpiece, but he got a bunch of extra laughs—I think he was happier with that at the end of the day."

Clint freely confesses his ulterior motives. While he's grateful that Ron gave him the choice of whether or not to wear the ugly toupee, he has also relished the opportunity to publicly rib his big brother for being tight-fisted.

Howard had attributed the success of *Ransom* to both skill and luck: "It was a solidly made story and we caught Mel Gibson at the perfect moment, after he'd won the Oscar for *Braveheart*." With *EDtv*, Howard's luck did not hold. When the film premiered in March 1999, most moviegoers could not resist comparing it to 1998's major hit, *The Truman Show*, which also told the story of a man who is televised twenty-four hours a day. Howard, who saw Peter Weir's film while putting the finishing touches on his own, emphasized that the two differ widely in tone and basic premise. Truman is unaware that his whole existence is a staged media event, while Ed's decision to live his life on camera is part of the point. Whereas *The Truman Show* aspires to be poignant, *EDtv* is designed as a rollicking comedy. Nonetheless, not even a lively marketing campaign that featured a huge lens staring out at the viewer, along with the catchphrase, "Fame on You!," could help *EDtv* come into its own. According to prevailing opinion, Howard's work was simply a pale copy of Weir's original. *EDtv* may be funnier than its predecessor, but this seemed to imply it was not worthy of serious regard.

Critics were divided about *EDtv*'s merits. Some called it glib and shallow, while others saw it as refreshing. Andrew O'Hehir of the Web magazine *Salon.com*, who had accused *The Truman Show* of being "sanctimonious," was not entirely satisfied with *EDtv*'s feel-good ending. But he called Howard's movie "a fast and funny ensemble comedy in the brainless, painless American tradition," adding that it could practically have been made in Hollywood's golden age: "Bleach out the colors, backdate the wardrobes, insert Gary Cooper and Rosalind Russell, and you've got one of Frank Capra's lesser films." Among audiences, however, *EDtv* quickly fizzled. Shot on a budget of more than $50 million, it grossed a mere $22.4 million, Howard's worst showing at the box office since *Night Shift*.

Howard's disappointment was tempered by an honor he had received just before *EDtv's* release. On March 23, 1999, wearing one of his trademark baseball caps and a huge grin, he embedded his hands and feet in wet cement in the forecourt of Hollywood's famous Grauman's Chinese Theatre. Boldly and legibly he wrote, "From in front of and behind the cameras . . . Thank you," then signed his name. (Howard's square is on the far left, next to the one where action hero Arnold Schwarzenegger has scrawled his signature line from *The Terminator*, "I'll be back!" Howard's former protégés, Michael Keaton and Tom Hanks, are nearby.)

To a crowd that included family, friends, and approximately a thousand fans, Howard made a brief speech that managed to incorporate memories of both the Apollo era and his own beginnings: "One small step in Hollywood, one great leap for Mayberry."

CHAPTER 14

A Green Christmas

(1999–2000)

"If you did something wrong, he would ask you to do it again in a way that made you want to do it right."
—GARV THORP, VISUAL EFFECTS
COORDINATOR, *DR. SEUSS' HOW
THE GRINCH STOLE CHRISTMAS*

IN 1999, THE YEAR HOWARD'S FOOTPRINTS TOOK UP residence in Hollywood cement, he encountered some of the other perks of stardom. On May 9 he appeared before an adoring group of drama students on cable network Bravo's *Inside the Actors Studio.* Casually dressed, Howard promptly and easily answered the questions posed by host James Lipton, admitting that his favorite word is *love* and his least favorite is *arrogance,* that he might have enjoyed becoming a high school basketball coach, and that (when feeling stressed) he sometimes finds it liberating to voice a certain four-letter word alluding to the sex act.

Other television tributes soon followed. One of the best was "Ron Howard: Hollywood's Favorite Son," which set ratings records when it debuted on A&E's *Biography* in September 1999. This appreciative survey of Howard's life featured family members and such guests as Tom Cruise, Nicole Kidman, Henry Winkler, and Tom Hanks. Andy Griffith and Don Knotts were on hand to reminisce about Ronny's early years. (Quipped Knotts, "We call him *Mister* Howard now!") Also in 1999 Robert J. Emery published, as part of a volume called *The Directors— Take One,* a lengthy (but typo-studded) conversation with Howard. Portions of the Emery interview were spliced together with film clips and celebrity quotes to form a one-hour documentary that frequently airs on *The Directors,* a series cosponsored by the American Film Institute and the Encore Movie Channel.

Though invariably genial during his public appearances, Howard showed a surprising flash of temper in a letter to the editors of *Newsweek,* published on February 1, 1999. He was responding to a gossipy item in *Newsweek*'s Periscope section, relaying what it called "buzz" and "counterbuzz" about George Lucas's upcoming *Star Wars Episode I: The Phantom Menace.* In his brief but powerful letter, Howard chided *Newsweek* for casting aspersions on an unfinished movie. He expressed outrage for the magazine's potshot at the new film's Anakin Skywalker, played by nine-year-old Jake Lloyd. (Periscope had claimed that insiders had dubbed Lloyd "Mannequin Skywalker," adding, "Word is that he stinks.") Identifying himself as someone who started acting professionally at an early age, Howard pointedly reminded the editors that "Jake is quite capable of reading, understanding, and feeling the full humiliation of a piece like that." He called *Newsweek*'s willingness to use hearsay as the basis for condemning Lloyd's performance "shameful."

Howard's scathing response to this frontal assault on a child actor reveals that, despite his mild-mannered persona, he is fully capable of becoming angry. Back when he coached Clint's basketball teams, he would go berserk over bad officiating. (He once theorized that, if he had settled on a coaching career, he might have been as volatile as Bobby Knight.) He is also liable to snap at people who yell at him. He admits, "That makes me crazy, and I will yell back. I have a very slow fuse, but it can go off." At home, his children have certainly seen Dad lose his temper, but in business situations he gets his way without resorting to tantrums. Grazer, who claims never to have had an argument with his

longtime partner, says Howard wins his points by sheer tenacity. Grazer
adds that getting into a fight with Howard can prove counterproductive:
Howard doesn't get angry when people push him too hard, but "he
makes a final judgment about them and becomes inflexible about it."

On the set, when faced with high-pressure, high-cost situations, many
directors are notorious for temperamental outbursts. A motion picture
executive who observed Howard's early directing efforts recalls that he
would "bark a few times" when a problem threatened to spin out of control. Such behavior seemed largely strategic: because he was not known
for screaming, his brief flare-ups "certainly [got] everybody's attention."
Though Howard prefers a peaceful set, he has zero tolerance for conduct
he deems unprofessional. During *Night Shift*, he quickly fired one actress
he felt wasn't doing her job. More recently, he has been able to avoid such
problems by handpicking a cast and crew in whom he can have complete
confidence. Many who are part of his inner circle—such as personal assistant Louisa Velis, first assistant director Aldric La'Auli Porter, and the
Oscar-winning editing team of Daniel P. Hanley and Mike Hill—have
been with him for decades. And those who have served on Howard production teams testify that the working atmosphere is unusually cordial.

One true believer is Garv Thorp, a veteran visual effects coordinator who was hired for Howard's *How the Grinch Stole Christmas*
(2000) after completing an Arnold Schwarzenegger action flick, *End of
Days* (1999). On the *End of Days* set, Thorp had found director Peter
Hyams no worse than most, "just a typical director being a typical
jerk." Hyams' way of taking charge was to disdain input from his crew,
even when their pointers might help him avoid costly mistakes. So
Thorp was not prepared for a preproduction meeting in which Howard
informed newcomers, "I want everybody with a suggestion to feel free
to pipe up and let me hear it, because that's why you're here."

Thorp was skeptical at first about Howard's friendly, egalitarian
manner: "Very few people of his stature are that nice. But *nobody's* that
nice. I just assumed it must be an act, and once the shit hits the fan we'll
see the real Ron, and that'll be fine." But even as the production passed
the six-month mark, when tempers normally tend to fray, Howard
pushed steadily forward, motivating cast and crew not through intimi-

dation but by making them truly want to do a good job. This left Thorp convinced that "he *is* the nicest man in Hollywood. There's no doubt. He's one of the nicest men I've ever met, which automatically makes him the nicest man in Hollywood, just 'cause Hollywood doesn't breed a whole lot of nice people."

In 1986, fresh from the success of *Splash* and *Cocoon*, Howard had told *Esquire* that someday he might want to make movies with more adult themes. When he reached fifty, he mused, it might seem foolish to be telling whimsical stories about aliens and mermaids. Nonetheless, he said, "the Peter Pan in me doesn't want to grow up yet. Once I cross the line, who knows? I may not be able to come back." When he made this statement, Howard was thirty-two years old. Over the next decade and a half, he would experiment with tougher, more realistic subject matter in *Backdraft* and *Ransom*, while also making forays into broad social satire with *The Paper* and *EDtv*. But his project for the year 2000 proved that, four years shy of his fiftieth birthday, he was still not quite ready to give up on his inner child.

The new project was *How the Grinch Stole Christmas*, based on the children's classic by Theodor Geisel, better known as Dr. Seuss. In 1966 the author himself had supervised a twenty-six-minute television version that featured the voice of Boris Karloff and animation work by Chuck Jones, but Geisel's deep-seated distrust of Hollywood had kept him from peddling the film rights to any of his forty-odd books. In 1998, however, his widow, Audrey Geisel, decided to open up bidding on some of her late husband's best-known stories. What followed was one of Hollywood's biggest-ever book auctions, with such hot creative forces as Tom Shadyac (*Liar Liar*), the Farrelly brothers (*There's Something About Mary*) and Gary Ross (*Pleasantville*) all clamoring to get their hands on *The Grinch*.

According to the ground rules, all prospective bidders had to commit to a minimum of $3 million before they could present their concepts to Audrey Geisel at her La Jolla, California, home. Universal Studios agreed to bid on behalf of Imagine Entertainment, by now its largest supplier of motion pictures. But Grazer's pitch to Geisel was a strikeout. He begged for a second chance, quickly phoned his partner, and suggested Howard catch a flight to the coast. After consulting with Cheryl, Howard shaped a new approach, one that would lampoon the mania surrounding Christmas while exploring the reasons behind the Grinch's antisocial behavior: "Why is he in a cave? Why is he living with a dog? . . . What's *that* all about?" Geisel immediately bought into Howard's vision, and by that evening Universal had arranged to pay $5 million for the right to make a full-length live-action version of *How the Grinch Stole Christmas*. (As the result of a separate deal, Imagine's screen adaptation of *The Cat in the Hat* is scheduled to appear in late 2003 with Grazer producing, Bo Welch directing, and Mike Myers in the title role.)

Audrey Geisel's concerns about preserving the integrity of her husband's work were eased when she met Jim Carrey and watched him transform into the Grinch before her eyes, without benefit of makeup. Howard had wanted to work with Carrey since 1997, when they discussed a possible screen adaptation of James Thurber's timeless story, "The Secret Life of Walter Mitty." Carrey's enthusiasm for the *Grinch* project clinched Howard's desire to direct it. "I wanted a front row seat for this one," he declared. Howard received $8 million up front; although he and Grazer reduced their usual back-end profit participation, both they and Carrey stood to benefit hugely from merchandising tie-ins. The fate of *Far and Away* had shown Howard that it's dangerous to anticipate a blockbuster. Nonetheless, everyone connected with *The Grinch* was thinking big. The film, budgeted at a whopping $123 million, was slated for a pre-Christmas release in the year 2000. The pressure was enormous: as Howard put it, "Who wants to be known as the people who ruined Dr. Seuss?"

Part of the challenge in filming *How the Grinch Stole Christmas* was developing a visual style that could convey Seuss's quirky two-dimensional world. Howard, who had never before made a fantasy of this magnitude, was by no means content with a "less is more" aesthetic. Instead, he opted for an eye-popping reimagining of the Seussian landscape, spread over eleven soundstages on the Universal lot. Though he had once referred to the story's Whoville as "a small town, kind of Mayberry-ish," Howard turned Seuss's simple hamlet into something far more elaborate: critic Bob Strauss of the *Daily News* noted that the film's outlandish sets look "like an unholy marriage of Frank Lloyd Wright and Rube Goldberg, honeymooning in Toontown." Publicity materials for *The Grinch* include mind-boggling numbers: 8,200 ornaments, 52,000 Christmas lights, 1,938 candy canes, 2 million linear feet of Styrofoam carved into fanciful shapes, and enough artificial snow to cover nine football fields.

Everyone in Hollywood seemed to stop by to admire Whoville in all its Yuletide glory. Crew member Garv Thorp recalls visits from Steven Spielberg, singer Garth Brooks, and actors from virtually all of Howard's previous films. The most memorable guest was Tom Hanks, who made a spur-of-the-moment decision to use the main Whoville set as the backdrop for his family holiday card. With Howard's blessings, he raced home to fetch his wife and children. Because some electricians were asked to stay late that evening to keep the Christmas lights blazing, Hanks found a way to show his appreciation. A few weeks later, an In-N-Out Burger catering truck drove onto the lot to provide an evening meal for all 130 members of the *Grinch* crew, with Hanks picking up the tab.

Howard wanted his spectacular set to be populated by equally spectacular-looking actors. To turn human beings into Seussian Whos, he relied on makeup wizard Rick Baker, who used a staff of sixty to glue foam rubber noses and upper lip appliances onto the ninety members of his cast. Costume designer Rita Ryack then dressed them all in elaborately whimsical clothing, so they resembled Christmas packages come to life. Howard also filled the backgrounds of his scenes with appropriately costumed Cirque du Soleil acrobats, whose odd postures and movements seemed to defy the laws of gravity. When the film was released, not everyone admired all this creative clutter. But the only three Oscar nominations for *How the Grinch Stole Christmas* were in art direction, makeup, and costume design.

While *The Grinch* was being shot, many Hollywood watchers wondered if Carrey's manic energy would add a new dimension to Howard's directorial style. David Sterritt of the *Christian Science Monitor* expressed the hope that by teaming with Carrey, Howard might move beyond what Sterritt called "safe, predictable, reliable entertainment," toward "something that will really have some edge and imagination." In fact, Howard did turn Carrey loose, giving him the freedom he had once granted such wildly inventive comic actors as Michael Keaton and John Candy, so Carrey could inhabit the character of the Grinch on his own terms. Carrey's improvisational talents helped to shape some of the film's more outrageous moments, like the Grinch chomping down on an onion and then briskly using it as underarm deodorant before paying a call on the residents of Whoville.

It was hard work for Carrey to exercise his spontaneity while encased in a costume and makeup he likened to "being buried alive on a daily basis." Rick Baker had devised special facial prosthetics and a head-to-toe body suit that combined Lycra Spandex with individually sewn yak hairs. The outfit was flexible enough to allow a full range of motion, but suiting up was not an easy matter. On each of the ninety-two days he worked, Carrey was immobilized for two-and-a-half hours while having his makeup applied. At the end of each day, it took another hour to turn him from Grinch back into Jim.

Carrey tried to be stoic, but the Grinch getup—and especially his thick yellow full-eyeball contact lenses—sometimes got him down. One afternoon, he became so acutely claustrophobic that shooting had to be halted hours earlier than planned. A few days later, when Carrey reported to the set, he found a second Grinch in residence. It was Howard, who had arrived extra early to be made up and outfitted in a costume identical to Carrey's own. It was his way of showing solidarity with his long-suffering star: for the rest of that day he directed in his Grinch suit. Bystanders still remember how outlandish it looked, between shots, to see two Grinches sitting side by side, discussing the upcoming scene. (Carrey returned the favor by miming a brief Ron-Howard-as-director imitation, complete with baseball cap, as part of an extemporized monologue that made it into the finished film.)

Carrey aimed to create audience sympathy for the Grinch by playing him as a social outcast, "a guy who wants to be invited to the party and isn't."

His approach was in keeping with Howard's notion that the Grinch's mean streak stems from childhood trauma. Howard's first major film, *Night Shift*, had dealt with a meek, repressed conformist who finally finds the courage to walk on the wild side. In *Splash*, love taught a mild-mannered hero to cast off the shackles of everyday life and plunge into uncharted waters. The Grinch's story is in a major sense the reverse of these. His frenzied rampages are not the behavior of a creature glad to be free of the strictures of a too-confining society. Instead, he acts against Whoville because Whoville has long since rejected him as too green and too hairy to be one of the gang. A flashback reveals that the breaking point came when the eight-year-old Grinch, trying to please little Martha May Who with a homemade Christmas gift, was laughed out of his classroom for his presumption. Since that young age, he has nursed his hurt feelings all alone (except for Max the dog), in his cave at the top of Mt. Crumpit. He pretends to hate Christmas, but craves the love, acceptance, and warm family feelings that the Christmas season is supposed to bring. The film's happy ending, then, signifies a homecoming.

So despite the barely contained anarchy of Carrey's performance, *How the Grinch Stole Christmas* communicates a familiar Howard message about the safe haven offered by home and family. Few can argue with this sentiment, but many critics took strong exception to the way Howard's film conveys it. Writing for the *New York Times*, Stephen Holden called *The Grinch* a "shrill, overstuffed, spiritless cinematic contraption," complaining that "the movie is so clogged with kooky gadgetry and special effects and glitter and goo that watching it feels like being gridlocked at Toys 'R' Us during the Christmas rush." At least some members of the viewing public agreed. Former Howard colleague Joe Dante confides that he could not bring himself to see this particular Howard opus: "The trailer was enough for me, thank you. The art direction just made my eyeballs ache, and so I couldn't watch it." Others have suggested that Tim Burton (*Batman*, *Sleepy Hollow*), a director far more accustomed than Howard to depicting self-contained fantasy worlds, might have been a better choice to bring *The Grinch* to the screen.

Amid all the critical drubbing, Roger Ebert predicted that children would view this version of the Seuss story "with perplexity and distaste."

Nonetheless, *How the Grinch Stole Christmas* broke box-office records from the first day of its release. Though Howard had brought it in over schedule and over budget, Universal quickly forgave him when *The Grinch* earned $55 million its opening weekend, and then became the top-grossing film of 2000, as well as one of Universal's top moneymakers of all time. By the following spring, it had racked up $260 million in domestic ticket sales; additional records were shattered in November 2001 when the first six days of the video and DVD release netted $145 million, second only to *Titanic*.

Before *The Grinch*'s theatrical release, Universal had spent a reported $40 million to $45 million on prints and advertising. It considerably lightened its financial burden by taking on a raft of "promotional partners," including Sprite, Wendy's, Wal-Mart, Toys 'R' Us, Visa, and Kellogg USA, to help spread the word about the movie. Even the U.S. Postal Service got into the act, agreeing to send out millions of Christmas 2000 cards, letters, and packages bearing a Grinch "Happy Wholidays" cancellation stamp. For the November 2001 video kickoff, Heinz linked the Grinch to its new green ketchup, and Grinch stickers appeared on 100 million supermarket bananas. The irony lies in how aggressively this film version of Dr. Seuss's original tale—which can be read as a fable about the overcommercialism of the holiday season—was turned into a marketing bonanza.

Howard is not unaware of the contradiction involved, but he doesn't complain about the ringing cash registers. His movie, he feels, still sends the message that Christmas means far more than lavish spending sprees. To him, there's nothing wrong with making money while reminding the public that compassion and love should be the hallmarks of the Christmas season. He's convinced his work serves the Seussian story, which for Howard "sort of has its cake and eats it too," by celebrating the true spirit of the holiday while making wacky comedy out of its excesses.

In early 1999, during the taping of *Inside the Actors Studio,* Howard admitted that it is in his nature "to want to try to entertain and please. Sometimes you can try too hard. And I'm guilty of that sometimes." This remark helps illustrate why those who dislike this movie feel so strongly on the subject. *The Grinch* contains much that is undeniably clever; its technical work is dazzling; Jim Carrey's contribution is often brilliant. But this is a film that is so eager to ingratiate its audience that it becomes weighted down by its own superabundance. Howard told his *Inside the Actors Studio* audience that in future he hoped to dedicate himself to challenging viewers as well as delighting them. One year after the release of *How the Grinch Stole Christmas*, his new film, *A Beautiful Mind*, would show how far he had traveled toward reaching this goal.

Howard has always been adamant about shielding his children from the glare of the media. That's one reason the 1999 A&E *Biography* tribute to Howard is memorable: it contains the first public conversation with Bryce Howard about her famous father. Bryce, a poised and pretty young lady of eighteen, candidly admits that her dad tends to be gullible when it comes to his three teenaged daughters, all of whom "give him a run for his money." She speaks admiringly of her parents as true "soul mates," who still enjoy movie dates three times a week. "They're not supposed to do that," she giggles, "They've been married for twenty years!" Bryce also confirms the reality of Howard's wholesome image: "He *is* sort of milk and cookies."

In high school, Bryce had proved far more socially adept than her once-shy parents had ever been. She also knew her own mind. After graduation, she landed a summer internship at *Vanity Fair* in New York City, then entered New York University, where she had been accepted into the prestigious Tisch School of the Arts with a major in theatre and a minor in writing. Blessed with acting talent as well as a beautiful singing voice, Bryce was eager to embark on the life of a performer. Although the Tisch School—alma mater of Alec Baldwin, Marcia Gay Harden, Ang Lee, and Oliver Stone—prides itself on training students who have chosen a professional arts career, she nonetheless questioned the whole point of higher education. On the set of *The Grinch*, where she played the tiny part of a "Surprised Who," Bryce pouted aloud about her father's insistence that she finish college before moving onto a path of her own choosing: "He's making me go to school and I can't convince him that I don't *need* to go to school." The irony is that

Howard, who never earned a college diploma, could not conceive of his daughter going out into the world without one.

Two years later, Bryce had adjusted to NYU, taking an active part in student productions (some of them controversial) and auditioning for the occasional professional job. She is not, however, the only Howard child to have been bitten by the acting bug. In summer 1999 when the family had temporarily relocated to Southern California for the filming of *The Grinch*, fourteen-year-old Paige enrolled in a drama class at L.A.'s Powerhouse Theatre. Classmates felt that the likable redhead was taking the class for fun rather than pursuing a serious career goal. They knew nothing about her family connections until a filmmaker with a balding pate and a gap-toothed grin showed up to watch the end-of-summer production. Thereafter Paige returned to her girls' boarding school near Boston. Meanwhile, as production on *The Grinch* continued, her twin and her younger brother enrolled in California schools, much to their grandparents' delight.

Between 1999 and 2000, while *How the Grinch Stole Christmas* moved through the production process, the honchos at Imagine Entertainment were also busy planning the company's future. The lucrative deal with Universal Studios was scheduled to end in 2001; a secondary arrangement with Disney (the chief backer of Imagine's television output) would terminate in 2000. For a while a serious possibility existed that Imagine would join forces with DreamWorks SKG, the entertainment company founded in 1994 by Howard's longtime friend Steven Spielberg, former Disney executive Jeffrey Katzenberg, and music mogul David Geffen. After a slow start, DreamWorks had hit its stride with such major hits as *Saving Private Ryan* (1998); through the terms of a proposed merger, Howard and Grazer would become part owners. This move could have given them additional Hollywood clout, along with tough new responsibilities. Ultimately, however, they chose to remain at Universal Studios, their home base for the previous fourteen years, under a revamped pact that would carry them through the year 2005.

One by-product of Imagine's negotiations with DreamWorks was the creation of Pop.com. The aim of this Internet company, founded in October 1999, was to provide an online showcase for short films and other features made by innovative thinkers from the entertainment world. DreamWorks and Imagine together owned half of Pop.com, with the other fifty percent controlled by Microsoft cofounder Paul Allen, who had bankrolled the new company to the tune of $50 million. The idea was that on-site advertising would eventually generate revenues. But Imagine and DreamWorks executives admitted that the financial prospects for Pop.com were uncertain and that they were backing the new venture largely out of "creative curiosity." As Howard himself explained, "It could be great business or not. But we are mainstream storytellers fascinated by the possibilities of this new medium."

The fanfare of the original announcement soon gave way to bitter disappointment. In September 2000, well before the long-awaited launch of the Pop.com Web site, the owners suddenly revealed they were pulling the plug. It's reported that the company's Web designers and other employees, furious at this callous disregard for their efforts, were given severance pay only if they promised not to take legal action. Howard has stayed mum about the fate of Pop.com, but its collapse seems one more example of a dot-com dream wilting beneath the harsh light of fiscal reality. To maintain a Web presence, Imagine and DreamWorks also established a stake in a far less ambitious movie fan site, CountingDown.com, where some of the content planned for Pop.com was eventually made available for public viewing.

On CountingDown.com the world could first see "The Clint Howard Variety Show," also known as "the shortest, cheapest variety show in the history of entertainment." The six two-minute video segments, originally intended for Pop.com, feature Clint in a tuxedo, welcoming visitors to a rundown set that purports to be a Burbank vacant lot. As host, Clint deliberately flies in the face of civility: his language is crude, and his guest artists range from the bizarre (a "dog act" made up of people dressed in dog costumes) to the grotesque (a chainsaw juggler who appears to slice off his forearm on camera).

A running theme is the stinginess of his Pop.com bosses, including brother Ron. The first episode features an interview with Henry Winkler: he and Clint perch uncomfortably on tiny beach chairs, discussing whether Ron is a cheapskate. (When asked if Ron ever picked up the check at lunch, Winkler deadpans, "No, but he would eat the most.") For episode six, Ron himself wanders by to check out the munchies on the set's snack table, then sticks around to be insulted by Clint for the show's deficiencies ("We don't have cash; you guys have squeezed us pretty good"). Though Ron angles to receive one of the gift turkeys to which all of Clint's guests are entitled, he ends up being foiled by his crafty sibling. Throughout, Clint presents himself as the little guy, going up against the greedy corporate giant who just happens to be his kin. Ron's participation here confirms that he stands behind Clint's endeavors, however outrageous these may be, and that he accepts brotherly teasing (as well as marginal humor) with good grace.

Also visible on CountingDown.com is a pair of short animated films, both directed by Howard, which hint at the secret fears of two of Hollywood's best-known directors. "Steven's Dream" is all about gluttony: a cartoon version of Steven Spielberg indulges in an orgy of overeating. In "Ron's Dream," Howard narrates a bizarre scenario about the filming of an important scene. The nightmare begins as he tells his leading actors that he needs a dramatic shot of a passionate nude embrace. When they balk at removing their clothing, he announces that he and his crew will strip to keep them company. (The film contains an amusing caricature of the director, wearing nothing but a baseball cap, his private parts hidden by a clipboard.) As the actors disrobe, Howard is in for a rude surprise. The handsome male lead has an "ass . . . the size of an ice cream truck," and the breasts of his female counterpart literally fall to the floor. Poor Howard is suddenly at a complete loss: "I got an actor hauling a trailer and an actress draggin' titty." Fortunately he awakens, realizing that what he's actually facing that day is a children's birthday party sequence.

If this goofy little cartoon derives from an actual Howard dream (perhaps from the time of *Parenthood*), it reinforces Howard's contention that, however calm he may seem, his nerves do play tricks when he's directing. The subject matter also hints that there's an adolescent side to Howard, a side that's childishly fascinated by the naked body. Such an attitude helps explain what Howard and writer Bob Dolman have called the "dick under the saucepan" scene in *Far and Away*, in which Shannon boldly peeks beneath the china bowl covering the genitalia of the otherwise nude Joseph. During the writing process, this odd and unlikely plot point reduced Howard and Dolman to giggling fits, but the scene made it into the movie. "Ron's Dream" is in its own way equally unlikely. It's surprising, given Howard's private nature, that he would willingly air his own psyche in public. This Internet experiment—like the whole notion behind Pop.com—confirms that Howard does not always play it safe. Though he's known for appealing to mainstream tastes, a part of him longs to explore the fringe.

At the dawn of the twenty-first century, while Ron was revealing flashes of his id and Clint was gleefully playing Mr. Hyde to his brother's Dr. Jekyll, their mother once again struggled with health problems. Despite two heart surgeries, the first in 1989, Jean had enjoyed a late-blooming acting career. In 1997, on her seventieth birthday, Ron and Clint threw a party at The Castaways, a Polynesian-themed hilltop restaurant in Burbank. Jean invited the scores of friends she felt had made a difference in her life. As always, Rance was the evening's chief raconteur, telling long and hilarious stories that had guests "rolling on the floor," according to Jean's longtime pal Phyllis Cohen. Despite the presence of such celebrities as Henry Winkler and Marion Ross, Cohen stresses that the event was not a glitzy Hollywood bash: "There were people from all walks of life, not necessarily theatre people or movie people. They had umpteen friends from all over, and everybody loved them."

Sadly, Jean's illness returned two years later. She regretfully retired from acting, proud that her years in the Screen Actors Guild had earned her medical benefits and a small pension. During a 1999 interview, Ron admitted that his mother's fight for life had taught him something about himself: "A lot of that drive and ambition I have, it turns out, comes from my mother." When her health allowed, Jean visited the *Grinch* set, pleased that both Rance and Clint had featured roles. Crew member Garv Thorp, who noticed the frail but cheery white-haired lady in the production office, mistook her for Ron's grandmother.

During filming of *The Grinch*, Thorp himself was diagnosed with a rare form of cancer that forced him to leave the production for three months. To his astonishment, his paychecks continued to arrive, even after he had been replaced on the crew. In March 2000 when he felt up to working part time, he was warmly welcomed back. Thorp is not sure who made these financial decisions, but credits Howard for being sensitive toward those facing serious health issues. When Thorp returned to the set, his head bald from his brush with mortality, he and Howard had a brief but moving conversation that touched on Jean's illness. Howard, it seemed, had by then made peace with the realization that his mother's time was almost up.

The end came on September 2, 2000. An obituary in the *Burbank Leader* stressed Jean's dedication to the local school system as well as her achievements as wife, mother, and performer. Rance told the paper, "She was a super actress, and she was a charming person without trying. It just bubbled out of her." Later, scores of friends gathered at Forest Lawn Memorial Park in the Hollywood Hills near Burbank to share in a celebration of Jean's life. Speakers included both of her sons, granddaughter Bryce, Marion Ross, and Andy Griffith. Teacher Steve Campbell described Jean's commitment to the Burbank schools: "She wanted the best for her boys and for all the other youngsters with whom they were growing up." Rance contributed a humorous rundown of Jean's seventy-three years, which he likened to the plot of a movie. He ended the informal service by asking the assembled to honor Jean's memory with a standing ovation. Campbell recalls, "I was right behind Ronny and Cheryl and the kids, and it was very very moving watching Ronny laughing and cheering and crying at the same time."

On display in the chapel during the service was a generous sampling of Jean's handiwork, including dainty doll clothes and fabulous holiday ribbons. Jean took special pleasure in adorning her house for the Christmas season. *How the Grinch Stole Christmas*, released a mere two months after her death, bears a tender dedication: to Jean Speegle Howard, "who loved Christmas the most."

CHAPTER 15

Mastermind

(2 0 0 0 – 2 0 0 2)

*"I'm not going to be able to be an asshole
with this guy."*
—RUSSELL CROWE, ACTOR, BEFORE
THE FILMING OF *A BEAUTIFUL MIND*

WHEN HE WAS EIGHT YEARS OLD, RONNY HOWARD SAW
a guest star have a nervous breakdown on the set of *The Andy Griffith
Show*. As the cameras rolled, the actor segued from his scripted lines
into a garbled diatribe. Suddenly he began sobbing, fell to the floor, and
curled into the fetal position. Howard remembers, "It was one of the
most extraordinary, intense, terrifying things I ever witnessed."

Brian Grazer too had long been fascinated by the mysteries of mental illness. In March 1996 the two Imagine partners were keen on
acquiring the movie rights to Michael B. Laudor's first-hand account of
graduating from Yale Law School while struggling with schizophrenia.
Others in Hollywood were also interested, with Disney bidding on
behalf of director Michael Mann, and Fox 2000 trying to get the rights
for Robert Redford. But Universal's offer of $1.5 million won the bid-
ding war for Imagine, which began developing *The Laws of Madness* in
hopes that Howard would direct.

In his preliminary research, Howard spoke at length to Laudor. He has tried to convey the young lawyer's unorthodox coping strategies by explaining that Laudor "viewed life as a television screen, and he would move his delusional lives to the corners of the screen, but he would have up to four hallucinations going at the same time. He began to trust what was in the center screen was real." For Howard it was gratifying to learn that a man so severely afflicted with hallucinations could still live productively. And Laudor's future looked bright: Scribner was paying a six-figure advance to publish his autobiography, and both Brad Pitt and Leonardo DiCaprio had expressed interest in playing him on film. Tragically, about the time that Howard decided to bypass *The Laws of Madness* in favor of *EDtv*, circumstances shook Laudor's fragile equilibrium. Following his father's death, he stopped taking his medication. In June 1998, a few months before Chris Gerolmo was to direct a screen adaptation of Laudor's story for Imagine, Laudor confessed to the brutal murder of his pregnant fiancée. She had been stabbed more than ten times with a chef's knife.

Though the Imagine development team was profoundly disheartened by Laudor's grim relapse, Grazer did not give up hope of finding a project involving mental illness with a happier outcome. In June 1998, coincidentally the same month as Laudor's confession, *Vanity Fair* published an excerpt from Sylvia Nasar's upcoming biography of John Forbes Nash Jr., a mathematical genius who survived schizophrenia and went on to win the Nobel Prize. Grazer was quickly drawn to Nasar's *A Beautiful Mind*, but had to overcome both the reluctance of the Nash family to consider a film version of their story and the efforts of rival producer Scott Rudin to outbid him. Finally, with the backing of Universal, Grazer gained control of the project for $1 million. In April 2000 the buzz in Hollywood was that Tom Cruise was up for the leading role, and that Robert Redford—whose directorial debut on *Ordinary People* (1980) had broached the subject of psychiatric disorder—was talking to Grazer about taking the helm.

Howard, aware of the new project from the start, was at first too deeply involved with *The Grinch* to be an active participant. The situation changed after screenwriter Akiva Goldsman came aboard.

Goldsman, whose parents were pioneers in the field of child psychology, literally grew up side by side with youngsters suffering from schizophrenic delusions. Before writing such Hollywood fare as *Batman and Robin* (1997), Goldsman had worked in the mental health field. From the first, his approach to John Nash's story was bold and original: he wanted to trick the audience into accepting as real the delusional world of the mentally ill. Goldsman's plan was to use Nasar's prize-winning biography as a point of departure, reasoning that within this perfectly detailed exterior life, he "could build an inner life, and in so doing give the audience a window into what it might feel like to suffer from this disease." Starting with what he calls the "architecture" of Nash's story—his genius, his schizophrenia, and his Nobel Prize—Goldsman proposed shaping a narrative that would be true to the spirit of Nash's emotional journey, though it might depart from the facts of Nash's life.

When, after much delay, Goldsman submitted a strong first draft of his screenplay, Howard was ready to make a commitment. He found himself attracted to *A Beautiful Mind* on many levels. It would be a radical departure from *How the Grinch Stole Christmas* and from the romances and action dramas for which he was best known. He also was fascinated by the tight, competitive world of higher mathematics during the Cold War period. Goldsman's witty DVD commentary makes clear that when Nash was at Princeton in 1950, "mathematicians were almost the rock stars of the era."

Howard, who has known stardom and is no stranger to the competitive urge, was intrigued about how these elements of his own youthful life would play out within the ivy-covered walls of an elite university. And having spent time on special effects projects, Howard was excited about returning to his first love: working closely with actors on emotionally challenging material. He was particularly pleased with the script's focus on the role played in Nash's recovery by the love and support of his wife, Alicia. Regarding what he calls the "really compelling adult love story" within *A Beautiful Mind*, Howard insists, "This is the real thing. This is the kind of love that lives are built on. And in this particular case I think a life was saved by it."

Goldsman gladly credits Howard's contributions to the final shooting script. Howard came up with the notion that visual patterns—on a crystal punchbowl, a stained glass window, or a gaudy necktie—be used to suggest the workings of Nash's mind. Howard also decided that the look of the film should gradually shift from the sunny "*Life* magazine–style" perfection of the early Princeton years into *film noir* shadows as Nash's paranoid delusions encroach. But Howard's ideas went far beyond stylistics. He worked closely with Goldsman over two drafts to enhance the film's basic story line. Howard insisted that the script show Nash proposing marriage to Alicia. At first Goldsman tried to resist what he saw as an impossible scene to write. Then he found a way to showcase both Nash's eccentricities and Alicia's strength of mind, by depicting her response to Nash's demand for "verifiable empirical data" that would justify a long-term commitment between them. Goldsman considers the resulting interchange a personal favorite.

Howard also enriched the screenplay with what he drew from his actors on the set. Goldsman, who was present throughout the three-month shoot, calls Howard "precise and tireless" in giving each scene just the right emotional pitch. In one sequence that illustrates the slow pace of Nash's recovery, Alicia overhears a one-sided conversation between John and a garbage man who seems to be illusory—but isn't. Goldsman had written the scene to end on a note of quiet sadness, with husband and wife both wracked with doubt about their future together. But Howard, shrewdly recognizing the audience's need for a shred of hope at this juncture, had the characters tacitly move from confusion to regret to an unexpected, but very welcome, shared amusement about their plight.

Goldsman and Howard agree that tough thinking went into the key scene in which Alicia walks out on Nash, but then returns. In real life their separation was considerably longer. In 1963 with Nash's behavior growing ever more erratic and hostile, Alicia divorced him after eight years of marriage. In 1970 she took him in when he had nowhere else to go. From then on, the two have remained devoted to one another, and remarried in 2001. Howard deeply regrets that his film lacked the time to show the full evolution of the Nash relationship, which he has called "powerful" and "heroic." That's why he expended so much mental energy on the short scene that contains "at least an acknowledgment, a nod, to the kind of difficult decision making that the real Alicia Nash had to deal with and make, in order to save this man."

The words Howard and Goldsman chose to cap the scene are Alicia's heartfelt "I need to believe . . . that something extraordinary is possible." Her line represents an almost exact parallel to the message Howard had long ago extracted from *Cocoon*, that "something extraordinary and unexpected can happen at any time."

Howard told the Directors Guild of America that one of his greatest challenges on this film was getting Alicia's "I need to believe" speech to ring true. In rehearsal, he tried out scores of ideas with actors Jennifer Connelly and Russell Crowe. Finally "Russell dropped to his knee and put his hand on my chest . . . he became Jennifer, and that's how we shot it." For Howard, this session represented "one of the most exciting days during the whole film." It inspired him to reflect, "This is what I love to do."

Back in 1991 Grazer had predicted that if his partner ever dared to reveal his darker side, "the moody dramatic actors he would like to work with would be attracted to him." On *A Beautiful Mind*, Grazer's words were triumphantly fulfilled: one of Howard's major achievements was casting the talented and prickly Crowe. Although by the time filming began, Crowe had won an Oscar for his starring role in the epic *Gladiator* (2000), Howard was most influenced by his understated power in *L.A. Confidential* (1997) and *The Insider* (1999). Seeing the latter film without opening credits, he literally did not recognize the pasty, middle-aged whistleblower who takes on the tobacco industry as Crowe. This experience convinced him that Crowe had the "chameleon" quality needed to submerge himself in the role of Nash. The Australian actor prepared for his first meeting with Howard by doing copious research, a sign that Crowe had the "truly ambitious sort of aggressive intellect that I thought really fit this character."

Crowe, who has been known to give directors a difficult time, immediately warmed to Howard's collaborative style. Howard "likes to use me as a sounding board for things he's thinking about," explained Crowe during production. "And I like that responsibility. It keeps me completely involved . . . . Have I made it clear that I'm really enjoying myself?" Once the film opened, Crowe summarized his experience: "Ron Howard, it seems to me, has got everybody in the world fooled that he's some kind of simple bloke. He's one of the most intense film-makers I've ever worked with." Crowe praised Howard for tempering his intensity with a gentle manner. Because Howard was also well organized and knew what he wanted, Crowe could put his own single-mindedness to work on the film's behalf.

Despite the strong subject matter and Crowe's passionate perform-ance style, a few lighthearted moments occurred on the set. At one piv-otal point in the story, Nash wakes from unconsciousness to stare into the face of a psychiatrist played by Christopher Plummer. The script requires the paranoid Nash to insist that Dr. Rosen is a Russian spy. But the first time Crowe played this wake-up scene, he made eye contact with his old friend Plummer and exclaimed, "I know you! You were in *Sound of Music*!" Mostly, however, filming was serious business. Because of the threat of a Screen Actors Guild strike, the production had no choice but to finish on schedule, and cast and crew would sometimes find themselves shooting twenty-four hours at a stretch. This additional pressure did not daunt Howard's actors. Plummer, a stage and screen veteran, credits Howard's ability to assemble a solid team: "He's like the old-fashioned director who trusts his company. I think the best directors are the ones who know how to cast. And once they've cast, they almost leave you alone because they've got the family, and they trust the family."

In some cases, of course, the actors *were* family. The administrator who welcomes Nash to the Harvard campus, and later stares in horror as he self-destructs, is Cheryl Howard, decked out in a French twist hairdo and a severe brown suit. Howard admits that his wife "did not like her look in this movie." He adds that after all these years she still does not consider herself an actress. Fortunately, "she . . . tolerates my need to have her in all the films." (In the same sequence, daughter Bryce is another appalled onlooker.) Later, in a scene on the lawn of a mental hospital, Rance Howard was to have played the small but vivid role of a mental patient who rants to empty air in full view of Nash and Dr. Rosen. This scene made useful points about the clinical aspects of schizophrenia, but because Howard decided that it interrupted the flow of the narrative, it was snipped from the film. It is entirely typical of Howard that he allows neither family feelings nor a sincere desire to educate the public to trump the dramatic needs of his story. Clint plays no on-camera role, and Ron admits that Clint's many fans have given him grief over this. But once principal photography ended, Clint participated in a looping session, and so—for those who listen hard—his voice can be recognized above the hubbub in a barroom scene.

Though Howard was so excited about this project that he claims he "ran to work every day," his nerves played their usual tricks on him. He confesses he particularly lost sleep over the details of the makeup that permits Crowe to age forty-seven years over the course of the film. The efforts of age-makeup specialist Greg Cannom, who had worked with Crowe on *The Insider* and Howard on *Cocoon*, proved invaluable. Howard also took the unusual (and costly) step of filming almost entirely in sequence, which both helped with the gradual age progression and allowed the actors to build upon the emotions of previous scenes. As director, Howard faced other nerve-wracking moments when planning logistically tricky sequences, such as the near drowning of the Nashes' baby in the bathtub. He especially agonized when filming scenes that might give away too soon the illusory nature of Nash's Cold War adventures. After staging the moment in which a futuristic radium diode is implanted in Nash's forearm, he passed yet another sleepless night.

Under the circumstances, it might seem that having the real John and Alicia Nash on the set would have added still more pressure. But Howard makes clear that their presence was a definite asset. From his brief conversations with Nash, Crowe was able to glean mannerisms, dialogue snippets, and ideas on how to integrate Nash's puckish sense of humor into the film. Howard invited Nash to be videotaped while he spelled out the findings that had earned him the 1994 Nobel Economics Prize for advancing the science of game theory, a discipline that explains interpersonal negotiations in mathematical terms. Watching Nash at the blackboard, Howard discovered a seventy-three-year-old man who was "really vibrant, really alive, interested," a far cry from the more guarded figure with whom he had previously chatted. Nash's zest for life made Howard appreciate more fully "the miracle of his recovery." He was also deeply moved by Alicia Nash; as he puts it, the script of A Beautiful Mind "continued to evolve and grow as I got to know the strength of this woman."

A Beautiful Mind—Howard's first real stab at an intimate psychological drama—covers far different ground than his previous films, but familiar themes continue to surface. When the audience first meets a twenty-year-old Princeton graduate student named John Nash, he already lives within a protective shell of his own making. Though intellectually gifted, he has no talent for personal relationships, and fends off social intimacies he can't handle by adopting a smug, haughty manner. His penchant for working math problems with a grease pencil on panes of window glass is explained by Akiva Goldsman as the filmmakers' "attempt to show that John sees the world through patterns." It is Nash's mental habit to superimpose these self-made patterns upon a reality that's cold and untidy, one that shows little respect for the unique creature he believes himself to be.

Like so many Howard characters, John Nash dares to make a giant leap, or several. Unfortunately, the intuitive leaps that confirm his mathematical genius parallel his psychological leap into an alternative world, a mysterious realm supercharged with global significance. By the film's midpoint, Nash has vaulted so far beyond the bounds of everyday existence that he is out of touch with the lives of those around him. Though he's convinced he is fending off dangerous forces, it is he who poses a threat, both to himself and to those he holds dear. What he cannot realize is that he has crossed the dividing line between sanity and paranoid schizophrenia.

It is not until Nash finally applies his powerfully logical mind to the illogic of his delusions that he can begin to chart his return to the land of the living. In this effort, Alicia is his guide and his inspiration. Nash's homecoming—his acceptance of a mundane life within a loving domestic environment—ultimately saves him. On the film's own terms, Nash's victory lies not so much in the winning of the Nobel Prize for work done forty years earlier, but in surviving long enough to transcend his illness and accept the recognition of his peers. Without the support of his wife and the mathematics community at Princeton, he would never have lived to see himself honored in his old age. So *A Beautiful Mind* sends a favorite Howard message: home and family are the source of salvation. Even those such as Nash, who take a giant step out into the uncharted universe, must at last come home again.

A Beautiful Mind was never pegged as a blockbuster in the making. In March 2001, nine months before the film's release, Grazer told the *New York Times,* "We had to find a way to make that story more accessible and entertaining. So we genrefied it, and turned John Nash's life into more of a compelling thriller. Because when you're schizophrenic, you're living in more than one reality." Though Grazer had a hunch that audiences would respond to a story of mental illness as long as it was sufficiently "genre-fied," Universal Studios required further convincing. Studio bosses decided *A Beautiful Mind* was an art film and thus a risky commercial prospect. As a result, Grazer (who personally has little interest in art films) agreed to forego his normal producer fee to get this movie made.

The film was reportedly budgeted at $60 million, with much of this dedicated to star salaries, and Russell Crowe earning somewhere around $15 million. Screenwriter Goldsman insists that production costs were deliberately kept low: even the involvement of Crowe, three-time Oscar nominee Ed Harris as a mysterious government agent, and director Howard could not guarantee a hit. Goldsman points out, "It's a movie about a mathematician with schizophrenia. Now, in retrospect that might seem like a commercial choice, but oh my god!" In March 2002 he told a radio host, "I think literally if you could have put our hands to Bibles and said, $150 million [domestic gross], we would have laughed."

When *A Beautiful Mind* opened in late December 2001, some early reviews predicted only modest success. But within five months the film had surpassed $170 million at the domestic box office and brought in well over $300 million worldwide, placing it among the 100 top-grossing films of all time. With its video and DVD release in early July 2002, *A Beautiful Mind* topped the charts for both sales and rentals. One woman who caught a first-run showing during the Christmas 2001 holidays typified the response among the ticket-buying public. Turning to her companion as the lights came up, she fervently exclaimed, "God, Ron Howard makes deeply moving movies!"

Some industry commentators took to *A Beautiful Mind* immediately. Peter Bart, a former studio executive and *Variety*'s editor in chief, published an open letter to Howard on December 3, three weeks before the film's official opening night. Candidly admitting that he had once considered Howard's new project a bad idea, Bart described his change of heart while watching a sneak preview: "Over the final credits I could visualize Oscars dancing by." Meanwhile, in the *Hollywood Reporter*, columnist Martin A. Grove announced that *A Beautiful Mind* "looks like the film to beat in this year's best picture race."

Among critics, opinions were slightly more mixed. *Variety*'s Todd McCarthy called *A Beautiful Mind* "consistently engrossing," and predicted that "the film's effective blend of intelligence and emotion will reach all manner of audiences." In *Time* magazine, Richard Schickel singled out for praise "the simple, elegant way Howard thrusts us into Nash's disastrously troubled mind." Schickel, a veteran critic who has not always been a Howard fan, hailed *A Beautiful Mind* as "mainstream filmmaking at its highest, most satisfying level." Howard's sometime nemesis, Kenneth Turan of the *Los Angeles Times*, admitted that *A Beautiful Mind* was Howard's most artistically successful serious film to date. But he still dismissed the film as "a too-tidy Ron Howard project," adding that "there is more to admire in *A Beautiful Mind* than you might expect, but less than its creators believe."

One of the film's most thoughtful critics was the *New York Times'* A. O. Scott, who seemed profoundly bothered by the liberties the filmmakers had taken with Nasar's source material. Citing the screenplay's many factual omissions (including Nash's apparent sexual interest in men and his fathering of a child out of wedlock before he married Alicia), Scott labeled the film version of *A Beautiful Mind* "a piece of historic revisionism on the order of *J.F.K.* or *Forrest Gump*." Still, there was much in the film that he could not resist admiring. Scott singled out a scene in which Alicia, as an MIT physics student, approaches Professor Nash with her solution to a famously difficult math problem. After glancing at her work, Nash brusquely rejects it as elegant but wrong. To Scott's way of thinking, Nash's comment here provides a fitting verdict for the film itself. Scott ended his review by saying, "The movie can—indeed should—be intellectually rejected, but you can't quite banish it from your mind."

Scott's review of *A Beautiful Mind* reflects his serious grappling with questions of historic accuracy and how these relate to aesthetic achievement. Certainly there is room, even for an admirer of the film, to ponder how Howard and company molded the messy realities of Nash's actual life into a full-fledged inspirational saga. But as *A Beautiful Mind* began winning major film awards, the allegations that it had dodged historical truth began to seem increasingly calculated to derail its chances of taking home the biggest cinematic prizes.

By the start of 2002, *A Beautiful Mind* was one of ten candidates for the American Film Institute's new award for best film of 2001. As January wore on, the movie picked up four Broadcast Critics Association trophies. (Howard tied with Baz Luhrman of *Moulin Rouge* for best director honors.) When Golden Globe winners were announced in a televised ceremony on January 20, 2002, *A Beautiful Mind* received four of the five awards for which it had been nominated: best motion picture drama, Russell Crowe as best dramatic actor, Jennifer Connelly as best supporting actress, and Akiva Goldsman as best screenwriter. Howard's own loss to Robert Altman, the seventy-five-year-old director of *Gosford Park*, was only a minor disappointment.

But while the awards and nominations continued to roll in, a controversy was brewing. In December, after Internet muckraker Matt Drudge complained that the film had omitted Nash's possibly unorthodox sexual appetites, a publicist from Miramax phoned a reporter on the Hollywood beat to alert him to the posting. Matters quickly escalated, with Universal accusing rival studios of spreading gossip about *A Beautiful Mind* to improve the Oscar chances for their own films. A brief but tense confrontation followed between Harvey Weinstein of Miramax and Universal chairman Stacey Snider.

Meanwhile, those responsible for promoting *A Beautiful Mind* were aggressive in countering the innuendo. In 1999 the Oscar hopes of a previous Universal biopic, *The Hurricane*, had apparently been dashed by charges of historic inaccuracy. So Universal's vice chairman of marketing and distribution, Marc Shmuger, masterfully deflected criticism of *A Beautiful Mind* by having the filmmakers reiterate that their movie was only *inspired* by the facts of Nash's life, and that its true intent was to convey the experience of mental illness. Shmuger's efforts were helped by the outpouring of support from the mental health community, which praised the film's authentic depiction of schizophrenia. Journalists soon received copies of a supplemental press kit on *A Beautiful Mind*. It featured an admiring *Newsweek* column by George Will, as well as a sheaf of letters sent to Howard by the families and caregivers of mental patients, all of them testifying that *A Beautiful Mind* is the rare movie that gets mental illness right. At about this time, the National Mental Health Awareness Campaign, chaired by Tipper Gore, presented Howard and Grazer with its first annual Awareness Award for their contribution to the public's understanding of mental health issues.

When Oscar nominations were announced in mid-February, *A Beautiful Mind* was on the list in eight categories, second only to *The Lord of the Ring*s. Howard got the good news about his best-director nomination while in Germany, where he and his lead actors had accompanied their film to the Berlin International Film Festival. Howard took time out to sympathize with those who might have been disappointed by the announcements—"Their names weren't called. I know how that feels"—but then celebrated his own good fortune by jumping onto the bar of a German pub to dance. As a nominee he was soon making the traditional rounds, even showing up at the Motion Picture and Television Home in California's San Fernando Valley to ingratiate himself with elderly Academy voters.

On a visit to the *Tonight Show*, Howard told host Jay Leno that he had mentally prepared himself for once again being overlooked. In fact, he admitted he had contemplated kicking over the television set if his name was not announced among the nominees. To which Leno quipped that he could not imagine Howard taking this violent step. Rather, "I see you movin' stuff out of the way so you could *push* the TV." Asked if he would vote for himself, Howard delighted the studio audience by moving from a polite explanation that voting is supposed to be secret to an emphatic "*Of course* I'm voting for myself. *Are you kidding?*"

Howard's exuberant manner on the Leno show could be seen as a deft performance by a shy man who knows the crowd loves extroverts. He hinted as much when Leno asked when he had last acted, by replying, "Well, outside of this appearance. . . ." But he gave a tiny glimpse of his personal life. He revealed that he had just spent his forty-eighth birthday watching daughter Paige in a production of *Dracula* that featured high school kids biting each other on the neck. The following day, Bryce turned twenty-one, celebrating with the whole family at an ice cream parlor she'd loved since childhood. That evening, Ron and Cheryl took in a play staged by Bryce's boyfriend (Ron described this as "intense young actors giving it everything"), then joined the young couple at a Manhattan technobar. Howard deadpanned that among the "freaks" with wild hair and piercings, "Cheryl and I fit right in." Finally, mercifully, they were allowed to go home.

While Howard was bringing his good-sport approach to the Oscar whirl, a second round of nastiness got underway. A month before the March 24 Oscar ceremony, Drudge and other commentators were accusing the real John Nash of being an anti-Semite, a charge that could potentially turn the Academy against *A Beautiful Mind*. In the wake of such attacks, Nasar wrote an op-ed piece in the *Los Angeles Times*, defending both Nash and the film that had used his life as a starting point. And on March 16 John and Alicia Nash appeared on *60 Minutes* to dispel the controversy. They denied Nash's alleged homosexuality, explained their involvement with the film as an attempt to provide financially for Nash's two sons, and insisted that any anti-Semitic statements by Nash had been made at the height of his delusions. (Said Nash to Mike Wallace, "I did have strange ideas during certain periods of time.")

Meanwhile *Time* magazine's exposé of the 2002 Oscar race

shenanigans focused on *A Beautiful Mind*. According to *Time*'s Richard Corliss, Universal spent as much as $15 million on the movie's Oscar push, including full-page ad inserts in major newspapers, in hopes of persuading the Academy's 5,739 voters to ignore all the badmouthing. Along the way *A Beautiful Mind* acquired its own public relations crisis manager, Allan Mayer of Sitrick and Company, to provide a counterbalance to the media's unrelenting stream of criticism.

Howard, as always, tried to take the high road. Having faced many critics during his four decades in show business, he normally remains philosophical about boos and bravos. As he once put it, "these are intelligent people who have a job to do." But in this high-stakes situation, his frustration occasionally showed. Before the traditional luncheon honoring Oscar nominees, he compared the calculated assaults against his film to the dirty tricks leveled at Democratic nominee Michael Dukakis during the 1988 presidential campaign. He lamented that Hollywood's newly intensified "attack strategy" is "not about reminding people of your virtues—it's attempting to undermine the other candidate's credibility. Well, that's a shame." Howard also decried the whispers against Nash, whom he characterized as "a noble figure." Toward those who would blame Nash for his behavior while caught in the grip of mental illness, Howard announced, "I have no respect for that whatsoever. To the extent that I feel some of that occurred, I take it personally."

Howard's righteous anger on behalf of Nash and *A Beautiful Mind* didn't, however, undercut his own good-guy image. One of the funniest pre-Oscar cartoons, by Robert Risko and Andy Borowitz, appeared in a late February edition of the *New Yorker*. It shows a parade of recognizable Academy Award hopefuls strolling the red carpet, with the musings of each spelled out in a thought balloon. A tuxedoed Howard is depicted as thinking, "Wish I'd win one, so I could stop acting so nice all the time."

At last the big night arrived. Host Whoopi Goldberg set the tone of the seventy-fourth annual Academy Awards ceremony by joking, "So much mud has been thrown this year—*all* the nominees look black."

Ultimately, the biggest story of the evening turned out to be the victories of Denzel Washington and Halle Berry, the first time in the history of the Oscars that two African-Americans triumphed in the best actor and best actress categories. But *A Beautiful Mind* wasn't forgotten. As John and Alicia Nash beamed from the balcony of Hollywood's new Kodak Theatre, Jennifer Connelly collected the Oscar for best supporting actress, and Akiva Goldsman won for his adapted screenplay. Goldsman's emotional speech included a special thank-you to Howard, "whose persistence of vision and unflagging grace are the movie's soul."

As the ceremony passed the four-hour mark, Mel Gibson read the names of the best director nominees, who included Robert Altman for *Gosford Park*, Peter Jackson for *The Lord of the Rings: The Fellowship of the Rings*, David Lynch for *Mulholland Drive*, and Ridley Scott for *Black Hawk Down*. The winner was Howard, who bounded to the stage to express his gratitude. Admitting that for years he had played out this moment in his mind, Howard began by acknowledging his parents. He noted that "before my mom passed away eighteen months ago, she predicted that this was going to happen for me on this film." Then, as the audience gasped and cheered, he added that Jean Howard had "also made that prediction on every movie that I've directed since 1983." Howard looked heavenward to salute his mother, then moved on to praise his family, cast, and crew, also thanking the Nashes for sharing their important story. Soon he was called back on stage, along with Grazer, to receive from Tom Hanks the Oscar for best picture of the year.

Backstage, Howard paid tribute to Grazer, whom he called the true producer of *A Beautiful Mind*, though they officially shared the credit and the best picture honors. One resourceful television entertainment program, *Access Hollywood*, hooked Howard up for a surprise telephone chat with Betty Trempe, his journalism teacher at Burroughs High. Trempe, who declared that her former pupil should have won an Oscar long ago, was clearly amused by Howard's confession that he often cut her class. (He was at pains to insist that "it wasn't out of disrespect.") The *Access Hollywood* segment ended with Howard being asked whether he planned to party the night away. His answer: "As long as the eyes can stay open."

The four Oscars did not end the debate about *A Beautiful Mind*. For weeks after the statuettes were handed out, detractors continued to gripe about the film's sins of omission. (The letters page in the *Los Angeles Times* for a while contained a lively exchange about Alicia Larde Nash, who although born in El Salvador was not portrayed on screen as a Latina.) In summing up all the controversy, the *Times'* Rachel Abramowitz spoke of the "wholesale attack on the Opie aesthetics, on Howard's facility for uplift, his penchant for optimism." But she also acknowledged the genuine popularity of both Howard and the message he has to offer. It seems clear that, despite all the naysaying by some, Howard has a gift for making a connection with movie fans around the globe. His promise of hope, presented with intelligence and artistic skill, resonates so loudly because people feel they can trust the messenger.

Is it because Howard is still Opie? Certainly, fans have not allowed the Mayberry kid to fade away. On January 27, 2002, Katie Maratta's "Talking Pictures" cartoon feature in the Sunday *Los Angeles Times* pointed out that three things make baby boomers feel their age: one is "seeing 'Opie' at awards shows." In a formal letter praising *A Beautiful Mind*, Dr. Ann Nolen of the National Alliance of the Mentally Ill couldn't resist signing off with the words, "Thanks, Opie." Even Russell Crowe, upon accepting a best-actor trophy from the Broadcast Film Critics Association, hailed his director with a cheeky "Opie done good!" And backstage after the Oscar broadcast, *Access Hollywood* reporter Pat O'Brien felt compelled to wonder, "What would Aunt Bee say now?"

It seems the nickname will haunt Howard for the rest of his days. "Opie" represents a part of him that apparently has not disappeared along with his hairline. He still has Opie's decency, optimism, and respect for those around him. But he's a little boy no longer. He has spread his wings, and there's no telling how far he'll fly.

Full Speed Ahead

(2002–)

"He is both Opie and as ruthless as he needs
to be to get the job done."
—A COLLEAGUE

RON HOWARD'S ACADEMY AWARDS FOR *A BEAUTIFUL MIND* crowned his efforts to win the respect of the Hollywood establishment. In recent years, Howard's reputation as something more than a cultural icon has been growing. In 1998 a *Hollywood Reporter* survey had ranked him ninth among mainstream Hollywood directors. By 2000 he had jumped to fourth place, preceded only by Steven Spielberg, James Cameron, and George Lucas, in terms of what the *Reporter* calls "bankability." International editor John Burman, who oversees the *Reporter*'s surveys, said of Howard in late 2002, "While he already sits in the top echelon of directors, the artistic and commercial success of *A Beautiful Mind* points to his global Director Power score rising even higher in the year to come."

Meanwhile, on *Premiere*'s Power List 2002, which came out shortly after the Oscar ceremony, Howard ranked twenty-ninth among Hollywood movers and shakers (including producers, studio bosses, and stars). Howard was labeled "A Beautiful Mensch" by *Premiere*,

which said he "made schizophrenia sympathetic, . . . sidestepping bisex-
uality issues and turning risky material into a class-act smash." In the
words of the wags on the *Premiere* staff, Howard's strength is that he's
"so nice, even Russell Crowe adores him." His weakness? That he's
"terminally square."

After winning the Oscar race, Howard was more in demand than
ever. Disney had long been wooing him to direct a big-budget action
drama about the Alamo, the Texas landmark that served as the focal
point of a John Wayne Western. Disney became interested in this project
in 1998, envisioning it as a stirring historical epic along the lines of
Braveheart. Three years later, in the aftermath of the September 11 ter-
rorist attacks against the United States, Disney studio chief Michael
Eisner put *The Alamo* on a fast track, reportedly paying screenwriter
John Sayles seven figures to supply a script for Howard to direct. Grazer,
who had signed on to produce the new film, explained its relevance in a
post-9/11 America: "It's not about patriotism so much as it's about individuals who take a stand. It's about how Americans struggled to survive."

As controversy raged about the historical inaccuracies of *A
Beautiful Mind*, Howard was at pains to inform the press that his version of *The Alamo* would be darker and more factual than the 1960
version on which Wayne was both director and star. It would, Howard
said, take into account the character flaws of the story's Texas heroes:
William Barret Travis was known for his marital infidelities, Jim Bowie
was a slave trader, and Davy Crockett lacked any vestige of political
correctness. Howard also vowed to incorporate the Mexican perspective into his film, along with that of the American settlers. As early as
March 2002, commentators were predicting that any attempt to tell the
story of the Alamo evenhandedly was doomed to failure. It was a wor-
risome sign when, in July 2002, a new high-profile writer was called in.
Stephen Gaghan, who had won the 2000 Oscar for his *Traffic* screenplay, was hired to rewrite a film now scheduled to start production in
December.

Shortly after the announcement of Gaghan's hiring came word that
Howard had stepped down as director of *The Alamo*. His official reason was that the project was too slow in coming together, but insiders

whispered about another set of issues, involving ratings, budgetary issues, and conflicting visions of what the film should be. Howard's new reluctance to do the Disney movie also put in jeopardy the participation of Crowe, who had rearranged a jam-packed schedule to play Sam Houston under Howard's direction. Some saw Howard's indecision as nothing more than a canny negotiating ploy. By late July the standoff ended with Howard no longer in the director's chair, though he and Grazer signaled their readiness to continue as producers. Disney, which had been facing a $125 million budget (with $30 million and a hefty percentage of the gross reportedly earmarked for Howard, Grazer, and Crowe), quickly took steps to hire a younger, lower-priced director, John Lee Hancock.

All the scuttlebutt about Howard's on-again–off-again commitment to *The Alamo* underscores the prominent place he now occupies in the Hollywood landscape. But high-level negotiations are hard on a man who prefers to avoid downtime between films. In January 2002, just after the release of *A Beautiful Mind*, Howard told one interviewer, "I'm working with some very fine writers on three or four different projects, and I haven't chosen yet. And I'd like to find something soon. I'm getting itchy to get back to work." Once he retreated from *The Alamo*, his name was often mentioned in conjunction with *Cinderella Man*, a Universal/Miramax film in which Crowe was slated to star as a Depression-era boxer. Howard also showed interest in *The Serpent and the Eagle*, the tale of how Spain's Hernando Cortez conquered Mexico with the help of an Aztec princess. Another possibility that surfaced late in 2002 was *Downtown*, a murder mystery with a gay cop as its hero. Based on an original script by Alan Ball (of *American Beauty* and television's *Six Feet Under*), *Downtown* had the potential to once again team Howard with Tom Hanks, who hoped to play the leading role. The nature of this project as well as the Hollywood hype surrounding it hints at how far the two men's careers have evolved since they filmed the light-hearted, unheralded *Splash* back in 1984.

It was not until the end of October 2002 that the press announced Howard's next firm directing venture: a psychological suspense drama based on Thomas Eidson's novel, *The Long Ride*. Critical favorites

Tommy Lee Jones and Cate Blanchett, both newcomers to Howard productions, agreed to portray a long-estranged father and daughter. The fact that this story, like *The Alamo*, is set in the Old West suggests Howard's eagerness to return to the territory he first explored in his boyhood 8mm movies, then re-visited on a much grander scale in the disappointing *Far and Away*.

The announcement of the new film, which was scheduled to go before the cameras in March, 2003, made the front page in all the Hollywood papers. With films directed by Howard having now racked up more than $1 billion at the domestic box office, his future choices will be equally big news for those who value mainstream entertainment. As Howard moves toward his second half century in show business, it seems clear that he will try to fulfill his vow to find projects that are, as he once put it, "a little braver." He will keep looking for new challenges, and for boundaries that he can transcend. But it's a good bet that he will not relinquish the basic humanity that marks his films as well as his approach to life.

Howard hopes for the longevity of a Robert Altman, still doing Oscar-caliber work at age seventy-five. However many productive years remain to him, Ron Howard is determined to use them well, extending what has always been a beautiful—and a memorable—career.

Timeline for Ron Howard

March 1, 1954	Ronald William Howard born, Duncan, Oklahoma
1955	Appears on screen as a baby in arms in *Frontier Woman*
1958	Rance, Jean, and Ronny Howard move to Burbank, California
1959	Professional acting debut in *The Journey*
April 1959	Clint Howard born
October 1960	First episode of *The Andy Griffith Show* airs
June 1962	*The Music Man* premieres
March 1963	*The Courtship of Eddie's Father* premieres
April 1968	*The Andy Griffith Show* ends after eight seasons
1971-1972	Howard is featured on *The Smith Family*, starring Henry Fonda
February 1972	"Love and the Happy Days" airs on *Love American Style*
June 1972	Graduates from Burroughs High School
September 1972	Enrolls in Cinema Division, University of Southern California
August 1973	*American Graffiti* premieres (last billing as "Ronny")
January 1974	First episode of *Happy Days* airs
February 1974	*The Migrants* airs
June 1975	Marries Cheryl Alley

August 1976	*The Shootist* premieres
June 1977	Howard makes directing debut with *Grand Theft Auto*
Summer 1980	Directs Bette Davis in television movie, *Skyward*
July 1980	Howard leaves *Happy Days* after 7 seasons
March 1981	Bryce Dallas Howard born
June 1981	Star on Hollywood Walk of Fame
July 1982	*Night Shift* premieres (first film with Brian Grazer)
March 1984	*Splash* premieres
Spring 1985	Paige Carlyle and Jocelyn Carlyle Howard born
June 1985	*Cocoon* premieres
Summer 1985	Howard family moves to Greenwich, Connecticut
March 1986	*Gung Ho* premieres
April 1986	*Return to Mayberry* airs (last major Ron Howard acting role)
August 1986	Newly founded Imagine Films Entertainment goes public
April 1987	Reed Cross Howard born during preproduction for *Willow*
May 1988	*Willow* premieres
August 1989	*Parenthood* premieres (first Ron Howard blockbuster)
May 1991	*Backdraft* premieres
May 1992	*Far and Away* premieres
Spring 1993	Imagine Entertainment becomes a privately held company
March 1994	*The Paper* premieres
June 1995	*Apollo 13* premieres
Spring 1996	Howard wins DGA Award for *Apollo 13*; the film is nominated for nine Oscars and wins two
November 1996	*Ransom* premieres
March 1999	*EDtv* premieres
March 1999	Footprints at Grauman's Chinese Theatre, Hollywood
November 2000	*How The Grinch Stole Christmas* premieres
December 2001	*A Beautiful Mind* premieres
Spring 2002	Awards season culminates in four Oscars for *A Beautiful Mind*, including best director and best picture
September 2002	*Apollo 13* rereleased in IMAX format

Filmography as an Actor

FEATURE FILMS

The Journey (1959), color, 122 minutes, not rated
PRODUCTION COMPANIES: Alby Pictures, MGM
PRODUCER AND DIRECTOR: Anatole Litvak
SCREENPLAY: George Tabori
ART DIRECTOR: Werner Schlichting, Isabella Schlichting
DIRECTOR OF PHOTOGRAPHY: Jack Hildyard
COSTUMES: Rene Hubert
MAKEUP: Eric Allwright, David Aylott
FILM EDITOR: Dorothy Spencer
MUSIC: Georges Auric, Michel Michelet
Cast: Deborah Kerr (Lady Diana Ashmore), Yul Brynner (Major Surov), Robert Morley (Hugh Deverill), Jason Robards Jr. (Paul Kedes/Fleming), E. G. Marshall (Harold Rhinelander), Anne Jackson (Mrs. Margie Rhinelander), Ronny Howard (Billy Rhinelander), Flip Mark (Flip Rhinelander), Kurt Kasznar (Czepege), David Kossoff (Simon Avron), Gerard Oury (Teklel Hafouli), Marie Daems (Francoise Hafouli), Anouk Aimee (Eva)

Five Minutes to Live (December 1961), black and white, 80 minutes, not rated
(Note: rereleased in November 1966 by American International Pictures as *Door-to-Door Maniac*. Running Time: 74 minutes. Robert L. Lippert added new footage, including a rape sequence, for this version.)
PRODUCTION COMPANIES: Somara Productions-Flower Film Productions
DISTRIBUTION COMPANIES: Sutton Pictures, Astor Pictures
PRODUCER: James Ellsworth
EXECUTIVE PRODUCER: Ludlow Flower

DIRECTOR: Bill Karn
STORY: Palmer Thompson
SCREENPLAY: Cay Forester
ART DIRECTOR: Edwin Shields
SET DECORATOR: Harry Reif
DIRECTOR OF PHOTOGRAPHY: Carl Guthrie
MAKEUP: Armand Del Mar
FILM EDITOR: Donald Nosseck
MUSIC: Gene Kauer, Johnny Cash

Cast: Johnny Cash (Johnny Cabot), Donald Woods (Ken Wilson), Cay Forester (Nancy Wilson), Pamela Mason (Ellen), Midge Ware (Doris), Victor Tayback (Fred Dorella), Ronny Howard (Bobby Wilson, credited as Ronnie Howard), Merle Travis (Max), Howard Wright (Pop), Norma Varden (Priscilla)

The Music Man (June 1962), color, 151 minutes, not rated
PRODUCTION COMPANY: Warner Bros. Pictures
DISTRIBUTION COMPANY: Warner Bros. Pictures
PRODUCER AND DIRECTOR: Morton DaCosta
SCREENPLAY: Marion Hargrove
(Based on the musical play by Meredith Willson and Franklin Lacey)
ART DIRECTOR: Paul Groesse
SET DECORATOR: George James Hopkins
DIRECTOR OF PHOTOGRAPHY: Robert Burks
COSTUMES: Dorothy Jeakins
MAKEUP: Gordon Bau
FILM EDITOR: William Ziegler
SOUND: M. A. Merrick, Dolph Thomas
MUSIC: Meredith Willson

Cast: Robert Preston (Harold Hill), Shirley Jones (Marian Paroo), Buddy Hackett (Marcellus Washburn), Hermione Gingold (Eulalie MacKecknie Shinn), Paul Ford (Mayor Shinn), Al Shea (Ewart Dunlop), Wayne Ward (Oliver Hix), Vern Reed (Jacey Squires), Bill Spangenberg (Olin Britt), Pert Kelton (Mrs. Paroo), Timmy Everett (Tommy Djilas), Susan Luckey (Zaneeta Shinn), Ronny Howard (Winthrop Paroo), Harry Hickox (Charlie Cowell), Charles Lane (Constable Locke), Mary Wickes (Mrs. Squires), Monique Vermont (Amaryllis), Rance Howard (Oscar Jackson)

The Courtship of Eddie's Father (March 1963), color, 117 minutes, not rated
PRODUCTION COMPANIES: Euterpe, Inc., Venice Productions
DISTRIBUTION COMPANY: MGM
PRODUCER: Joe Pasternak
DIRECTOR: Vincente Minnelli
SCREENPLAY: John Gay
(Based on the novel by Mark Toby)

ART DIRECTORS: George W. Davis, Urie McCleary
SET DECORATORS: Henry Grace, Keogh Gleason
DIRECTOR OF PHOTOGRAPHY: Milton Krasner
SPECIAL VISUAL EFFECTS: Robert R. Hoag
COSTUMES: Helen Rose
MAKEUP: William Tuttle
FILM EDITOR: Adrienne Fazan
MUSIC: George Stoll

Cast: Glenn Ford (Tom Corbett), Shirley Jones (Elizabeth Marten), Stella Stevens (Dollye Daly), Dina Merrill (Rita Behrens), Roberta Sherwood (Mrs. Livingston), Ronny Howard (Eddie), Jerry Van Dyke (Norman Jones)

Village of the Giants (October 1965), color, 80 minutes, not rated
PRODUCTION COMPANIES: Berkeley Productions, Embassy Pictures
DISTRIBUTION COMPANY: Embassy Pictures
PRODUCER AND DIRECTOR: Bert I. Gordon
STORY: Bert I. Gordon
SCREENPLAY: Alan Caillou
(Based on the novel *The Food of the Gods*
by H. G. Wells)
ART DIRECTOR: Franz Bachelin
SET DECORATOR: Robert R. Benton
DIRECTOR OF PHOTOGRAPHY: Paul C. Vogel
SPECIAL VISUAL EFFECTS: Bert I. Gordon, Flora Gordon
COSTUMES: Leah Rhodes, Frank Richardson
MAKEUP: Wally Westmore
FILM EDITOR: John Bushelman
SOUND: John Carter, Charles Grenzbach
MUSIC: Jack Nitzsche

Cast: Tommy Kirk (Mike), Johnny Crawford (Horsey), Beau Bridges (Fred), Ronny Howard (Genius), Joy Harmon (Merrie), Bob Random (Rick), Tisha Sterling (Jean), Charla Doherty (Nancy), Tim Rooney (Pete), Kevin O'Neal (Harry)

The Wild Country (February 1971), color, 100 minutes, G
PRODUCTION COMPANY: Walt Disney Productions
DISTRIBUTION COMPANY: Buena Vista
PRODUCER: Ron Miller
DIRECTOR: Robert Totten
SCREENPLAY: Calvin Clements Jr., Paul Savage
(Based on the novel *Little Britches*
by Ralph Moody)
PRODUCTION DESIGNER: Robert Clatsworthy
ART DIRECTOR: John B. Mansbridge
SET DECORATORS: Emile Kuri, Hal Gausman

DIRECTOR OF PHOTOGRAPHY: Frank Phillips
SPECIAL VISUAL EFFECTS: Robert A. Mattey
COSTUMES: Chuck Keehne, Emily Sundby
MAKEUP: Robert J. Schiffer
FILM EDITOR: Robert Stafford
SOUND: Robert O. Cook
MUSIC EDITOR: Evelyn Kennedy
MUSIC: Robert F. Brunner

Cast: Steve Forrest (Jim Tanner), Vera Miles (Kate), Jack Elam (Thompson), Ronny Howard (Virgil), Frank de Kova (Two Dog), Morgan Woodward (Ab Cross), Clint Howard (Andrew), Dub Taylor (Phil), Woodrow Chambliss (Dakota), Karl Swenson (Jensen), Mills Watson (Feathers)

American Graffiti (August 1973), color, 110 minutes, PG
PRODUCTION COMPANY: Lucasfilm Ltd./Coppola Company
DISTRIBUTION COMPANY: Universal
PRODUCERS: Francis Ford Coppola, Gary Kurtz
DIRECTOR: George Lucas
SCREENPLAY: George Lucas, Gloria Katz, Willard Huyck
ART DIRECTOR: Dennis Clark
SET DECORATOR: Douglas Freeman
DIRECTOR OF PHOTOGRAPHY: Haskell Wexler
COSTUMES: Aggie Guerard Rodgers
FILM EDITORS: Verna Fields, Marcia Lucas
SUPERVISING SOUND EDITOR: James Nelson
SOUND: Walter Murch, Arthur Rochester
MUSIC COORDINATOR: Karin Green

Cast: Richard Dreyfuss (Curt), Ronny Howard (Steve), Paul Le Mat (John), Charlie Martin Smith (Terry), Cindy Williams (Laurie), Candy Clark (Debbie), Mackenzie Phillips (Carol), Wolfman Jack (Disc Jockey), Harrison Ford (Bob Falfa), Suzanne Somers (Blonde in T-Bird), Kathleen Quinlan (Peg, credited as Kathy Quinlan)

Happy Mother's Day, Love George (August 1973), color, 90 minutes, PG
(aka *Run Stranger, Run*)
PRODUCTION COMPANY: Taurean Films
DISTRIBUTION COMPANY: Cinema 5
PRODUCER AND DIRECTOR: Darren McGavin
SCREENPLAY: Robert Clouse
DIRECTOR OF PHOTOGRAPHY: Walter Lassally
COSTUMES: Robert Anton, Anne Klein, Pierre Cardin
FILM EDITOR: George Grenville
SOUND: Hal Lewis, Richard Portman, Evelyn Rutledge
MUSIC: Don Vincent

Cast: Patricia Neal (Cara), Cloris Leachman (Ronda), Bobby Darin (Eddie), Tessa Dahl (Celia), Ron Howard (Johnny), Kathie Browne (Crystal), Joe Mascolo (Piccolo), Simon Oakland (Police Chief), Thayer David (Minister Pollard), Gale Garnett (Yolanda)

The Spikes Gang (April 1974), color, 96 minutes, PG

PRODUCTION COMPANY:	Walter Mirisch–Richard Fleischer Productions
DISTRIBUTION COMPANY:	United Artists
PRODUCER:	Walter Mirisch
DIRECTOR:	Richard Fleischer
SCREENPLAY:	Irving Ravetch, Harriet Frank Jr. (Based on the novel *The Bank Robber* by Giles Tippette)
ART DIRECTOR:	Julio Molino
SET DECORATOR:	Antonios Mateos
DIRECTOR OF PHOTOGRAPHY:	Brian West
SPECIAL VISUAL EFFECTS:	Antonio Parra
FILM EDITORS:	Ralph Winters, Frank J. Urioste
SOUND:	George Stephenson
MUSIC:	Fred Karlin

Cast: Lee Marvin (Harry Spikes), Gary Grimes (Will Young), Ron Howard (Les Richter), Charlie Martin Smith (Tod Mayhew), Arthur Hunnicutt (Kid White), Noah Beery (Jack Basset), Marc Smith (Abel Young), Don Fellows (Cowboy, hamlet), Elliott Sullivan (Billy), Robert Beatty (Sheriff, cemetery)

The First Nudie Musical (March 1976), color, 90 minutes, R

PRODUCTION COMPANY:	Paramount
DISTRIBUTION COMPANY:	Paramount
PRODUCER:	Jack Reeves
DIRECTORS:	Mark Haggard, Bruce Kimmel
SCREENPLAY:	Bruce Kimmel
ART DIRECTOR:	Tom Rassmussen
SET DESIGNER:	Timothy J. Bloch
DIRECTOR OF PHOTOGRAPHY:	Douglas H. Knapp
COSTUMES:	Tom Rassmussen
FILM EDITOR:	Allen Peluso
MUSIC:	Bruce Kimmel

Cast: Stephen Nathan (Harry Schechter), Cindy Williams (Rosie), Bruce Kimmel (John Smithee), Leslie Ackerman (Susie), Alan Abelew (George Brenner), Diana Canova (Juanita), Alexandra Morgan (Mary La Rue), Frank Doubleday (Arvin), Kathleen Hietala (Eunice), Art Marino (Eddie), Ron Howard (Actor at Audition, uncredited)

Eat My Dust! (April 1976), color, 89 minutes, PG

PRODUCTION COMPANY:	New World Pictures

DISTRIBUTION COMPANY: New World Pictures
PRODUCER: Roger Corman
DIRECTOR: Charles B. Griffith
SCREENPLAY: Charles B. Griffith
ART DIRECTOR: Peter Jamison
SET DECORATOR: Bill Paxton
DIRECTOR OF PHOTOGRAPHY: Eric Saarinen
COSTUME SUPERVISOR: Jane Ruhm
FILM EDITOR: Tina Hirsch
MUSIC: David Grisman

Cast: Ron Howard (Hoover), Christopher Norris (Darlene), Warren Kemmerling (Harry Niebold), Dave Madden (Big Bubba Jones), Robert Broyles (Bud), Evelyn Russel (Delores Westerby), Rance Howard (Deputy Clark), Jessica Potter (Lallie), Charles Howerton (J. B.), Kathy O'Dare (Miranda), Clint Howard (Georgie), Paul Bartel (cameo appearance), Corbin Bernsen (cameo appearance)

The Shootist (August 1976), color, 100 minutes, G
PRODUCTION COMPANY: Dino De Laurentiis
DISTRIBUTION COMPANY: Paramount
PRODUCERS: M. J. Frankovich, William Self
DIRECTOR: Don Siegel
SCREENPLAY: Miles Hood Swarthout, Scott Hale
(Based on the novel by Glendon Swarthout)
PRODUCTION DESIGNER: Robert Boyle
SET DECORATOR: Arthur Parker
DIRECTOR OF PHOTOGRAPHY: Bruce Surtees
SPECIAL VISUAL EFFECTS: Augie Lohman
COSTUMES: Moss Mabry
MAKEUP: Dave Grayson, Joe Di Bella
FILM EDITOR: Douglas Stewart
SOUND: Alfred J. Overton
MUSIC: Elmer Bernstein

Cast: John Wayne (J. B. Books), Lauren Bacall (Bond Rogers), Ron Howard (Gillom Rogers), James Stewart (Dr. Hostetler), Richard Boone (Sweeney), Hugh O'Brian (Pulford), Bill McKinney (Cobb), Harry Morgan (Marshal Thibido), John Carradine (Beckum), Sheree North (Serepta), Richard Lenz (Dobkins), Scatman Crothers (Moses)

Grand Theft Auto (June 1977), color, 89 minutes, PG
PRODUCTION COMPANY: New World Pictures
DISTRIBUTION COMPANY: New World Pictures
PRODUCER: Jon Davison
EXECUTIVE PRODUCER: Roger Corman
DIRECTOR: Ron Howard
SCREENPLAY: Rance Howard, Ron Howard

ART DIRECTOR:	Keith Michaels
SET DESIGNER:	Charles Nixon
DIRECTOR OF PHOTOGRAPHY:	Gary Graver
SPECIAL VISUAL EFFECTS:	Roger George
COSTUMES:	Jane Ruhm, Linda Pearl
MAKEUP:	Leigh Mitchell
FILM EDITOR:	Joe Dante
MUSIC:	Peter Ivers

Cast: Ron Howard (Sam Freeman), Nancy Morgan (Paula Powers), Marion Ross (Vivian Hedgeworth), Pete Isacksen (Sparky), Barry Cahill (Bigby Powers), Hoke Howell (Preacher), Lew Brown (Jack Klepper), Elizabeth Rogers (Priscilla Powers), Rance Howard (Ned Slinker), Don Steele (Curley Q. Brown), Clint Howard (Ace), Garry Marshall (Underworld Boss, credited as Garry K. Marshall), Paul Bartel (Groom)

More American Graffiti (August 1979), color, 111 minutes, PG

PRODUCTION COMPANY:	Lucasfilm Ltd./Universal Production
DISTRIBUTION COMPANY:	Universal
PRODUCER:	Howard Kazanjian
EXECUTIVE PRODUCER:	George Lucas
DIRECTOR:	B. W. L. Norton
SCREENPLAY:	B. W. L. Norton
	(Based on the characters created by George Lucas, Gloria Katz, Willard Huyck)
ART DIRECTOR:	Ray Storey
SET DECORATOR:	Doug von Koss
DIRECTOR OF PHOTOGRAPHY:	Caleb Deschanel
COSTUMES:	Agnes Rodgers
FILM EDITOR:	Tina Hirsch
SUPERVISING SOUND EDITOR:	Ben Burtt

Cast: Candy Clark (Debbie Dunham), Bo Hopkins (Little Joe Young, Chopper Gunner), Ron Howard (Steve Bolander), Paul Le Mat (John Milner), Mackenzie Phillips (Carol/Rainbow), Charles Martin Smith (Warrant Officer Terry "The Toad" Fields), Cindy Williams (Laurie Bolander), Anna Bjorn (Eva), Richard Bradford (Major Creech), John Brent (Ralph, Club Owner), Harrison Ford (Officer Bob Falfa, uncredited)

Frank Capra's American Dream (September 1997), B&W and color, 109 minutes, G (documentary)

PRODUCTION COMPANIES:	Sony Pictures Television, Frank Capra Productions
DISTRIBUTION COMPANY:	Sony Pictures
PRODUCER:	Charles A. Duncombe Jr.
EXECUTIVE PRODUCERS:	Tom Capra, Frank Capra Jr., George Zaloom, Les Mayfield, Jean-Michel Michenaud

DIRECTOR: Kenneth Bowser
WRITTEN BY: Kenneth Bowser
PRODUCTION DESIGNER: Dan Butts
DIRECTOR OF PHOTOGRAPHY: Richard Pendleton
MAKEUP: Teri Groves
FILM EDITOR: Arnold Glassman
PRODUCTION SOUND MIXER: Rob Scott
MUSIC: John Hodian

Cast: Ron Howard (narrator), Robert Altman, Jeanine Basinger, Edward Bernds, Frank Capra Jr., Tom Capra, Allen Daviau, Andre De Toth, Richard Dreyfuss, Bill Duke, Peter Falk, Amy Heckerling, Marshall Herskovitz, Arthur Hiller, Michael Keaton, Angela Lansbury, Garry Marshall, Joseph McBride, John Milius, Martin Scorsese, Richard Schickel, Oliver Stone, Bob Thomas, Fay Wray, Jane Wyatt, Edward Zwick (interview subjects)

Welcome to Hollywood, color, 89 minutes, R
PREMIERED AT AFI FILM FESTIVAL: 10/28/98
PRODUCTION COMPANIES: Stone Canyon Entertainment, Crystal Springs Productions, Filmsmith Productions, Blump International Films
DISTRIBUTION COMPANIES: PM Entertainment Group, Inc., Phaedra Cinema
PRODUCERS: Zachary Matz, Tony Markes
EXECUTIVE PRODUCERS: Jim Lampley, Bree Walker, Brad Schlei
DIRECTORS: Tony Markes, Adam Rifkin
SCREENPLAY: Shawn Ryan, Tony Markes
CAMERA: Kramer Morganthau, Rob Bennett, Nick Mendoza, Howard Wexler
FILM EDITOR: Jane Kurson
SOUND: Richard Mercado
MUSIC: Justin Reinhardt

Cast: Tony Markes (Anton Markwell, aka Nick Decker), Adam Rifkin (Adam Rifkin), Angie Everhart (Angie Everhart), David Andriole (David Lake). Cameo appearances include: Sandra Bullock, Nicolas Cage, Cameron Crowe, Jeff Goldblum, Cuba Gooding Jr., David Hasselhoff, Ron Howard, Will Smith, John Travolta, John Waters (all playing themselves)

Osmosis Jones (August 2001), color, 95 minutes, PG
PRODUCTION COMPANY: Conundrum Entertainment
DISTRIBUTION COMPANY: Warner Bros.
PRODUCERS: Bradley Thomas, Peter Farrelly, Bobby Farrelly, Zak Penn, Dennis Edwards
DIRECTORS: Peter Farrelly, Bobby Farrelly
ANIMATION DIRECTORS: Piet Kroon, Tom Sito

SCREENPLAY: Marc Hyman
PRODUCTION DESIGNER: Sidney Jackson Bartholomew Jr.
DIRECTOR OF PHOTOGRAPHY: Mark Irwin
COSTUMES: Pamela Ball Withers
FILM EDITORS: Lois Freeman-Fox, Stephen R. Schaeffer, Sam Seig
MUSIC SUPERVISOR: Ken Ross

Cast: Bill Murray (Frank), Molly Shannon (Mrs. Boyd), Chris Elliott (Bob), Elena Franklin (Shane). Character voices: Chris Rock (Osmosis Jones), Laurence Fishburne (Thrax), David Hyde-Pierce (Drix), Brandy Norwood (Leah), William Shatner (The Mayor), Ron Howard (Tom Colonic)

The Independent (December 2001), color, 85 minutes, R
PRODUCTION COMPANY: United Lotus Group
DISTRIBUTION COMPANY: Arrow Releasing
PRODUCER: Mike Wilkins
EXECUTIVE PRODUCER: Jerry Weintraub
DIRECTOR: Stephen Kessler
SCREENPLAY: Mike Wilkins, Stephen Kessler
PRODUCTION DESIGNER: Russell Christian
DIRECTOR OF PHOTOGRAPHY: Amir Hamed
COSTUMES: Yoona Kwak
FILM EDITOR: Chris Franklin
MUSIC: Ben Vaughn

Cast: Jerry Stiller (Morty Fineman), Janeane Garofolo (Paloma Fineman), Max Perlich (Ivan), Ginger Lynn Allen (Mayor Kitty Storm), and Ron Howard, Peter Bogdanovich, Roger Corman, and Karen Black, among others, as themselves

TELEVISION MOVIES

The Migrants, color, 90 minutes, PBS
FIRST AIRED: 2/3/74
PRODUCTION COMPANY: CBS Entertainment
PRODUCER AND DIRECTOR: Tom Gries
TELEPLAY: Lanford Wilson
(Based on a story by Tennessee Williams)
DIRECTOR OF PHOTOGRAPHY: Dick Kratina
EDITOR: Bud S. Isaacs
MUSIC: Billy Goldenberg

Cast: Cloris Leachman (Viola Barlow), Ron Howard (Lyle Barlow), Sissy Spacek (Wanda Trimpin), Cindy Williams (Betty), Ed Lauter (Mr. Barlow), Lisa Lucas (Molly Barlow), Mills Watson (Hec Campbell), David Clennon (Tom Trimpin), Dinah Englund (Billie Jean Barlow), Brad Sullivan (Johnson)

RON HOWARD

Locusts, color, 90 minutes, ABC

FIRST AIRED: 10/9/74
PRODUCTION COMPANY: Carson Productions
DISTRIBUTION COMPANY: Paramount Pictures Television
PRODUCER: Herbert J.Wright
EXECUTIVE PRODUCER: Michael Donohew
DIRECTOR: Richard T. Heffron
TELEPLAY: Robert Malcom Young
DIRECTOR OF PHOTOGRAPHY: Jack Woolf
EDITOR: Neil MacDonald
MUSIC: Mike Post, Peter Carpenter

Cast: Ben Johnson (Amos Fletcher), Ron Howard (Donny Fletcher), Katherine Helmond (Claire Fletcher), Lisa Gerritsen (Sissy Fletcher), Belinda Balaski (Janet Willimer), Rance Howard (Aaron), Robert Cruse (Cully Cullitan), William Speerstra (Ace Teverley), Bob Koons (Blauser), Robert Hoffman (Tom)

Huckleberry Finn, color, 90 minutes, ABC

FIRST AIRED: 3/25/75
PRODUCTION COMPANY: ABC Circle Films
PRODUCER: Steven North
DIRECTOR: Robert Totten
TELEPLAY: Jean Holloway
(Based on the novel by Mark Twain)
ART DIRECTOR: Peter M. Wooley
DIRECTOR OF PHOTOGRAPHY: Andrew Jackson
EDITORS: Diane Adler, Marsh Hendry
MUSIC: Earl Robinson

Cast: Ron Howard (Huckleberry Finn), Donny Most (Tom Sawyer), Royal Dano (Mark Twain), Antonio Fargas (Jim Watson), Jack Elam (King), Merle Haggard (Duke), Rance Howard (Pap Finn), Jean Howard (Widow Douglas), Clint Howard (Arch), George "Shug" Fisher (Old Doc)

I'm a Fool, color, 36 minutes, PBS

FIRST AIRED: 4/6/77 (as part of *The American Short Story* series)
PRODUCTION COMPANIES: Learning in Focus, South Carolina Television Network
PRODUCER: Dann McCann
EXECUTIVE PRODUCER: Robert Geller
DIRECTOR: Noel Black
TELEPLAY: Ron Cowen
(Based on the short story by Sherwood Anderson)

Cast: Ron Howard, Santiago Gonzalez, Amy Irving, Otis Calef, Randi Kallan, John Light, John Tidwell

Act of Love, color, 120 minutes, NBC

FIRST AIRED:	9/24/80
PRODUCTION COMPANY:	Cypress Point Productions
DISTRIBUTION COMPANY:	Paramount Pictures Television
PRODUCER:	Bruce J. Sallan
EXECUTIVE PRODUCER:	Gerald W. Abrams
DIRECTOR:	Jud Taylor
TELEPLAY:	Michael DeGuzman
	(Based on the novel by Paige Mitchell)
ART DIRECTOR:	John Vallone
DIRECTOR OF PHOTOGRAPHY:	Michael Margulies
EDITOR:	Gregory Prange
MUSIC:	Billy Goldenberg

Cast: Ron Howard (Leon Cybulkowski), Robert Foxworth (Andrew Rose), Mickey Rourke (Joseph Cybulkowski), David Spielberg (Victor Burton), Jacqueline Brookes (Eugenia Cybulkowski), Sondra West (Margaret Cybulkowski), Gail Youngs (Joan Gruber), Mary Kay Place (Becky Wiggins), Dr. Warren Fitzpatrick (Peter Michael Goetz), Peter Hobbs (Judge Traviera)

Bitter Harvest, color, 120 minutes, NBC

FIRST AIRED:	5/18/81
PRODUCTION COMPANY:	Charles Fries Productions
PRODUCER:	Tony Ganz
EXECUTIVE PRODUCER:	Charles Fries
DIRECTOR:	Roger Young
TELEPLAY:	Richard Friedenberg
	(Based on the book by Frederic Halbert, Sandra Halbert)
ART DIRECTOR:	Bryan Ryman
DIRECTOR OF PHOTOGRAPHY:	Gayne Rescher
EDITOR:	Thomas Fries
MUSIC:	Fred Karlin

Cast: Ron Howard (Ned De Vries), Art Carney (Walter Peary), Tarah Nutter (Kate De Vries), David Knell (Brandon), Barry Corbin (Dr. Agajanian), Richard Dysart (Dr. Morton Freeman), Michael Bond (Dr. Bill DeJong), Jim Haynie (Doc Vandecamp), Robert Hirschfeld (Harold), G. W. Bailey (Jim Lazlo)

Fire on the Mountain, color, 120 minutes, NBC

FIRST AIRED:	11/23/81
PRODUCTION COMPANIES:	River City Productions, Carson Productions
PRODUCERS:	Robert Lovenheim, Richard Rosenthal

EXECUTIVE PRODUCER: John J. McMahon
DIRECTOR: Donald Wrye
TELEPLAY: John Sacret Young
(Based on the novel by Edward Abbey)
ART DIRECTOR: Beala Neel
DIRECTOR OF PHOTOGRAPHY: Woody Omens
EDITOR: Ronald J. Fagan
MUSIC: Basil Poledouris

Cast: Buddy Ebsen (John Vogelin), Ron Howard (Lee Mackie), Julie Carmen (Cruza Peralta), Ross Harris (Billy Starr), Ed Brodow (Major Parrell), Michael Conrad (Colonel Desalius), Gary Graham (Marshal Burr), Harvey Vernon (Bartender), Will Hare (Hayduke)

Return to Mayberry, color, 120 minutes, NBC
FIRST AIRED: 4/13/86
PRODUCTION COMPANIES: Viacom Productions, Strathmore Productions
PRODUCERS: Dean Hargrove, Robin S. Clark
EXECUTIVE PRODUCERS: Andy Griffith, Richard O. Linke
DIRECTOR: Bob Sweeney
TELEPLAY: Harvey Bullock, Everett Greenbaum
PRODUCTION DESIGNER: Ray Storey
ART DIRECTOR: Dale Allan Pelton
DIRECTOR OF PHOTOGRAPHY: Richard C. Glouner
EDITOR: David Solomon
MUSIC: Earle Hagen

Cast: Andy Griffith (Andy Taylor), Ron Howard (Opie Taylor), Don Knotts (Barney Fife), Jim Nabors (Gomer Pyle), George Lindsey (Goober Pyle), Aneta Corsaut (Helen Crump Taylor), Betty Lynn (Thelma Lou), Jack Dodson (Howard Sprague), Hal Smith (Otis Campbell), Howard Morris (Ernest T. Bass), Denver Pyle (Briscoe Darling), Maggie Peterson-Mancuso (Charlene Darling), Karlene Crockett (Eunice Taylor), Allen Williams (Lloyd Fox), Paul Willson (Ben Woods), Rance Howard (Preacher)

TELEVISION SERIES
Note: Credits for long-running series reflect the premiere episode.

Barnaby and Mr. O'Malley (pilot for unsold series), black and white, 30 minutes, CBS
FIRST AIRED: 12/20/59 (Episode of G. E. Theatre)
PRODUCER: Stanley Rubin
DIRECTOR: Sherman Marks
WRITERS: Louis Pelletier

Cast: Bert Lahr (Mr. O'Malley), Ronny Howard (Barnaby Baxter), June Dayton (Alice Baxter), William Redfield (George Baxter), Mel Blanc (Leprechaun Voice), Debbie Megowan (Janie), Don Beddoe (Dr. Harvey)

The Andy Griffith Show, black and white, then color, CBS
Air dates: 10/3/60 to 4/1/68 (pilot aired on *The Danny Thomas Show* on 2/15/60)

PRODUCTION COMPANY: Danny Thomas Productions
PRODUCER: Aaron Ruben
EXECUTIVE PRODUCER: Sheldon Leonard
DIRECTOR: Sheldon Leonard
WRITERS: Jack Elinson, Charles Stewart
ART DIRECTORS: Ralph Bergen, Ken Reid
DIRECTOR OF PHOTOGRAPHY: Sid Hickox
EDITOR: Joe Gluck

Cast: Andy Griffith (Andy Taylor), Don Knotts (Deputy Barney Fife), Ronny Howard (Opie Taylor), Frances Bavier (Bee Taylor).

Over the course of the series, additional regulars included: Elinor Donahue (Ellie Walker), Aneta Corsaut (Helen Crump), Sue Ane Langdon (Mary Simpson), Betty Lynn (Thelma Lou), Hal Smith (Otis Campbell), Jack Dodson (Howard Sprague), Howard McNear (Floyd Lawson), Jim Nabors (Gomer Pyle), George Lindsey (Goober Pyle), Jack Burns (Warren Ferguson), Howard Morris (Ernest T. Bass), Ken Berry (Sam Jones), Arlene Golonka (Millie Swanson), Denver Pyle (Briscoe Darling), Cheerio Meredith (Emma Brand), Buddy Foster (Mike Jones), Mary Lansing (Martha Clark), Dick Elliott (Mayor Pike), Parley Baer (Mayor Stoner), Julie Adams (Mary Simpson, in later episodes), Nina Shipman (Irene Fairchild), Mary Treen (Rose), Clint Howard (Leon)

The Smith Family, color, 30 minutes, ABC

AIRED: 1/20/71 to 9/8/71, 4/12/72 to 6/14/72
EXECUTIVE PRODUCER: Don Fedderson
PRODUCER AND WRITER: Edmund Hartmann
DIRECTOR: Herschel Daugherty
MUSIC: Mike Minor

Cast: Henry Fonda (Chad Smith), Janet Blair (Betty Smith), Darleen Carr (Cindy Smith), Ronny Howard (Bob Smith), James-Michael Wixted (Brian Smith), John Carter (Ray Martin), Charles McGraw (Capt. Hughes)

Happy Days, color, 30 minutes, ABC

AIRED: 1/15/74 to 7/19/84 (A pilot episode, entitled "Love and the Happy Days," aired on ABC's *Love American Style* on February 25, 1972, but the show was significantly revamped before it became a series. Ron Howard was no longer a regular after 1980.)
PRODUCTION COMPANIES: Paramount TV, Miller-Milkis Productions
PRODUCERS: William S. Bickley, Thomas L. Miller, Edward K. Milkis

RON HOWARD

DIRECTOR: Mel Ferber
WRITERS: Rob Reiner, Philip Mishkin, Garry Marshall
Cast: Ron Howard (Richie Cunningham), Anson Williams (Warren "Potsie" Weber), Marion Ross (Marion Cunningham), Tom Bosley (Howard Cunningham), Henry Winkler (Arthur "Fonz" Fonzarelli), Donny Most (Ralph Malph), Erin Moran (Joanie Cunningham)

Over the course of the series, additional regulars included Scott Baio (Charles "Chachi" Arcola), Ellen Travolta (Louisa Arcola), Lynda Goodfriend (Lori Beth Allen), Linda Purl (Ashley Pfister), Heather O'Rourke (Heather Pfister), Pat Morita (Arnold Takahashi), Al Molinaro (Al Delvecchio), Penny Marshall (Laverne DeFazio), Cindy Williams (Shirley Feeney), Robin Williams (Mork). Jerry Paris was the director of the vast majority of episodes, and Garry Marshall is considered the show's creator

Fonz and The Happy Days Gang, color, 30 minutes (animation), ABC
AIR DATES: 11/8/80 to 9/18/82
PRODUCTION COMPANY: ABC
PRODUCERS: William Hanna, Joseph Barbera
Cast: Henry Winkler (voice of Fonzie), Ron Howard (voice of Richie), Donny Most (voice of Ralph), Didi Conn (voice of Cup Cake), Frank Welker (voice of Mr. Cool), Wolfman Jack (announcer)

Filmography as a Director and Producer

FEATURE FILMS

Grand Theft Auto (June 1977), color, 89 minutes, PG

PRODUCTION COMPANY:	New World Pictures
DISTRIBUTION COMPANY:	New World Pictures
PRODUCER:	Jon Davison
EXECUTIVE PRODUCER:	Roger Corman
DIRECTOR:	Ron Howard
SCREENPLAY:	Rance Howard, Ron Howard
ART DIRECTOR:	Keith Michaels
SET DESIGNER:	Charles Nixon
DIRECTOR OF PHOTOGRAPHY:	Gary Graver
SPECIAL VISUAL EFFECTS:	Roger George
COSTUMES:	Jane Ruhm, Linda Pearl
MAKEUP:	Leigh Mitchell
FILM EDITOR:	Joe Dante
MUSIC:	Peter Ivers

Cast: Ron Howard (Sam Freeman), Nancy Morgan (Paula Powers), Marion Ross (Vivian Hedgeworth), Pete Isacksen (Sparky), Barry Cahill (Bigby Powers), Hoke Howell (Preacher), Lew Brown (Jack Klepper), Elizabeth Rogers (Priscilla Powers), Rance Howard (Ned Slinker), Don Steele (Curley Q. Brown), Clint Howard (Ace), Garry Marshall (Underworld Boss, as Garry K. Marshall), Paul Bartel (Groom)

Leo and Loree (April 1980), color, 97 minutes, PG

PRODUCTION COMPANY:	Jerry Paris Film Production
DISTRIBUTION COMPANY:	United Artists
PRODUCER:	Jim Begg
EXECUTIVE PRODUCER:	Ron Howard
DIRECTOR:	Jerry Paris
STORY:	James Ritz, Ron Howard
SCREENPLAY:	James Ritz
ART DIRECTOR:	Linda Pearl
DIRECTOR OF PHOTOGRAPHY:	Costa Petalas
FILM EDITOR:	Ed Cotter
MUSIC:	Jay Asher

Cast: Donny Most (Leo), Linda Purl (Loree), David Huffman (Dennis), Jerry Paris (Tony), Shannon Farnon (Christina Harper), Allan Rich (Jarvis), Susan Lawrence (Cindy)

Night Shift (July 1982), color, 105 minutes, R

PRODUCTION COMPANY:	Ladd Company
DISTRIBUTION COMPANY:	Warner Bros.
PRODUCER:	Brian Grazer
EXECUTIVE PRODUCER:	Don Kranze
DIRECTOR:	Ron Howard
SCREENPLAY:	Lowell Ganz, Babaloo Mandel
PRODUCTION DESIGNER:	Jack Taylor Collis
ART DIRECTOR:	Pete Smith
SET DECORATOR:	Richard Goddard
DIRECTOR OF PHOTOGRAPHY:	James Crabe
FILM EDITORS:	Robert J. Kern, Daniel P. Hanley, Mike Hill
SOUND EDITORS:	Jack Schrader, Laurel Ladevich, Joey Ippolito
MUSIC:	Burt Bacharach, Carole Bayer Sager

Cast: Henry Winkler (Chuck Lumley), Michael Keaton (Bill Blazejowski), Shelley Long (Belinda Keaton), Gina Hecht (Charlotte Koogle), Pat Corley (Edward Koogle), Bobby Di Cicco (Leonard), Nita Talbot (Vivian), Basil Hoffman (Drollhauser), Tim Rossovich (Luke), Clint Howard (Jeffrey)

Splash (March 1984), color, 109 minutes, PG

PRODUCTION COMPANY:	Touchstone Films
DISTRIBUTION COMPANY:	Buena Vista
PRODUCER:	Brian Grazer
EXECUTIVE PRODUCER:	John Thomas Lenox
DIRECTOR:	Ron Howard
STORY:	Bruce Jay Friedman
SCREENPLAY:	Lowell Ganz, Babaloo Mandel, Bruce Jay Friedman (Based on a story by Brian Grazer)

PRODUCTION DESIGNER: Jack T. Collis
ART DIRECTOR: John B. Mansbridge
SET DECORATOR: Norman Rockett
DIRECTOR OF PHOTOGRAPHY: Don Peterman
COSTUMES: May Routh
FILM EDITORS: Daniel P. Hanley, Michael Hill
SOUND MIXER: Richard S. Church
MUSIC EDITOR: Richard S. Luckey
MUSIC: Lee Holdridge

Cast: Tom Hanks (Allen Bauer), Daryl Hannah (Madison), Eugene Levy (Walter Kornbluth), John Candy (Freddie Bauer), Dody Goodman (Mrs. Stimler), Shecky Greene (Mr. Buyrite), Richard B. Shull (Dr. Ross), Bobby Di Cicco (Jerry), Howard Morris (Dr. Zidell), Tony DiBenedetto (Tim, the Doorman), Rance Howard (McCullough), Corki Corman-Grazer (Wife), Cheryl Howard (Girl at Wedding), Clint Howard (Wedding Guest)

Cocoon (June 1985), color, 158 minutes, PG-13
PRODUCTION COMPANY: Fox-Zanuck/Brown Productions
DISTRIBUTION COMPANY: 20th Century Fox
PRODUCERS: Richard D. Zanuck, David Brown, Lili Fini Zanuck
DIRECTOR: Ron Howard
STORY: David Saperstein
SCREENPLAY: Tom Benedek
PRODUCTION DESIGNER: Jack T. Collis
SET DECORATOR: Jim Duffy
DIRECTOR OF PHOTOGRAPHY: Don Peterman
SPECIAL VISUAL EFFECTS: Greg Cannom, Rick Baker
COSTUME DESIGNER: Aggie Guerard Rodgers
COSTUME SUPERVISOR: Edward Marks
MAKEUP: Robert Norin, Kevin Haney
FILM EDITORS: Michael Hill, Daniel Hanley
SOUND EDITORS: William Hartman, Michael Corrigan
SOUND MIXER: Richard Church
MUSIC: James Horner

Cast: Don Ameche (Art Selwyn), Wilford Brimley (Ben Luckett), Hume Cronyn (Joe Finley), Brian Dennehy (Walter), Jack Gilford (Bernie Lefkowitz), Steve Guttenberg (Jack Bonner), Maureen Stapleton (Mary Luckett), Jessica Tandy (Alma Finley), Gwen Verdon (Bess McCarthy), Herta Ware (Rose Lefkowitz), Tahnee Welch (Kitty), Clint Howard (John Dexter), Rance Howard (Detective), Jean Speegle (Woman)

Gung Ho (March 1986), color, 111 minutes, PG-13
PRODUCTION COMPANY: Ron Howard Productions
DISTRIBUTION COMPANY: Paramount

PRODUCERS:	Tony Ganz, Deborah Blum
EXECUTIVE PRODUCER:	Ron Howard
DIRECTOR:	Ron Howard
STORY:	Edwin Blum, Lowell Ganz, Babaloo Mandel
SCREENPLAY:	Lowell Ganz, Babaloo Mandel
PRODUCTION DESIGNER:	James Schoppe
ART DIRECTOR:	Jack G. Taylor Jr.
SET DECORATOR:	John Anderson
DIRECTOR OF PHOTOGRAPHY:	Don Peterman
COSTUMES:	Betsy Cox
MAKEUP:	Ric Sagliani, Janet Flora
FILM EDITORS:	Daniel Hanley, Michael Hill
SOUND EDITORS:	Harriet Fidlow, Jeffrey Stern, Robert Hein
SOUND MIXER:	Richard S. Church
MUSIC EDITOR:	Kenneth Karman
MUSIC:	Thomas Newman

Cast: Michael Keaton (Hunt Stevenson), Gedde Watanabe (Kazihiro), George Wendt (Buster), Mimi Rogers (Audrey), John Turturro (Willie), Soh Yamamura (Mr. Sakamoto), Sab Shimono (Saito), Rick Overton (Googie), Clint Howard (Paul), Jihmi Kennedy (Junior), Rance Howard (Mayor Zwart), Jean Speegle (Lady in Market)

No Man's Land (October 1987), color, 107 minutes, R

PRODUCTION COMPANY:	Orion Pictures
DISTRIBUTION COMPANY:	Orion Pictures
PRODUCERS:	Joseph Stern, Dick Wolf
EXECUTIVE PRODUCERS:	Ron Howard, Tony Ganz
DIRECTOR:	Pete Werner
SCREENPLAY:	Dick Wolf
PRODUCTION DESIGNER:	Paul Peters
SET DECORATOR:	Ethel Robins Richards
DIRECTOR OF PHOTOGRAPHY:	Hiro Narita
SPECIAL VISUAL EFFECTS:	Dennis Peterson
COSTUME DESIGNER:	Jodie Tillen
COSTUME SUPERVISOR:	Robert Chase
MAKEUP:	Susan A. Cabral
FILM EDITOR:	Steve Cohen
SUPERVISING SOUND EDITOR:	Tom C. McCarthy
SOUND EDITORS:	Fred Judkins, Roxanne Jones, Jimmy Ling, Howard S. M. Neiman, Don Walden
MUSIC:	Basil Poledouris

Cast: D. B. Sweeney (Benjy Taylor), Charlie Sheen (Varrick), Lara Harris (Ann Varick), Randy Quaid (Lt. Vincent Bracey), Bill Duke (Malcom), R. D. Call (Frank Martin), Arlen Dean Snyder (Lt. Curtis Loos), M. Emmet Walsh (Captain Haun), Jenny Gago (Tory Bracey), Lori Butler (Suzanne)

Willow (April 1988), color, 126 minutes, PG

PRODUCTION COMPANY:	Lucasfilm Ltd., in association with Imagine Entertainment
DISTRIBUTION COMPANY:	MGM
PRODUCER:	Nigel Wooll
EXECUTIVE PRODUCER:	George Lucas
DIRECTOR:	Ron Howard
STORY:	George Lucas
SCREENPLAY:	Bob Dolman
PRODUCTION DESIGNER:	Allan Cameron
ART DIRECTORS:	Tim Hutchinson, Tony Reading, Malcolm Stone
DIRECTOR OF PHOTOGRAPHY:	Adrian Biddle
SPECIAL VISUAL EFFECTS:	Dennis Muren, Michael McAlister, Phil Tippett, John Richardson
COSTUME DESIGNER:	Barbara Lane
COSTUME SUPERVISOR:	Rosemary Burrows
MAKEUP:	Nick Dudman, Alan Boyle, Tommie Manderson, Eddie Knight, Amanda Knight
FILM EDITORS:	Daniel Hanley, Michael Hill, Richard Hiscott
SUPERVISING SOUND EDITOR:	Richard Hymns
SOUND:	Teresa Eckton, David Stone, Sandina Bailo-Lape
MUSIC EDITOR:	Jim Henrikson
MUSIC:	James Horner

Cast: Val Kilmer (Madmartigan), Joanne Whalley (Sorsha), Warwick Davis (Willow), Jean Marsh (Queen Bavmorda), Patricia Hayes (Raziel), Billy Barty (High Aldwin), Pat Roach (Kael), Gavan O'Herlihy (Airk), David Steinberg (Meegosh), Phil Fondacaro (Vohnkar)

Clean and Sober (August 1988), color, 124 minutes, R

PRODUCTION COMPANY:	Imagine Entertainment
DISTRIBUTION COMPANY:	Warner Bros.
PRODUCERS:	Tony Ganz, Deborah Blum
EXECUTIVE PRODUCER:	Ron Howard
DIRECTOR:	Glen Gordon Caron
SCREENPLAY:	Tod Carroll
PRODUCTION DESIGNER:	Joel Schiller
ART DIRECTOR:	Eric W. Orbom
SET DECORATOR:	Don Remacle
DIRECTOR OF PHOTOGRAPHY:	Jan Kiesser
COSTUMES:	Robert Turturice
MAKEUP:	Robert Mills

FILM EDITOR: Richard Chew
SUPERVISING SOUND EDITOR: Lon E. Bender
SOUND: Dan Rich, Frank Smathers,
Linda Whittlesey
MUSIC EDITOR: Jim Harrison
MUSIC: Gabriel Yared

Cast: Michael Keaton (Daryl Poynter), Kathy Baker (Charlie Standers), Morgan Freeman (Craig), Tate Donovan (Donald Towle), M. Emmet Walsh (Richard Dirks), Luca Bercovici (Lenny), Brian Benben (Martin Laux), Ben Piazza (Kramer), Henry Judd Baker (Xavier), Claudia Christian (Iris)

Vibes (August 1988), color, 99 minutes, PG
PRODUCTION COMPANY: Imagine Entertainment
DISTRIBUTION COMPANY: Columbia
PRODUCERS: Deborah Blum, Tony Ganz
EXECUTIVE PRODUCER: Ron Howard
DIRECTOR: Ken Kwapis
STORY: Deborah Blum, Lowell Ganz,
Babaloo Mandel
SCREENPLAY: Lowell Ganz, Babaloo Mandel
PRODUCTION DESIGNER: Richard Sawyer
ART DIRECTORS: Gregory Pickrell, Eugene Gurlitz
SET DECORATOR: George R. Nelson
DIRECTORS OF PHOTOGRAPHY: John Bailey, Neil Krepela
COSTUMES: Ruth Myers, John Boxer
MAKEUP: Alan Friedman, Peter Wrona Jr.
FILM EDITOR: Carol Littleman
SUPERVISING SOUND EDITOR: Dennis Drummond
SOUND: George H. Anderson, Cindy Marty, Roxanne
Jones, Jeffrey Rosen
MUSIC EDITOR: Jim Henrikson
MUSIC: James Horner

Cast: Cyndi Lauper (Sylvia Pickel), Jeff Goldblum (Nick Deezy), Julian Sands (Dr. Harrison Steele), Googy Gress (Ingo Swedlin), Elizabeth Pena (Consuelo), Michael Lerner (Burt Wilder), Aharon Ipale (Alejandro de la Vivar), Ronald G. Joseph (Carl), Peter Falk (Harry Buscafusco), Ramon Bieri (Eli Diamond)

Parenthood (August 1989), color, 124 minutes, PG-13
PRODUCTION COMPANY: Imagine Entertainment
DISTRIBUTION COMPANY: Universal
PRODUCER: Brian Grazer
EXECUTIVE PRODUCER: Joseph M. Caracciolo
DIRECTOR: Ron Howard

STORY:	Lowell Ganz, Babaloo Mandel, Ron Howard
SCREENPLAY:	Lowell Ganz, Babaloo Mandel
PRODUCTION DESIGNER:	Todd Hallowell
ART DIRECTOR:	Christopher Nowak
SET DECORATOR:	Nina F. Ramsey
DIRECTOR OF PHOTOGRAPHY:	Donald McAlpine
COSTUMES:	Ruth Morley
MAKEUP:	Fern Buchner, Peter Wrona Jr., Frank H. Griffin Jr.
FILM EDITORS:	Michael Hill, Daniel Hanley
SUPERVISING SOUND EDITOR:	Anthony S. Ciccolini III
SOUND:	Ron Kalish, Bitty O'Sullivan-Smith
MUSIC EDITOR:	Dan Carlin Sr.
MUSIC:	Randy Newman

Cast: Steve Martin (Gil), Mary Steenburgen (Karen), Dianne Wiest (Helen), Jason Robards (Frank), Rick Moranis (Nathan), Tom Hulce (Larry), Martha Plimpton (Julie), Keanu Reeves (Tod), Harley Kozak (Susan), Dennis Dugan (David Brodsky), Joaquin Phoenix (Garry, credited as Leaf Phoenix), Rance Howard (dean at college), Clint Howard (Lou)

Closet Land (March 1991), color, 120 minutes, R

PRODUCTION COMPANY:	Imagine Entertainment
DISTRIBUTION COMPANY:	Universal
PRODUCER:	Janet Meyers
EXECUTIVE PRODUCERS:	Brian Grazer, Ron Howard
DIRECTOR:	Radha Bharadwaj
SCREENPLAY:	Radha Bharadwaj
PRODUCTION DESIGNER:	Eiko Ishioka
ART DIRECTOR:	Kenneth A. Hardy
SET DECORATOR:	Gary Matteson
DIRECTOR OF PHOTOGRAPHY:	Bill Pope
COSTUMES:	Eiko Ishioka
MAKEUP:	Frances Mathias
FILM EDITOR:	Lisa Churgin
SOUND:	Douglas Murray
MUSIC:	Richard Einhorn

Cast: Madeleine Stowe (Woman), Alan Rickman (Man)

Backdraft (May 1991), color, 136 minutes, R

PRODUCTION COMPANIES:	Imagine Entertainment, Trilogy Entertainment Group
DISTRIBUTION COMPANY:	Universal

RON HOWARD

PRODUCERS:	Richard B. Lewis, Pen Densham, John Watson
EXECUTIVE PRODUCERS:	Brian Grazer, Raffaella De Laurentiis
DIRECTOR:	Ron Howard
SCREENPLAY:	Gregory Widen
PRODUCTION DESIGNER:	Albert Brenner
ART DIRECTOR:	Carol Wood
SET DECORATOR:	Garrett Lewis
SET DESIGNERS:	William B. Fosser, Harold L. Fuhrman
DIRECTOR OF PHOTOGRAPHY:	Mikael Salomon
SPECIAL VISUAL EFFECTS:	Scott Farrar
COSTUME DESIGNER:	Jodie Tillen
COSTUME SUPERVISOR:	John Casey
FILM EDITORS:	Daniel Hanley, Michael Hill
SUPERVISING SOUND EDITOR:	Richard Hymns
SOUND:	Gary Summers, Randy Thom, Gary Rydstrom, Tom Johnson
MUSIC:	Hans Zimmer

Cast: Kurt Russell (Stephen McCaffrey), William Baldwin (Brian McCaffrey), Scott Glenn (John Adcox), Jennifer Jason Leigh (Jennifer Vaitkus), Donald Sutherland (Ronald Bartel), Rebecca De Mornay (Helen McCaffrey), Jason Gedrick (Tim Krizminski), J. T. Walsh (Martin Swayzak), Clint Howard (Ricco), Cedric Young (Grindle), Tony Mockus Sr. (Chief John Fitzgerald), Jack McGee (Schmidt), Mark Wheeler (Pengelly), Robert De Niro (Donald Rimgale)

Far and Away (May 1992), color, 140 minutes, PG-13

PRODUCTION COMPANY:	Imagine Entertainment
DISTRIBUTION COMPANY:	Universal
PRODUCERS:	Brian Grazer, Ron Howard
EXECUTIVE PRODUCER:	Todd Hallowell
DIRECTOR:	Ron Howard
STORY:	Bob Dolman, Ron Howard
SCREENPLAY:	Bob Dolman
PRODUCTION DESIGNERS:	Allan Cameron, Jack T. Collis
ART DIRECTORS:	Jack Senter, Steve Spence, Tony Reading
SET DECORATORS:	Josie MacAvin, Richard Goddard
SET DESIGNERS:	Joseph Hubbard, Robert M. Beall
DIRECTOR OF PHOTOGRAPHY:	Mikael Salomon
COSTUME DESIGNER:	Joanna Johnston
COSTUME SUPERVISORS:	Pam Wise, James Tyson, Rhonda McGuirke
MAKEUP:	Richard Dean, Edouard F. Henriques III
FILM EDITORS:	Michael Hill, Daniel Hanley
SUPERVISING SOUND EDITOR:	Anthony Ciccolini III

SOUND DESIGNERS: Anthony Ciccolini III, Lou Cerborino
MUSIC: John Williams

Cast: Tom Cruise (Joseph), Nicole Kidman (Shannon), Thomas Gibson (Stephen), Robert Prosky (Christie), Barbara Babcock (Nora Christie), Colm Meany (Kelly), Eileen Pollock (Molly Kay), Michelle Johnson (Grace), Douglas Gillison (Dermody), Wayne Grace (Bourke), Rance Howard (Tomlin), Clint Howard (Flynn)

The Paper (March 1994), color, 112 minutes, R

PRODUCTION COMPANY: Imagine Entertainment
DISTRIBUTION COMPANY: Universal
PRODUCERS: Brian Grazer, Frederick Zollo
EXECUTIVE PRODUCERS: Dylan Sellers, Todd Hallowell
DIRECTOR: Ron Howard
SCREENPLAY: David Koepp, Stephen Koepp
PRODUCTION DESIGNER: Todd Hallowell
ART DIRECTOR: Maher Ahmad
SET DECORATOR: Debra Schutt
DIRECTOR OF PHOTOGRAPHY: John Seale
COSTUMES: Rita Ryack
MAKEUP: Allen Weisinger, Jean Luc Russier, Manlio Rocchetti, Fern Buchner, Craig Lyman, Michael Laudati, Neal Martz
FILM EDITORS: Daniel Hanley, Michael Hill
SUPERVISING SOUND EDITORS: Anthony Ciccolini III, Lou Cerborino
SOUND: Maurice Schell
MUSIC: Randy Newman

Cast: Michael Keaton (Henry Hackett), Robert Duvall (Bernie White), Glenn Close (Alicia Clark), Marisa Tomei (Martha Hackett), Randy Quaid (McDougal), Jason Robards (Graham Keighley), Jason Alexander (Marion Sandusky), Spalding Gray (Paul Bladden), Catherine O'Hara (Susan), Lynne Thigpen (Janet), Clint Howard (Ray Blaisch), Rance Howard (Alicia's doctor), Cheryl Howard (Redheaded barmaid)

Apollo 13 (June 1995), color, 139 minutes, PG

PRODUCTION COMPANIES: Imagine Entertainment, Universal Pictures
DISTRIBUTION COMPANY: Universal
PRODUCER: Brian Grazer
EXECUTIVE PRODUCER: Todd Hallowell
DIRECTOR: Ron Howard
SCREENPLAY: William Broyles Jr., Al Reinert (Based on the book *Lost Moon* by Jim Lovell and Jeffrey Kluger)
PRODUCTION DESIGNER: Michael Corenblith

ART DIRECTORS:	David Bomba, Bruce Alan Miller
SET DECORATOR:	Merideth Boswell
DIRECTOR OF PHOTOGRAPHY:	Dean Cundey
SPECIAL VISUAL EFFECTS:	Robert Legato, Erik Nash
COSTUME DESIGNER:	Rita Ryack
COSTUME SUPERVISOR:	Dan Bronson
MAKEUP:	Daniel C. Striepeke, Hallie D'Amore, Larry Abbott, Michael Lorenz
FILM EDITORS:	Mike Hill, Dan Hanley
SOUND:	Rick Dior, Steve Pederson, Scott Millan, Ezra Dweck, Bob Chefalas
SUPERVISING SOUND EFFECTS EDITOR:	Stephen Hunter Flick
MUSIC EDITORS:	Thomas Drescher, Jim Henrikson
MUSIC:	James Horner

Cast: Tom Hanks (Jim Lovell), Kevin Bacon (Jack Swigert), Bill Paxton (Fred Haise), Gary Sinise (Ken Mattingly), Ed Harris (Gene Kranz), Kathleen Quinlan (Marilyn Lovell), David Andrews (Pete Conrad), Xander Berkeley (Henry Hurt), Christian Clemenson (Dr. Chuck), Brett Cullen (Capcom One), Clint Howard (EECOM White), Jean Speegle Howard (Blanch Lovell), Rance Howard (Reverend), Roger Corman (Congressman)

The Chamber (October 1996), color, 113 minutes, R

PRODUCTION COMPANIES:	Universal Pictures, Imagine Entertainment
DISTRIBUTION COMPANY:	Universal
PRODUCERS:	John Davis, Brian Grazer, Ron Howard
EXECUTIVE PRODUCERS:	David T. Friendly, Ric Kidney, Karen Kehela
DIRECTOR:	James Foley
SCREENPLAY:	William Goldman, Chris Reese (Based on the novel by John Grisham)
PRODUCTION DESIGNER:	David Brisbin
ART DIRECTOR:	Mark Worthington
SET DECORATOR:	Lisa Fischer
DIRECTOR OF PHOTOGRAPHY:	Ian Baker
COSTUME DESIGNER:	Tracy Tynan
COSTUME SUPERVISOR:	Susie Money
MAKEUP:	Lance Anderson
FILM EDITOR:	Mark Warner
SUPERVISING SOUND EDITORS:	Wylie Stateman, Paul Timothy Carden
SOUND:	Tony Lamberti, Hector C. Gika
MUSIC EDITORS:	Adam Smalley, J. J. George
MUSIC:	Carter Burwell

Cast: Chris O'Donnell (Adam Hall), Gene Hackman (Sam Cayhall), Faye Dunaway (Lee Bowen), Robert Prosky (E. Garner Goodman), Raymond Barry (Rollie Wedge),

Bo Jackson (Sgt. Packer), Lela Rochon (Nora Stark), David Marshall Grant (Governor McAllister), Nicholas Pyror (Judge Slattery), Harve Presnell (Attorney General Roxburgh)

Ransom (November 1996), color, 121 minutes, R

PRODUCTION COMPANIES:	Imagine Entertainment, Touchstone Pictures
DISTRIBUTION COMPANY:	Buena Vista
PRODUCERS:	Scott Rudin, Brian Grazer, B. Kipling Hagopian
EXECUTIVE PRODUCER:	Todd Hallowell
DIRECTOR:	Ron Howard
STORY:	Cyril Hume, Richard Maibaum
SCREENPLAY:	Richard Price, Alexander Ignon
	(Based on the previous film version of *Ransom* as well as the teleplay *Fearful Decision*, by Cyril Hume, Richard Maibum)
PRODUCTION DESIGNER:	Michael Corenblith
ART DIRECTOR:	John Kasarda
SET DECORATOR:	Susan Bode
DIRECTOR OF PHOTOGRAPHY:	Piotr Sobocinski
COSTUMES:	Rita Ryack
MAKEUP:	Allen Weisinger
FILM EDITORS:	Dan Hanley, Mike Hill
SUPERVISING SOUND EDITOR:	Anthony "Chic" Ciccolini III
SOUND:	Glenn Auchinachie, Dan Sable, Jason Canovas
MUSIC EDITORS:	Jim Henrikson, Suzana Peric
MUSIC:	James Horner

Cast: Mel Gibson (Tom Mullen), Rene Russo (Kate Mullen), Gary Sinise (Jimmy Shaker), Delroy Lindo (Agent Lonnie Hawkins), Lili Taylor (Maris Connor), Liev Schreiber (Clark Barnes), Evan Handler (Miles Roberts), Donnie Wahlberg (Cubby Barnes), Brawley Nolte (Sean Mullen), Dan Hedaya (Jackie Brown), Cheryl Howard (Science Fair Coordinator)

Inventing the Abbotts (April 1997), color, 107 minutes, R

PRODUCTION COMPANY:	Imagine Entertainment
DISTRIBUTION COMPANY:	20th Century Fox
PRODUCERS:	Ron Howard, Brian Grazer, Janet Meyers
EXECUTIVE PRODUCERS:	Karen Kehela, Jack Cummins
DIRECTOR:	Pat O'Connor
SCREENPLAY:	Ken Hixon
	(Based on the story by Sue Miller)
PRODUCTION DESIGNER:	Gary Frutkoff
ART DIRECTOR:	William V. Ryder
SET DECORATOR:	Kathryn Peters

SET DESIGNERS:	Louisa S. Bonnie, Steve Cooper
DIRECTOR OF PHOTOGRAPHY:	Kenneth MacMillan
COSTUME DESIGNER:	Aggie Guerard Rodgers
COSTUME SUPERVISOR:	Winnie Brown-Willis
MAKEUP:	Julie Hewett
FILM EDITOR:	Ray Lovejoy
SUPERVISING SOUND EDITOR:	Don Sharpe
SOUND:	Rocky Phelan
MUSIC EDITORS:	Graham Sutton, Michael Connell, Steve Lotwis
MUSIC:	Michael Kamen

Cast: Joaquin Phoenix (Doug Holt), Billy Crudup (Jacey Holt), Will Patton (Lloyd Abbott), Kathy Baker (Helen Holt), Jennifer Connelly (Eleanor Abbott), Michael Sutton (Steve), Liv Tyler (Pamela Abbott), Joanna Going (Alice Abbott), Barbara Williams (Joan Abbott), Alessandro Nivola (Peter Vanlaningham)

EDtv (March 1999), color, 123 minutes, PG-13

PRODUCTION COMPANIES:	Universal Pictures, Imagine Entertainment
DISTRIBUTION COMPANY:	Universal
PRODUCERS:	Brian Grazer, Ron Howard
EXECUTIVE PRODUCERS:	Todd Hallowell, Michel Roy, Richard Sadler
DIRECTOR:	Ron Howard
SCREENPLAY:	Lowell Ganz, Babaloo Mandel (Based on the film *Louis 19, le roi des ondes* by Emile Gaudreault, Sylvie Bouchard)
PRODUCTION DESIGNER:	Michael Corenblith
ART DIRECTOR:	Dan Webster
SET DECORATOR:	Merideth Boswell
DIRECTOR OF PHOTOGRAPHY:	John Schwartzman
COSTUMES:	Rita Ryack
MAKEUP:	Fred C. Blau, Ken Chase, Kimberly Greene, Ann Lee Masterson, Elaine Offers
FILM EDITORS:	Mike Hill, Dan Hanley
SUPERVISING SOUND EDITOR:	Chic Ciccolini III
SOUND:	Daniel Pagan
MUSIC:	Randy Edelman

Cast: Matthew McConaughey (Ed), Jenna Elfman (Shari), Woody Harrelson (Ray), Sally Kirkland (Jeanette), Martin Landau (Al), Ellen DeGeneres (Cynthia), Rob Reiner (Mr. Whitaker), Dennis Hopper (Hank), Elizabeth Hurley (Jill), Adam Goldberg (John), Clint Howard (Ken), Cheryl Howard (Party Girl)

Beyond the Mat (October 1999), color, 102 minutes, R (documentary)

PRODUCTION COMPANIES:	Imagine Entertainment; I, I, Me, Me Productions
DISTRIBUTION COMPANY:	Universal
PRODUCERS:	Brian Grazer, Ron Howard, Michael Rosenberg, Barry Bloom, Barry W. Blaustein
DIRECTOR:	Barry W. Blaustein
WRITER:	Barry W. Blaustein
PRODUCTION DESIGNER:	Jake Kline
DIRECTORS OF PHOTOGRAPHY:	Michael Grady, Mitchell Amundsen
MAKEUP:	Ania M. Harasimiak
FILM EDITOR:	Jeff Werner
PRODUCTION SOUND MIXERS:	Shawn Holden, Peter Verrando
MUSIC:	Nathan Barr

Dr. Seuss' How the Grinch Stole Christmas (November 2000), color, 105 minutes, PG

PRODUCTION COMPANIES:	Universal Pictures, Imagine Entertainment
DISTRIBUTION COMPANY:	Universal
PRODUCERS:	Brian Grazer, Ron Howard
EXECUTIVE PRODUCER:	Todd Hallowell
DIRECTOR:	Ron Howard
SCREENPLAY:	Jeffrey Price, Peter S. Seaman (Based on the children's book by Dr. Seuss)
PRODUCTION DESIGNER:	Michael Corenblith
ART DIRECTOR:	Lauren Polizzi
SET DECORATOR:	Merideth Boswell
DIRECTOR OF PHOTOGRAPHY:	Don Peterman
SPECIAL VISUAL EFFECTS:	Kevin Mack, Matthew Butler, Bryan Grill
COSTUME DESIGNER:	Rita Ryack
COSTUME SUPERVISOR:	Dan Bronson
MAKEUP:	Toni G., Alex Proctor, Kazuhiro Tsuji, Lance Anderson, Jane Aull, Kate Biscoe, John Blake, Fred Blau, Barney Burman, Bill Corso, Wade Daily, Zoltan Elek, Earl Ellis, Leonard Engelman, Jane Galli, Kevin Haney, Isabel Harkins, Joel Harlow, Donna-Lou Henderson, Will Huff, Karen Iverson, Jamie Kelman, Michael Key, Heather Koontz-Eaton, Toby Lamm, Mark Landon, Steve La Porte, Margie Latinopoulous, Judy Lovell, Bart Mixon, Gil Mosko, Kenny Myers, Geneva Nash-Morgan, Ve Neill, Greg Nelson, Deborah Patino, Joe Podnar, Margaret Prentice, Vincent Prentice,

	Steve Prouty, Jerry Quist, Bernd Rantscheff, Craig Reardon, Jill Rockow, Robert Romero, Sandra Rowden, Robert Ryan, Amy Schmiederer, Mark Shostrom, Robin Slater, Mike Smithson, Richard Snell, Rick Stratton, Thom Surprenant, Jackie Tichenor, Christien Tinsley, June Westmore, Monty Westmore, Karen Westerfield
SPECIAL EFFECTS MAKEUP:	Rick Baker
FILM EDITORS:	Dan Hanley, Mike Hill
SUPERVISING SOUND EDITORS:	Scott Hecker, Michael M. Geisler
SOUND:	Eric A. Norris, Brian Thomas Nist, Kenneth L. Johnson
MUSIC:	James Horner

Cast: Jim Carrey (The Grinch), Jeffrey Tambor (Mayor Augustus Maywho), Christine Baranski (Martha May Whovier), Bill Irwin (Lou Lou Who), Molly Shannon (Betty Lou Who), Clint Howard (Whobris), Taylor Momsen (Cindy Lou Who), Anthony Hopkins (Narrator), Josh Ryan Evans (8-year-old Grinch), Mindy Sterling (Clarnella), Rachel Winfree (Rose), Rance Howard (Elderly Timekeeper), Bryce Howard (Surprised Who)

A Beautiful Mind (December 2001), color, 134 minutes, PG-13

PRODUCTION COMPANIES:	Universal Pictures, DreamWorks Pictures, Imagine Entertainment
DISTRIBUTION COMPANY:	Universal
PRODUCERS:	Brian Grazer, Ron Howard
EXECUTIVE PRODUCERS:	Karen Kehela, Todd Hallowell
DIRECTOR:	Ron Howard
SCREENPLAY:	Akiva Goldsman (Based on the book by Sylvia Nasar)
PRODUCTION DESIGNER:	Wynn Thomas
ART DIRECTOR:	Robert Guerra
SET DECORATOR:	Leslie Rollins
DIRECTOR OF PHOTOGRAPHY:	Roger Deakins
SPECIAL VISUAL EFFECTS:	Kevin Mack
COSTUME DESIGNER:	Rita Ryack
COSTUME SUPERVISORS:	Bill Campbell, Winsome G. McKoy
MAKEUP:	Neal Martz, Todd Kleitsch, Kymbra Callaghan, Linda Lazar
FILM EDITORS:	Mike Hill, Dan Hanley
SUPERVISING SOUND EDITOR:	Chic Ciccolini III
MUSIC EDITOR:	Jim Henrikson
MUSIC:	James Horner

Cast: Russell Crowe (John Nash), Ed Harris (Parcher), Jennifer Connelly (Alicia Nash), Christopher Plummer (Dr. Rosen), Paul Bettany (Charles), Adam Goldberg (Sol), John Lucas (Hansen), Vivien Cardone (Marcee), Anthony Rapp (Bender), Jason Gray-Stanford (Ainsley), Judd Hirsch (Helinger), Cheryl Howard (Harvard Administrator), Rance Howard (White-haired patient)

TELEVISION MOVIES

Cotton Candy (1978), color, 120 minutes, NBC

FIRST AIRED:	10/26/78
PRODUCTION COMPANY:	Major H Productions
PRODUCER:	John Thomas Lenox
DIRECTOR:	Ron Howard
TELEPLAY:	Ron Howard, Clint Howard
ART DIRECTOR:	Cyndy Severson
DIRECTOR OF PHOTOGRAPHY:	Robert Jessup
EDITOR:	Robert Kern Jr.
MUSIC:	Joe Renzetti

Cast: Charlie Martin Smith (George Smally), Clint Howard (Corky MacFearson), Leslie E. King (Brenda Mathews), Kevin Lee Miller (Barry Bates), Manuel Padilla Jr. (Julio Guererro), Dino Scofield (Bart Bates), Mark Wheeler (Torbin Bequette), Alvy Moore (George's Father), Joan Crosby (George's Mother), Ray LePere (Coach Grimes), Rance Howard (Bremmercamp)

Skyward (1980), color, 120 minutes, NBC

FIRST AIRED:	11/20/80
PRODUCTION COMPANY:	Major H/Anson Productions
PRODUCER:	John A. Kuri
EXECUTIVE PRODUCERS:	Ron Howard, Anson Williams
DIRECTOR:	Ron Howard
STORY:	Anson Williams
TELEPLAY:	Nancy Sackett
ART DIRECTOR:	Jack Morley
DIRECTOR OF PHOTOGRAPHY:	Robert Jessup
EDITOR:	Robert Kern Jr.
MUSIC:	Lee Holdridge
ASSISTANT TO THE PRODUCER:	Cheryl Howard

Cast: Bette Davis (Billie Dupree), Howard Hesseman (Coop Trenton), Marion Ross (Natalie Ward), Clu Gulager (Steve Ward), Ben Marley (Scott Billings), Lisa Whelchel (Lisa Ward), Suzy Gilstrap (Julie Ward), Jana Hall (Miss Sinclair), Rance Howard (Pilot #2), Cheryl Howard, Clint Howard

Skyward Christmas (1981), color, 60 minutes, NBC
FIRST AIRED: 12/3/81
PRODUCTION COMPANY: Major H/Anson Productions
PRODUCERS: Joe Pope, John Kuri
EXECUTIVE PRODUCERS: Ron Howard, Anson Williams
DIRECTOR: Vincent McEveety
TELEPLAY: Craig Buck
MUSIC: Lee Holdridge
Cast: Suzy Gilstrap (Julie Ward), Bibi Besch (Natalie Ward), Christopher Connelly
(Steve Ward), Kelly Ann Conn (Lisa Ward), Audra Lindley (Billie Dupree), Geoffrey
Lewis (Coop Trenton), Jack Elam (Clay Haller), Justin Dana (Billy Ward), Harold
Scruggs (Leo)

Through the Magic Pyramid (1981), color, 120 minutes, NBC
FIRST AIRED IN TWO PARTS: 12/6/81, 12/13/81
PRODUCTION COMPANY: Major H Productions
PRODUCERS: Rance Howard, Herbert J. Wright
EXECUTIVE PRODUCER: Ron Howard
DIRECTOR: Ron Howard
TELEPLAY: Rance Howard, Herbert J. Wright
ART DIRECTOR: John A. Kuri
DIRECTOR OF PHOTOGRAPHY: Gary Graver
EDITOR: Robert Kern Jr.
MUSIC: Joe Renzetti
Cast: Chris Barnes (Bobby Tuttle), Hans Conried (Ay, Mr. Mantley), Vic Tayback
(Horembeb), Olivia Barash (Princess Baket), Betty Beaird (Eleanor Tuttle), Gino
Conforti (Hotep), Elaine Giftos (Nefertiti), James Hampton (Sam Tuttle), Robbie Rist
(Bonkers), Kario Salem (Akhenaten), Eric Greene (Tut), Jo Anne Worley (Moontdeme),
Sydney Penny (Princess Ankelsen)

When Your Lover Leaves (1983), color, 120 minutes, NBC
FIRST AIRED: 10/31/83
PRODUCTION COMPANIES: Major H Productions, Fair Dinkum
Productions, NBC Entertainment
PRODUCERS: Roger Birnbaum, Ervin Zavada
EXECUTIVE PRODUCERS: Henry Winkler, Ron Howard
DIRECTOR: Jeff Bleckner
TELEPLAY: Terence Mulcahy, B. R. Maxfield
ART DIRECTOR: Dave L. Love
DIRECTOR OF PHOTOGRAPHY: Reed Smoot
EDITOR: Artie Mandelberg
MUSIC: Randy Edelman
Cast: Valerie Perrine (Ronda Thompson), Betty Thomas (Maude), David Ackroyd (Joe
Waterson), Ed O'Neill (Mack Shore), Merritt Butrick (Aaron), Dwight Schultz

(Richard Reese), Richard Hamilton (Gramps), Shannon Wilcox (Louise), Jack Riley (Ralph), Lucille Benson (Greta)

Into Thin Air (1985), color, 120 minutes, CBS

FIRST AIRED:	10/29/85
PRODUCTION COMPANYIES:	Major H Productions, Tony Ganz Productions
PRODUCER:	Joseph Stern
EXECUTIVE PRODUCERS:	Ron Howard, Tony Ganz, Irv Wilson
DIRECTOR:	Roger Young
TELEPLAY:	George Rubino
ART DIRECTOR:	Douglas Higgins
DIRECTOR OF PHOTOGRAPHY:	Charles Correll
EDITOR:	Eric Sears
MUSIC:	Brad Fiedel

Cast: Ellen Burstyn (Joan Walker), Robert Prosky (Jim Conway), Sam Robards (Stephen Walker), Nicholas Pryor (Larry Walker), John Dennis Johnston (Earl Pike), Patricia Smith (Olga Conway), Tate Donovan (Brian Walker), Caroline McWilliams (Assistant District Attorney Towler), J. P. Bumstead (Agent Cameron), Bill Calvert (Rob Walker)

Lone Star Kid (1988), color, 55 minutes, E! Network

PRODUCTION COMPANY:	Wonderworks
PRODUCER:	Barbara Hiser
EXECUTIVE PRODUCERS:	Anson Williams, Ron Howard, Fred Tatashore
DIRECTOR:	Anson Williams
TELEPLAY:	Barbara Hiser, Anson Williams
DIRECTOR OF PHOTOGRAPHY:	Stephen L. Posey
MUSIC:	Charlie Daniels

Cast: James Earl Jones, Chad Sheets, Charlie Daniels, Rodger Boyce, Tom Capps, Michael Costello, James N. Harrell, Rhashell Hunter, John Martin, Jo Carol Moffett

TELEVISION SERIES
Note: credits for long-running series reflect the premiere episode.

Littleshots, color, 30 minutes (pilot for unsold series)

FIRST AIRED:	6/25/83
PRODUCTION COMPANIES:	Major H Productions, Anson Productions, Paramount TV
PRODUCER:	Bruce Johnson
EXECUTIVE PRODUCERS:	Ron Howard, Anson Williams
DIRECTOR:	Ron Howard
WRITER:	Bob Dolman

PRODUCTION DESIGNER: John A. Kuri
MUSIC: John Beal
Cast: Joey Lawrence (Pete), Robbie Kiger (Spetter), Keri Houlihan (Greddy), Maya Akerling (Linda). Others include: Soleil Moon Frye (Samantha)

Maximum Security (1985), color, 30 minutes (6-part miniseries), HBO
FIRST AIRED: 3/13/85
PRODUCTION COMPANIES: Major H Productions, New World TV
PRODUCERS: Jim Begg, Jeffrey Ganz
EXECUTIVE PRODUCERS: Tony Ganz, Ron Howard
DIRECTOR: Sharron Miller
WRITER: Ari Jubelirer
DIRECTOR OF PHOTOGRAPHY: Stephen L. Posey
MUSIC: David Frank, Jay Asher
Cast: Robert Desiderio, Geoffrey Lewis, Jean Smart, Trinidad Silva, Stan Shaw, Caroline McWilliams, Stephen Elliott, Teddy Wilson, Kerry Sherman, Jeff Ware, Ponchita Gomez

Dick Van Dyke Show, color, 30 minutes (pilot for unsold series, 1986-87)
PRODUCTION COMPANY: New World Television
PRODUCERS: Anson Williams, Ron Howard
CAST: Dick Van Dyke

Take Five (1987), color, 30 minutes, CBS
FIRST AIRED: 4/8/87
PRODUCTION COMPANIES: Imagine Television, Empire City Productions, Tri-Star Television
PRODUCERS: David Misch, Todd Stevens
EXECUTIVE PRODUCERS: Brian Grazer, Ron Howard
DIRECTOR: Barnet Kellman
WRITERS: Lowell Ganz, Babaloo Mandel
MUSIC: David Frank
Cast: George Segal, Derek McGrath, Bruce Jarchow, Jim Haynie, Melanie Chartoff, Todd Field, Severn Darden, Eugene Roche, Patti Yasutake

Smart Guys, color, 30 minutes (pilot for unsold series, 1988-89)
PRODUCTION COMPANY: Imagine Entertainment
EXECUTIVE PRODUCERS: Ron Howard, Brian Grazer, Dori Weiss
DIRECTOR: Jonathan Lynn
WRITERS: Michael DiGaetano, Larry Gay
Cast: Chris Rich (Ned), Anthony Starke (Tommy), John Pinette (Nick), Constance Shulman (Arlene)

Parenthood (1990), color, 30 minutes, NBC (pilot was 60 minutes)
FIRST AIRED: 8/20/90
PRODUCTION COMPANY: Universal Television
PRODUCER: Sascha Schneider
EXECUTIVE PRODUCERS: Ron Howard, Brian Grazer, Lowell Ganz, Babaloo Mandel
DIRECTOR: Allan Arkush
WRITER: Lowell Ganz, Babaloo Mandel
PRODUCTION DESIGN: Curtis A. Schnell
EDITOR: Joanne D'Antonio

Cast: Ed Begley Jr. (Gil Buckman), William Windom (Frank Buckman), Jayne Atkinson (Karen Buckman), Sheila MacRae (Marilyn Buckman), Maryedith Burrell (Helen Buckman), Leonardo DiCaprio (Garry Buckman), Bess Meyer (Julie Buckman Hawks), David Arquette (Tod Hawks), Max Elliott Slade (Kevin Buckman), Thora Birch (Taylor Buckman), Zachary Lavoy (Justin Buckman)

Hiller and Diller (1997), color, 30 minutes, ABC
FIRST AIRED: 9/23/97
PRODUCTION COMPANIES: Imagine Television, Touchstone Television
PRODUCER: Stephen C. Grossman
EXECUTIVE PRODUCERS: Brian Grazer, Ron Howard, Tony Krantz, Lowell Ganz, Babaloo Mandel, Tracy Newman, Jonathan Stark
DIRECTOR: Gil Junger
WRITERS: Lowell Ganz, Babaloo Mandel
PRODUCTION DESIGNER: Bill Brzeski
DIRECTOR OF PHOTOGRAPHY: Joe Pennella
EDITOR: Kris Trexler
SOUND: Larry Stephens
MUSIC: Ray Colcord

Cast: Richard Lewis (Neil Diller), Kevin Nealon (Ted Hiller), Jordan Baker (Jeanne Hiller), Allison Mack (Brooke), Kyle Sabihy (Zane Diller), Jillian Berard (Allison Hiller), Faryn Einhorn (Lizzie Hiller), Jonathan Osser (Josh Hiller), Danny Zorn, Bodhi Pine Elfman, Eugene Levy (Gordon Schermerhorn)

From the Earth to the Moon (1998), color, 60 minutes (12-part miniseries), HBO
FIRST AIRED: 4/5/98
PRODUCTION COMPANIES: HBO Original Programming, Imagine Entertainment, Clavius Base
PRODUCERS: Brian Grazer, Ron Howard, Michael Bostick
EXECUTIVE PRODUCER: Tom Hanks
DIRECTORS: Tom Hanks, David Frankel, Lili Fini Zanuck, and others

WRITER: Steven Katz, Graham Yost, Remi Aubuchon, Al Reinert, and others

PRODUCTION DESIGNER: Richard Toyon

ART DIRECTOR: Seth Reid

DIRECTOR OF PHOTOGRAPHY: Gale Tattersall

SPECIAL VISUAL EFFECTS: Ernest Farino

EDITORS: Laurie Grotstein, Lisa Zeno Churgin, Richard Pearson

SOUND: Joe Foglia

MUSIC: Michael Kamen, Mark Mancina, Mark Isham

Cast includes: David Andrews (Frank Borman), Tim Daly (Jim Lovell), Al Franken (Jerome Weisner), Tony Goldwyn (Neil Armstrong), Cary Elwes (Michael Collins), Nick Searcy (Deke Slayton), Dan Lauria (James Webb), Kevin Pollak (Joseph Shea), Ted Levine (Alan Shepard), James Rebhorn (Harrison Storms)

Sports Night (1998-2000), color, 30 minutes, ABC

FIRST AIRED: 9/22/98

PRODUCTION COMPANIES: Imagine Television, Touchstone Television

PRODUCERS: John Amodeo, Tracey Stern, Rachel Sweet

EXECUTIVE PRODUCERS: Aaron Sorkin, Brian Grazer, Ron Howard, Tony Krantz, Thomas Schlamme, Rob Scheidlinger

DIRECTOR: Thomas Schlamme

WRITER: Aaron Sorkin

PRODUCTION DESIGNER: Thomas E. Azzari

SET DECORATOR: Mark Johnson

DIRECTOR OF PHOTOGRAPHY: Peter Smokler

COSTUMES: Maureen Gates

EDITOR: Janet Ashikaga

SOUND: Larry La Sota

MUSIC: W. G. Snuffy Walden

Cast: Josh Charles (Dan Rydell), Peter Krause (Casey McCall), Felicity Huffman (Dana Whitaker), Robert Guillaume (Isaac Jaffe), Joshua Malina (Jeremy Goodwin), Sabrina Lloyd (Natalie Hurley), Robert Mailhouse (J. J.), Kayla Blake (Kim), Greg Baker (Elliott), Timothy Davis-Reed (Chris)

Felicity (1998-2002), color, 60 minutes, WB

FIRST AIRED: 9/29/98

PRODUCTION COMPANIES: Imagine Television, Touchstone Television

PRODUCER: Anthony Santa Croce

EXECUTIVE PRODUCERS: Brian Grazer, Ron Howard, Tony Krantz, J. J. Abrams, Matt Reeves

DIRECTOR: Matt Reeves

WRITER:	J. J. Abrams
PRODUCTION DESIGNER:	Woody Crocker
DIRECTOR OF PHOTOGRAPHY:	Richard Fannin
EDITOR:	Stan Salfas
SOUND:	Ed White
MUSIC:	W. G. Snuffy Walden

Cast: Keri Russell (Felicity Porter), Scott Speedman (Ben Covington), Amy Jo Johnson (Julie Emrick), Scott Foley (Noel Crane), William Monaghan (George Rogalsky), Darnell Williams (Joe Papaleo), Erich Anderson (Edward Porter), Eve Gordon (Barbara Porter), Amanda Foreman (Meghan), Norma Maldonado (Principal)

The PJs (1999–2001), color, 30 minutes (animation), WB

FIRST AIRED:	1/10/99
PRODUCTION COMPANIES:	Imagine Television, Eddie Murphy Productions, Will Vinton Studios, Touchstone Television
PRODUCERS:	Mike Mendel, Mike Price
EXECUTIVE PRODUCERS:	Larry Wilmore, Steve Tompkins, Brian Grazer, Ron Howard, Tony Krantz, Eddie Murphy, Will Vinton, Tom Turpin
DIRECTOR:	Mark Gustafson
WRITER:	Don Beck
ART DIRECTOR:	Paul Harrod
DIRECTOR OF PHOTOGRAPHY:	Tim McGilvry
EDITOR:	Maria Ramirez
SOUND:	Beau Biggart, John Asman, Sam Black
MUSIC:	Mark Bonilla

Cast (voice only): Eddie Murphy (Thurgood Stubbs), Loretta Devine (Muriel Stubbs), James Black (Tarnell), Michael Paul Chan (Jimmy Ho), Ja'net DuBois (Mrs. Avery), Cheryl Francis Harrington (Haiti Lady), Shawn Michael Howard (Smokey), Jenifer Lewis (Bebe), Pepe Serna (Sanchez), Crystal Scales (Calvin)

Wonderland (2000), color, 60 minutes, ABC

FIRST AIRED:	3/30/00
PRODUCTION COMPANIES:	Touchstone Televison, Imagine Television
EXECUTIVE PRODUCERS:	Peter Berg, Ron Howard, Brian Grazer, Tony Krantz
DIRECTOR AND WRITER:	Peter Berg
SET DESIGNER:	Michael Boonstra
DIRECTOR OF PHOTOGRAPHY:	Ron Fortunato
EDITOR:	Dan Lebental
MUSIC:	Craig Wedren

Cast: Ted Levine (Dr. Robert Banger), Martin Donovan (Dr. Neil Harrison), Michelle Forbes (Dr. Lyla Garrity), Billy Burke (Dr. Abe Matthews), Michael Jai White (Dr. Derrick Hatcher), Joelle Carter (Heather Miles), Patricia Clarkson (Tammy Banger)

The Beast (2001), color, 60 minutes, ABC

FIRST AIRED:	6/13/01
PRODUCTION COMPANY:	Imagine Television, Touchstone Television
EXECUTIVE PRODUCERS:	Mimi Leder, Kario Salem, Ian Sander, Kim Moses, Brian Grazer, Ron Howard, Tony Krantz
DIRECTOR:	Mimi Leder
WRITER:	Kario Salem
PRODUCTION DESIGNER:	James Spencer
DIRECTOR OF PHOTOGRAPHY:	Charles Minsky
EDITOR:	Martin Nicholson
MUSIC:	Joseph Vitarelli

Cast: Frank Langella (Jackson Burns), Jason Gedrick (Reese McFadden), Peter Riegert (Ted Fisher), Elizabeth Mitchell (Alice Allenby), Naveen Andrews (Tamir Naipaul), Harriet Sansom Harris (Mrs. Sweeney), April Grace (Sonya Topple), Wendy Crewson (Maggie Steech)

24 (2001-), color, 60 minutes, Fox

FIRST AIRED:	11/6/01
PRODUCTION COMPANIES:	Imagine Television, 20th Century Fox Television
PRODUCER:	Cyrus Yavneh
EXECUTIVE PRODUCERS:	Joel Surnow, Robert Cochran, Ron Howard, Brian Grazer, Tony Krantz
DIRECTOR:	Stephen Hopkins
WRITER:	Robert Cochran, Joel Surnow
PRODUCTION DESIGNER:	Carlos Barbosa
DIRECTOR OF PHOTOGRAPHY:	Peter Levy
EDITOR:	David Thompson
MUSIC:	Sean Callery

Cast: Kiefer Sutherland (Jack Bauer), Leslie Hope (Teri Bauer), Elisha Cuthbert (Kimberly Bauer), Sarah Clarke (Nina Myers), Dennis Haybert (David Palmer), Penny Johnson Jerald (Sherry Palmer), Tanya Wright (Patty Brooks)

Major Awards and Honors for Films Directed by Ron Howard

Through the Magic Pyramid (1981)
Emmy Awards
    Outstanding Children's Program: Rance Howard and Herbert Wright, producers;
    Ron Howard, executive producer (nominated)

Night Shift (1982)
Golden Globes
    Best Actor in a Motion Picture—Comedy/Musical: Henry Winkler (nominated)

Splash (1984)
Academy Awards
    Best Writing, Screenplay Written Directly for the Screen: Bruce Jay Friedman,
    Lowell Ganz, Brian Grazer, Babaloo Mandel (nominated)

Golden Globes
    Best Motion Picture—Comedy/Musical (nominated)

NSFC Awards (National Society of Film Critics)
    Best Screenplay: Bruce Jay Friedman, Lowell Ganz, Babaloo Mandel (won)

Saturn Awards (Academy of Science Fiction, Fantasy & Horror Films)
    Best Actress: Daryl Hannah (won)

WGA Screen Awards (Writers Guild of America)
    Best Screenplay Written Directly for the Screen: Bruce Jay Friedman, Lowell Ganz,
    Babaloo Mandel (nominated)

YOUNG ARTIST AWARDS
Best Family Motion Picture—Musical or Comedy (nominated)

Cocoon (1985)

ACADEMY AWARDS
Best Actor in a Supporting Role: Don Ameche (won)
Best Effects—Visual Effects: David Berry, Scott Farrar, Ralph McQuarrie, Ken Ralston (won)

ARTIOS AWARDS (CASTING SOCIETY OF AMERICA)
Best Casting for Feature Film—Drama: Penny Perry (nominated)

DGA AWARDS (DIRECTORS GUILD OF AMERICA)
Outstanding Directorial Achievement in Motion Pictures: Ron Howard (nominated)

GOLDEN GLOBES
Best Motion Picture—Comedy/Musical (nominated)

HUGO AWARDS
Best Dramatic Presentation (nominated)

SATURN AWARDS (ACADEMY OF SCIENCE FICTION, FANTASY & HORROR FILMS)
Best Director: Ron Howard (won)

WGA SCREEN AWARDS (WRITERS GUILD OF AMERICA)
Best Screenplay Written Directly for the Screen: Tom Benedek (nominated)

YOUNG ARTIST AWARDS
Best Family Motion Picture—Drama (won)

Willow (1988)

ACADEMY AWARDS
Best Sound Effects Editing: Ben Burtt, Richard Hymns (nominated)
Best Visual Effects: Christopher Evans, Michael J. McAlister, Dennis Muren, Phil Tippett (nominated)

HUGO AWARDS
Best Dramatic Presentation (nominated)

RAZZIE AWARDS
Worst Screenplay: Bob Dolman; George Lucas, story (nominated)
Worst Supporting Actor: Billy Barty (nominated)

SATURN AWARDS (ACADEMY OF SCIENCE FICTION, FANTASY & HORROR FILMS)
Best Costumes: Barbara Lane (won)

YOUNG ARTIST AWARDS
Best Family Motion Picture—Drama (nominated)
Best Young Actor in a Motion Picture: Warwick Davis (nominated)

Parenthood (1989)

ARTIOS AWARDS (CASTING SOCIETY OF AMERICA)
Best Casting for Feature Film—Comedy: Janet Hirshenson, Jane Jenkins (won)

ASCAP FILM AND TELEVISION MUSIC AWARDS (AMERICAN SOCIETY OF COMPOSERS, AUTHORS, AND PUBLISHERS)
Top Box Office Films: Randy Newman (won)

ACADEMY AWARDS
Best Actress in a Supporting Role: Dianne Wiest (nominated)
Best Music—Song: Randy Newman, for "I Love to See You Smile" (nominated)

AMERICAN COMEDY AWARDS
Funniest Supporting Actor in a Motion Picture: Rick Moranis (won)

GOLDEN GLOBES
Best Original Song—Motion Picture: Randy Newman, for "I Love to See You Smile" (nominated)
Best Performance by an Actor in a Motion Picture—Comedy/Musical: Steve Martin (nominated)
Best Performance by an Actress in a Supporting Role in a Motion Picture: Dianne Wiest (nominated)

YOUNG ARTIST AWARDS
Best Family Motion Picture—Comedy (won)
Best Young Actor Starring in a Motion Picture: Joaquin Phoenix (nominated)
Best Young Actor in a Supporting Role in a Motion Picture: Jasen Fisher (nominated)
Outstanding Performance by an Actor under 9 years of Age: Zachary Lavoy (nominated)

Backdraft (1991)

ACADEMY AWARDS
Best Effects—Sound Effects Editing: Richard Hymns, Gary Rydstrom (nominated)
Best Effects—Visual Effects Editing: Scott Farrar, Allen Hall, Clay Pinney, Mikael Salomon (nominated)
Best Sound—Gary Rydstrom, Gary Summers, Randy Thom, Glenn Williams (nominated)

BAFTA FILM AWARDS (BRITISH ACADEMY OF FILM AND TELEVISION ARTS)
Best Special Visual Effects— Scott Farrar, Allen Hall, Clay Pinney, Mikael Salomon (nominated)

MTV MOVIE AWARDS
Best Action Sequence (nominated)
Best Movie (nominated)

RON HOWARD

Far and Away (1992)
MTV MOVIE AWARDS
  Best Action Sequence (nominated)
  Best On-Screen Duo: Tom Cruise, Nicole Kidman (nominated)

RAZZIE AWARDS
  Worst Original Song: Enya, music; Roma Ryan, lyrics, for "Book of Days"
    (nominated)

The Paper (1994)
ACADEMY AWARDS
  Best Music—Song: Randy Newman, for "Make Up Your Mind" (nominated)

Apollo 13 (1995)
ASCAP FILM AND TELEVISION MUSIC AWARDS (AMERICAN SOCIETY OF COMPOSERS,
  AUTHORS, AND PUBLISHERS)
  Top Box Office Films: James Horner (won)

ACADEMY AWARDS
  Best Actor in a Supporting Role: Ed Harris (nominated)
  Best Actress in a Supporting Role: Kathleen Quinlan (nominated)
  Best Art Direction—Set Decoration: Merideth Boswell, Michael Corenblith
    (nominated)
  Best Visual Effects: Leslie Ekker, Michael Kanfer, Robert Legato, Matt Sweeney
    (nominated)
  Best Film Editing: Daniel P. Hanley, Mike Hill (won)
  Best Music—Original Dramatic Score: James Horner (nominated)
  Best Picture: Brian Grazer (nominated)
  Best Sound: Rick Dior, David MacMillan, Scott Millan, Steve Pederson (won)
  Best Screenplay Based on Material from Another Medium:William Broyles Jr.,
    Al Reinert (nominated)

ARTIOS AWARDS (CASTING SOCIETY OF AMERICA)
  Best Casting for Feature Film—Drama: Jane Hirshenson, Jane Jenkins (nominated)

ASC AWARDS (AMERICAN SOCIETY OF CINEMATOGRAPHERS)
  Outstanding Achievement in Cinematography in Theatrical Releases: Dean Cundey
    (nominated)

BAFTA FILM AWARDS (BRITISH ACADEMY OF FILM AND TELEVISION ARTS)
  Best Achievement in Special Effects: Leslie Ekker, Michael Kanfer, Robert Legato,
    Matt Sweeney (won)
  Best Cinematography: Dean Cundey (nominated)
  Best Editing: Daniel P. Hanley, Mike Hill (nominated)
  Best Sound: Rick Dior, David MacMillan, Scott Millan, Steve Pederson
    (nominated)

Best Production Design: Michael Corenblith (won)

BRITISH SOCIETY OF CINEMATOGRAPHERS
Best Cinematography: Dean Cundey (nominated)

CFCA AWARDS (CHICAGO FILM CRITICS ASSOCIATION)
Best Picture (won)

DGA AWARDS (DIRECTORS GUILD OF AMERICA)
Outstanding Directorial Achievement in Motion Pictures: Ron Howard, director; Aldric La'Auli Porter, first assistant director; Jane Paul, second assistant director; Carl Clifford, unit production manager (won)

EDDIE AWARDS (AMERICAN CINEMA EDITORS)
Best Edited Feature Film: Daniel P. Hanley, Mike Hill (nominated)

GOLDEN GLOBES
Best Director: Ron Howard (nominated)
Best Motion Picture—Drama (nominated)
Best Performance by an Actor in a Supporting Role in a Motion Picture: Ed Harris (nominated)
Best Performance by an Actress in a Supporting Role in a Motion Picture: Kathleen Quinlan (nominated)

HUGO AWARDS
Best Dramatic Presentation (nominated)

MTV MOVIE AWARDS
Best Male Performer: Tom Hanks (nominated)
Best Movie (nominated)

PGA GOLDEN LAUREL AWARDS (PRODUCERS GUILD OF AMERICA)
Motion Picture Producer of the Year: Brian Grazer, Todd Hallowell (won)

SCREEN ACTORS GUILD AWARDS
Outstanding Performance by a Cast (won)
Outstanding Performance by a Male Actor in a Supporting Role: Ed Harris (won)

SEFCA AWARDS (SOUTHEASTERN FILM CRITICS ASSOCIATION)
Best Director: Ron Howard (won)
Best Picture (won)
Best Supporting Actor: Ed Harris (won)

WGA SCREEN AWARDS (WRITERS GUILD OF AMERICA)
Best Screenplay Based on Material Previously Produced or Published: William Broyles Jr., Al Reinert (nominated)

YOUNG ARTIST AWARDS
Best Family Feature—Drama (nominated)

Ransom (1996)

ASCAP FILM AND TELEVISION MUSIC AWARDS (AMERICAN SOCIETY OF COMPOSERS, AUTHORS, AND PUBLISHERS)
Top Box Office Films: James Horner (won)

BLOCKBUSTER ENTERTAINMENT AWARDS
Favorite Actor—Suspense: Mel Gibson (won)
Favorite Supporting Actress—Suspense: Lili Taylor (won)

GOLDEN GLOBES
Best Performance by an Actor in a Motion Picture—Drama: Mel Gibson (nominated)

IMAGE AWARDS
Outstanding Supporting Actor in a Motion Picture: Delroy Lindo (nominated)

YOUNG ARTIST AWARDS
Best Performance in a Feature Film—Supporting Young Actor: Brawley Nolte (nominated)

How the Grinch Stole Christmas (2000)

ASCAP FILM AND TELEVISION MUSIC AWARDS (AMERICAN SOCIETY OF COMPOSERS, AUTHORS, AND PUBLISHERS)
Top Box Office Films: James Horner (won)

ACADEMY AWARDS
Best Art Direction—Set Decoration: Merideth Boswell, set director; Michael Corenblith, art director (nominated)
Best Costume Design: Rita Ryack (nominated)
Best Makeup: Rick Baker, Gail Rowell-Ryan (won)

ALFS AWARDS (LONDON FILM CRITICS CIRCLE)
Actor of the Year: Jim Carrey, also for Man in the Moon (1999) (nominated)

AWARDS FOR EXCELLENCE IN PRODUCTION DESIGN (SOCIETY OF MOTION PICTURE AND TELEVISION ART DIRECTORS)
Feature Film—Period or Fantasy Films: Michael Corenblith (won)

BAFTA FILM AWARDS (BRITISH ACADEMY OF FILM AND TELEVISION ARTS)
Best Makeup/Hair: Rick Baker, Toni G. Sylvia Nava, Gail Rowell-Ryan, Kazuhiro Tsuji (won)

BLIMP AWARDS (KIDS' CHOICE AWARDS)
Favorite Movie (won)
Favorite Movie Actor: Jim Carrey (won)

BLOCKBUSTER ENTERTAINMENT AWARDS
Favorite Actor—Comedy: Jim Carrey (won)
Favorite Female—Newcomer: Taylor Momsen (nominated)
Favorite Supporting Actor—Comedy: Jeffrey Tambor (nominated)

Favorite Supporting Actress—Comedy: Christine Baranski, Molly Shannon (nominated)

CANADIAN COMEDY AWARDS
Film—Pretty Funny Male Performance: Jim Carrey (nominated)

CDG AWARDS (COSTUME DESIGNERS GUILD)
Excellence for Costume Design for Film—Period/Fantasy: Rita Ryack (won)

EMPIRE AWARDS (UNITED KINGDOM)
Best Actor: Jim Carrey (nominated)

GOLDEN GLOBES
Best Performance by an Actor in a Motion Picture—Comedy/Musical: Jim Carrey (nominated)

GOLDEN SATELLITE AWARDS
Best Art Direction: Michael Corenblith (nominated)
Best Costume Design: Rita Ryack (won)
Best Visual Effects: Kevin Scott Mack (nominated)

HOLLYWOOD MAKEUP ARTIST AND HAIR STYLIST GUILD AWARDS
Best Innovative Hair Styling—Feature: Terry Baliel, Patricia Miller, Gail Rowell-Ryan (won)
Best Special Makeup Effects—Feature: Rick Baker, Tony G. Kazuhiro Tsuji (won)

MTV MOVIE AWARDS
Best Villain: Jim Carrey (won)

RAZZIE AWARDS
Worst Remake or Sequel (nominated)
Worst Screenplay: Jeffrey Price, Peter S. Seaman (nominated)

SATURN AWARDS (ACADEMY OF SCIENCE FICTION, FANTASY & HORROR FILMS)
Best Actor: Jim Carrey (nominated)
Best Costume: David Page, Rita Ryack (nominated)
Best Director: Ron Howard (nominated)
Best Fantasy Film (nominated)
Best Makeup: Rick Baker, Gail Rowell-Ryan (won)
Best Music: James Horner (won)
Best Performance by a Younger Actor: Taylor Momsen (nominated)
Best Special Effects: Matthew E. Butler, Bryan Grill, Allen Hall, Kevin Scott Mack (nominated)
Best DVD Special Edition Release (nominated, 2002)

SIERRA AWARDS (LAS VEGAS FILM CRITICS SOCIETY)
Best Costume Design: Rita Ryack (nominated)
Best Family Film (nominated)

VIDEO PREMIERE AWARDS
Best Overall New Extra Features, New Release: Colleen A. Benn, Marian Mansi (nominated)

YOUNG ARTIST AWARDS (UNITED STATES)
Best Family Feature Film—Comedy (won)
Best Performance in a Feature Film—Young Actress Age Ten or Under: Taylor Momsen (nominated)

A Beautiful Mind (2001)

AFI FILM AWARDS (AMERICAN FILM INSTITUTE)
AFI Actor of the Year—Male—Movies: Russell Crowe (nominated)
AFI Featured Actor of the Year—Female—Movies: Jennifer Connelly (won)
AFI Movie of the Year: Brian Grazer, Ron Howard (nominated)
AFI Screenwriter of the Year: Akiva Goldsman (nominated)

ACADEMY AWARDS
Best Actor in a Leading Role: Russell Crowe (nominated)
Best Actress in a Supporting Role: Jennifer Connelly (won)
Best Director: Ron Howard (won)
Best Editing: Daniel P. Hanley, Mike Hill (nominated)
Best Makeup: Colleen Callaghan, Greg Cannom (nominated)
Best Music—Original Score: James Horner (nominated)
Best Picture: Brian Grazer, Ron Howard (won)
Best Screenplay Based on Material Previously Produced or Published: Akiva Goldsman (won)

ARTIOS AWARDS (CASTING SOCIETY OF AMERICA)
Feature Film Casting—Drama: Jane Jenkins, Janet Hirshenson (nominated)

BAFTA FILM AWARDS (BRITISH ACADEMY OF FILM AND TELEVISION ARTS)
Best Film: Brian Grazer, Ron Howard (nominated)
Best Performance by an Actor in a Leading Role: Russell Crowe (won)
Best Performance by an Actress in a Supporting Role: Jennifer Connelly (won)
Best Screenplay—Adapted: Akiva Goldsman (nominated)

DAVID LEAN AWARD FOR DIRECTION
Ron Howard (nominated)

BFCA AWARDS (BROADCAST FILM CRITICS ASSOCIATION)
Best Actor: Russell Crowe (won)
Best Director: Ron Howard (tied with Baz Luhrmann for *Moulin Rouge*)
Best Picture (won)
Best Supporting Actress: Jennifer Connelly (won)

CFCA AWARDS (CHICAGO FILM CRITICS ASSOCIATION)
Best Actor: Russell Crowe (nominated)
Best Director: Ron Howard (nominated)

Best Original Score: James Horner (nominated)
Best Picture (nominated)
Best Screenplay: Akiva Goldsman (nominated)
Best Supporting Actress: Jennifer Connelly (nominated)

DGA AWARDS (DIRECTORS GUILD OF AMERICA)
Outstanding Directorial Achievement in Motion Pictures: Ron Howard, director; Aldric La'Auli Porter, first assistant director; Kristen Bernstein, second assistant director; Noreen R. Cheleden, second second assistant director; Kathleen McGill, unit production manager; Jane Ferguson, DGA trainee (won)

EDDIE AWARDS (AMERICAN CINEMA EDITORS)
Best Edited Feature Film—Dramatic: Daniel P. Hanley, Mike Hill (nominated)

GOLDEN GLOBES
Best Director—Motion Picture: Ron Howard (nominated)
Best Motion Picture—Drama (won)
Best Original Score—Motion Picture: James Horner (nominated)
Best Performance by an Actor in a Motion Picture—Drama: Russell Crowe (won)
Best Performance by an Actress in a Supporting Role in a Motion Picture—Drama: Jennifer Connelly (won)
Best Screenplay—Motion Picture: Akiva Goldsman (won)

GOLDEN SATELLITE AWARDS
Best Film Editing: Daniel P. Hanley, Mike Hill (nominated)
Best Original Score: James Horner (nominated)
Best Original Song: James Horner, music; Will Jennings, lyrics; for "All Love Can Be" (won)
Best Performance by an Actor in a Motion Picture—Drama: Russell Crowe (nominated)
Best Performance by an Actor in a Supporting Role—Drama: Ed Harris (nominated)
Best Performance by an Actress in a Supporting Role—Drama: Jennifer Connelly (won)
Best Screenplay—Adapted: Akiva Goldsman (nominated)

GOLDEN REEL AWARDS (MOTION PICTURE SOUND EDITORS)
Best Sound Editing—Dialogue and A.D.R., Domestic Feature Film: Stan Bochner, dialogue editor; Allan Byer, production mixer; Louis Cerborino, dialogue editor; Anthony J. Ciccolini III, supervising sound editor; Kenna Doeringer, assistant ADR editor; Dean Drabin, ADR mixer; Chris Jenkins, re-recording mixer; Marc Laub, dialogue editor; Douglas Murray, ADR recordist; Don Peebles, assistant dialogue editor; Lynne Redding, voice casting; Deborah Wallach, supervising ADR editor; Paul J. Zydel, ADR mixer (won)
Best Sound Editing—Music—Feature Film: Jim Henrikson, music editor (nominated)

RON HOWARD

HUMANITAS PRIZE
Feature Film Screenplay that "honestly explores the complexities of the human experience and sheds light on the positive values of life": Akiva Goldsman (nominated)

KCFCC AWARDS (KANSAS CITY FILM CRITICS CIRCLE)
Best Supporting Actress: Jennifer Connelly (tied with Maggie Smith for *Gosford Park*)

MTV MOVIE AWARDS
Best Male Performance: Russell Crowe (nominated)

OFCS AWARDS (ONLINE FILM CRITICS SOCIETY)
Best Actor: Russell Crowe (nominated)
Best Supporting Actress: Jennifer Connelly (won)

PGA GOLDEN LAUREL AWARDS (PRODUCERS GUILD OF AMERICA)
Motion Picture Producer of the Year: Brian Grazer, Ron Howard (nominated)

SCREEN ACTORS GUILD AWARDS
Outstanding Performance by a Female Actor in a Leading Role: Jennifer Connelly (nominated)
Outstanding Performance by a Male Actor in a Leading Role: Russell Crowe (won)
Outstanding Performance by the Cast of a Theatrical Motion Picture: Paul Bettany, Jennifer Connelly, Russell Crowe, Adam Goldberg, Ed Harris, Judd Hirsch, Josh Lucas, Christopher Plummer, Anthony Rapp (nominated)

SEFCA AWARDS (SOUTHEASTERN FILM CRITICS ASSOCIATION)
Best Supporting Actress: Jennifer Connelly (tied with Maggie Smith for *Gosford Park* and Marisa Tomei for *In the Bedroom*)

USC SCRIPTER AWARD
Best Adaptation of a Book to an English-Language Film: Akiva Goldsman, screen writer; Sylvia Nasar, author (won)

WGA SCREEN AWARD (WRITERS GUILD OF AMERICA)
Best Screenplay Based on Material Previously Produced or Published: Akiva Goldsman (won)

ADDITIONAL AWARDS AND HONORS

LAUREL AWARDS (1963)
Best New Personality (nominated—placed ninth)

GOLDEN GLOBES (1977)
Best Motion Picture Actor in a Supporting Role: *The Shootist* (nominated)

MAJOR AWARDS AND HONORS FOR FILMS DIRECTED BY RON HOWARD

GOLDEN GLOBES (1978)
Best TV Actor—Music/Comedy: *Happy Days* (nominated)

STAR (FOR TELEVISION) DEDICATED IN HIS HONOR AT 6838 HOLLYWOOD BOULEVARD, ON THE HOLLYWOOD WALK OF FAME (1981)

AMERICAN CINEMATHEQUE GALA TRIBUTE (1999)

EMMY AWARDS (1998)
Outstanding Miniseries: *From the Earth to the Moon* (won)

PGA GOLDEN LAUREL AWARDS (1999)
Television Producer of the Year Award in Longform: *From the Earth to the Moon* (won)

EMMY AWARDS (1999)
Outstanding Animated Program (for programming one hour or less): *The PJs* (nominated as a producer)

HANDPRINT/ FOOTPRINT CEREMONY, GRAUMAN'S CHINESE THEATRE (1999)

PGA GOLDEN LAUREL AWARDS (2000)
Television Producer of the Year Award in Episodic: *Sports Night* (nominated)

SHOWEST AWARDS (SHOWEST CONVENTION, NATIONAL ASSOCIATION OF THEATRE OWNERS, 2002)
Director of the Year Award (won)

Source Notes for Chapter Opening Quotes

1. Jean Howard, interviewed by Matt Lauer, *Headliners and Legends*, MSNBC, 2000.
2. Ron Howard, in Beck, Ken and Jim Clark, *Mayberry Memories* (Nashville, Tennessee: Rutledge Hill Press, 2000), 8.
3. Ron Howard, in Johnson, Ross, "Howard's Run," *The Hollywood Reporter Salutes 1995 Showeast Honorees* (October 18, 1995), S-10.
4. Ron Howard, in Rosenfield, Paul, "Life Begins After High School," *Los Angeles Times* (August 19, 1977), 13.
5. Ron Howard, in Emery, Robert J., *The Directors—Take One: In Their Own Words* (New York: TV Books, 1999), 51.
6. Ron Howard, in Ressner, Jeffrey, "Nice Guy at Mission Control," *Time* (July 3, 1995), 53.
7. Ron Howard, in Blowen, Michael, "He's Not Opie Anymore," *L.A. Life, Daily News* (June 21, 1985), 5.
8. Don Ameche, *Ibid.*
9. Ron Howard, in Birnbach, Lisa, "The Man Who Makes 'Normal' Trendy," *Parade Magazine* (April 7, 1985), 5.
10. Lowell Ganz, in Rechtshaffen, Michael, "Talk of the Town," *Hollywood Reporter, ShoWest: Ron Howard* (March 5-11, 2002), S-4.
11. Brian Grazer, in Holson, Laura M., "Producers Who Measure Profits Against Beautiful Odds," *New York Times* (March 22, 2002).
12. Ron Howard, in Nelson, Jill, "Star Man," *USA Weekend* (June 23-25, 1995), 6.
13. Ron Howard, in Birnbach, Lisa, "The Man Who Makes 'Normal' Trendy," *Parade Magazine* (April 7, 1985), 5.
14. Garv Thorp, taped telephone conversation with the author, November 9, 2001.
15. Russell Crowe, in "The 2001 Power List," *Premiere* (May 2001), 62.
Epilogue An unnamed production associate in Greenberg, James, "Ron Howard Plays with Fire," *Los Angeles Times Magazine* (May 12, 1991), 13.

Selected Bibliography

BOOKS

Andersen, Christopher B. *The Book of People*. A Perigee Book. New York: G. P. Putnam's Sons, 1981.

Beck, Ken, and Jim Clark. *Mayberry Memories: The Andy Griffith Show Photo Album*. Nashville, Tennessee: Rutledge Hill Press, 2000.

Dolman, Bob, and Ron Howard. *Far and Away: The Illustrated Story of a Journey from Ireland to America in the 1890s*. London: Boxtree Limited, 1992.

Ebsen, Buddy. *The Other Side of Oz*. Newport Beach, California: Donovan Publishing, 1993.

Emery, Robert J. *The Directors—Take One: In Their Own Words*. New York: TV Books, 1999.

Gehring, Wes D. *Populism and the Capra Legacy*. Westport, Connecticut: Greenwood Press, 1995.

Goldsman, Akiva. *A Beautiful Mind: The Shooting Script*. A Newmarket Shooting Script® Series Book. New York: Newmarket, 2002.

Holt, Georgia and Phyllis Quinn with Sue Russell. *Star Mothers: The Moms Behind the Celebrities*. New York: Simon and Schuster, 1988.

Kael, Pauline. *Hooked*. New York: E. P. Dutton, 1989.

Kael, Pauline. *State of the Art*. New York: E. P. Dutton, 1985.

Kael, Pauline. *Taking It All In*. New York: Holt, Rinehart and Winston, 1984.

Kluger, Jeffrey, with foreword by Ron Howard. *The Apollo Adventure: The Making of the Apollo Space Program and the Movie Apollo 13*. New York: Pocket Books, 1995.

Knotts, Don, with Robert Metz. *Barney Fife, and Other Characters I Have Known*. Thorndike, Maine: G. K. Hall and Company, 1999.

Kramer, Barbara. *Ron Howard: Child Star & Hollywood Director*. People to Know series. Springfield, New Jersey: Enslow Publishers, Inc., 1998.

Nasar, Sylvia. *A Beautiful Mind: The Life of Mathematical Genius and Nobel Laureate John Nash*. A Touchstone Book. New York: Simon and Schuster, 1998.

Pollock, Dale. *Skywalking: The Life and Films of George Lucas*. New York: Harmony Books, 1973.

Ryan, Joal. *Former Child Stars: The Story of Hollywood's Least Wanted*. Toronto: ECW Press, 2000.

Thomson, David. *A Biographical Dictionary of Film*. New York: Alfred A. Knopf, 1994.

ARTICLES

Abramowitz, Rachel. "In a Crisis, It was a 'Beautiful' Job." *Los Angeles Times*, March 25, 2002.

Andrews, Nigel. "The Arts Interview: Ron Howard." *Financial Times* (London), February 16-17, 2002.

Armstrong, Lois. "Happy Days Are Here Forever, As Ron Howard Plays Cecil B. in the Big D." *People*, June 12, 1978.

"A Small Boy with a Modest Outlook." *TV Guide*, July 13-19, 1963.

Attanasio, Paul. "Ron Howard's Happy Days." *Washington Post*, June 21, 1985.

Barra, Allen. "The Nation; Alamo Redux: A Mission Impossible." *New York Times*, March 10, 2002.

Bart, Peter. "Happy Days." *GQ*, May 1999.

Berkman, Meredith. "Paper Boy." *Entertainment Weekly*, April 1, 1994.

Birnbach, Lisa. "The Man Who Makes 'Normal' Trendy." *Parade Magazine*, April 7, 1985.

Blair, Iain. "EDtv: The Media Is the Message." *Film and Video*, March 1999.

Blowen, Michael. "He's Not Opie Anymore." *L.A. Life, Daily News*, June 21, 1985.

Bond, Paul. "Pop.com Wraps Before It Starts." *Hollywood Reporter*, September 6, 2000.

Bull, Debby. "Ron Howard." *Us*, April 7, 1986.

Burman, John. "Director Power '98." *Hollywood Reporter*, October 20-26, 1998.

——. "Director Power 2000." *Hollywood Reporter*, November 14–20, 2000.

Calvo, Dana. "'Beautiful Mind' Over the Usual Hollywood Matter." *Los Angeles Times*, January 15, 2002.

Case, Brian. "Friends and Relations." *Time Out* (London), January 3-10, 1990.

Champlin, Charles. "Ron Howard: The Gratifying Growth of a Director." *Los Angeles Times*, January 4, 1990.

Corliss, Richard. "Inside the Oscar Wars." *Time*, March 25, 2002.

Darnton, Nina. "A Portrait of John Forbes Nash Jr.'s Shattered Brilliance." *New York Times*, June 3, 2001.

Dawes, Amy. "Tribute to Howard a Page from H'wood Family Album." *Daily Variety*, March 26, 1990.

Du Brow, Rick. "Are Happy Days Over for NBC?" *Los Angeles Herald-Examiner*, July 23, 1980.

Edwards, Nadine M. "A House to Grow With." *Los Angeles Times Home*, December 27, 1981.

Eller, Claudia. "Imagine That: Movie-Making Duo Has One of Industry's Best Track Records." *Los Angeles Times*, October 22, 1996.

Eller, Claudia. "Reeling in the Years." *Los Angeles Times*, February 27, 1994.

Eller, Claudia, and Andy Marx. "Imagine Toppers Like Their Privacy." *Weekly Variety*, May 3, 1993.

Eller, Claudia, and Andy Marx. "It's Just Their Imagination: Howard and Grazer Back in Business—of Making Movies." *Daily Variety*, January 15, 1993.

Fleming, Michael. "Disney Gives 'Rookie' Ace 'Alamo' Reins." *Variety.com*, July 29, 2002.

Fleming, Michael. "Howard Off 'Alamo.'" *Variety.com*, July 7, 2002.

Friendly, David T. "A 'Coming Out' for Howard and 'Cocoon.'" *Los Angeles Times*, June 12, 1985.

Gethers, Peter. "A Night of Vice with Mr. Nice." *Esquire*, December 1986.

Ginsberg, Merle. "Grazer's Edge." *W*, October 1996.

Givens, Ron, with Charles Leerhsen. "The Nice Guy Rides Again." *Newsweek*, August 28, 1989.

Goldstein, Patrick. "'Beautiful Mind' Script Was a Tortuous Journey for Its Screenwriter." *Los Angeles Times*, February 13, 2002.

Goldstein, Patrick. "Playing 'Mind' Games." *Los Angeles Times*, January 22, 2002.

Goldstein, Patrick. "Ron Howard Making a Big 'Splash.'" *Los Angeles Times*, March 26, 1984.

Grant, Hank. "Ronny Howard: Natural Actor and a Real Boy." *Kansas City Star*, June 2, 1963.

Grove, Martin A. "Howard & Grazer's 'Mind' Looks Like Film to Beat for Best Picture." *Hollywood Reporter*, December 12, 2001.

Greenberg, James. "Grazer and Howard Going Public with Imagine Films." *Daily Variety*, May 22, 1986.

Greenberg, James. "Ron Howard Plays with Fire." *Los Angeles Times Magazine*, May 12, 1991.

Hachem, Samir. "The Metamorphosis of Ron Howard." *Horizon*, June 1985.

Harmetz, Aljean. "How to Be a Hot Hollywood Producer." *New York Times*, March 10, 1985.

Henry, William A., III. "Ron Howard Is No Splash in the Pan." *GQ*, July 1985.

Hochman, David. "Ron." *Us*, November 1996.

Hochman, Steve. "This Clint Makes His Own Day." *Los Angeles Times*, July 5, 1995.

Holson, Laura M. "Producers Who Measure Profits Against Beautiful Odds." *New York Times*, March 22, 2002.

Hopper, Hedda. "No One Gets into the Act when Ronny, 8, Performs." *Los Angeles Times,* March 17, 1963.

Horn, John. "Ron Howard's Last Stand at the Alamo." *Newsweek*, July 29, 2002.

Hruska, Bronwen. "They Can't Buy a Break." *Los Angeles Times Calendar*, April 21, 1996.

Jerome, Jim. "A Whale of a Tail." *People*, April 9, 1984.

Johnson, Ross. "Howard's Run." *The Hollywood Reporter Salutes 1995 Showeast Honorees*, October 18, 1995.

Kalbacker, Warren. "Playboy Interview: Ron Howard." *Playboy*, May 1994.

Keslar, Linda. "Imagine Bid by Howard, Grazer OK'd." *Daily Variety*, January 13, 1993.

Kilday, Gregg, and Zorianna Kit. "Good Will on Oscar Lunch Menu." *Hollywood Reporter*, March 12-18, 2002.

King, Andrea. "Grazer's Edge." *Hollywood Reporter Producer of the Year Salute*, February 20, 1992.

Kit, Zorianna, and Beth Laski. "Imagine That: Uni Re-ups Grazer, Howard to 2005." *Hollywood Reporter*, October 19, 2000.

Kligman, David. "Live on RONtv." *Entertainment Today*, April 2-8, 1999.

Koltnow, Barry. "Yes, I Haven't a Clue Who You Are." *Orange County Register*, February 3, 2002.

Landesman, Cosmo. "The King of Corn." *Sunday Times* (London), September 10, 1995.

Laski, Beth. "The Cat in the Hat." *Cinescape*, November/December 2000.

Lyman, Rick. "Ron Howard: Here's to You, Mrs. Robinson." *New York Times*, November 3, 2000.

MacFarquhar, Larissa. "The Producer." *New Yorker*, October 15, 2001.

Margulies, Lee. "Will Star's Loss Hurt 'Happy Days'?" *Los Angeles Times*, July 23, 1980.

McBride, Joseph. "TV's Pace Is Fast But Ron Howard Amazed by Whirlwind 'Pic' Sked." *Daily Variety*, April 22, 1977.

McCarthy, Todd. "Auteur Opie." *Film Comment*, vol. 20, no. 3, June 1984.

McClung, Paul. "Even Fate Can't Stop OU's Jean." *Oklahoma Daily*, March 18, 1948.

Meador, Mitch. "Ron Howard Has Deep Roots in Duncan." *Lawton Constitution*, March 13, 1999.

Michaelson, Judith. "Imagine That." *Los Angeles Times*, February 16, 1992.

Miller, Greg. "DreamWorks, Imagine in Venture to Showcase Online Programming." *Los Angeles Times*, October 26, 1999.

Miller, Samantha, with Vicki Sheff-Cahan. "Scene Stealer." *People*, November 23, 1998.

Morice, Laura. "Burn Baby Burn." *Us*, June 27, 1991.

Mosley, Walter. "On Ron Howard." In *Writers on Directors*, conceived and photographed by Susan Gray. New York: Watson-Guptill Publications, 1999.

Nasar, Sylvia. "A Beautiful Mind Is Besmirched by Enquiring Minds." *Los Angeles Times*, March 13, 2002.

Nelson, Jill. "Star Man." *USA Weekend*, June 23-25, 1995.

Oppenheimer, Jean. "Read All About It." *L. A. Village View*, March 26-31, 1994.

Page, Don. "Howard Family Still Has Time to Act." *Los Angeles Times*, May 9, 1968.

Perez, Christopher. "Planning Parenthood." *Village View*, August 11-17, 1989.

"Power List 2002." *Premiere*, May 2002.

Puig, Claudia. "Ron Howard's Moving Tribute to Familyhood." *Los Angeles Times*, March 26, 1990.

Rader, Dotson. "A Nice Guy and a Winner." *Parade Magazine*, November 10, 1996.

Rechtshaffen, Michael. "A Beautiful Calling." *Hollywood Reporter*, *ShoWest: Ron Howard*, March 5-11, 2002.

Rensin, David. "20 Questions: Ron Howard." *Playboy*, August 1985.

Ressner, Jeffrey. "Nice Guy at Mission Control." *Time*, July 3, 1995.

Roberts, Jerry. "Imagine Co-Chairs Travel Different Paths to the Top." *Daily Variety*, March 19, 1998.

Rosenfield, Paul. "Life Begins After High School." *Los Angeles Times*, August 19, 1977.

Royal, Susan. "Parenthood: An Interview with Ron Howard." *American Premiere*, August/September 1989.

Sandlin, Elizabeth. "Young Actor Scores." *Duncan Banner*, April 28, 1960.

Satzman, Darrell. "Actress Jean Howard dies at 73." *Burbank Leader*, September 6, 2000.

Scott, A. O. "A 'Mind' Is a Hazardous Thing to Distort." *New York Times*, March 21, 2002.

Smith, Cecil. "Howard, 26, Directs Bette Davis, Legend." *Los Angeles Times*, November 18, 1980.

Stevenson, Richard W. "Ron Howard: A Wall St. Star, Too." *New York Times*, August 25, 1989.

Strauss, Bob. "'Grinch' Cast and Crew Deliver with Charm." *L.A. Life, Daily News*, November 17, 2000.

Turan, Kenneth. "Ron Howard May Work in Hollywood But He Doesn't Really Live There." *Family Weekly*, June 30, 1985.

Weinraub, Bernard. "The Dark Underbelly of Ron Howard." *New York Times*, November 12, 1996.

Whipp, Glenn. "In the Spirit." *L.A. Life, Daily News*, November 17, 2000.

Whipp, Glenn. "Mind Games." *L.A. Life, Daily News*, December 27, 2001.

Wilson, Craig. "The Happy Days of a Happy Man." *USA Weekend*, March 28-30, 1986.

INTERVIEWS AND DOCUMENTARIES

The Directors: The Films of Ron Howard, for Encore, 1997, updated 2001. Also released in a videocassette version as *The Directors: Ron Howard* by Media Entertainment in cooperation with the American Film Institute, 1999.

James Horner and Akiva Goldsman interviews with Larry Mantle, *AirTalk*, radio station KPCC-FM, March 5, 2002.

John and Alicia Nash interview with Mike Wallace, *60 Minutes*, CBS, March 16, 2002.

Passions and Achievements: A 20-Year Retrospective of Soundtracks from the Films of Director Ron Howard, notes by Daniel Schweiger. Compact disc from Milan Entertainment, Inc., 1997.

Ron Howard appearance on *The Tonight Show with Jay Leno*, NBC, March 6, 2002.

Ron Howard interview with James Lipton, *Inside the Actors Studio*, Bravo, 1999.

Ron Howard interview with Nic Harcourt, *Morning Becomes Eclectic*, radio station KCRW-FM, January 8, 2002.

Ron Howard interview with Terry Gross, *Fresh Air*, National Public Radio, 1995.

Ron Howard segment of *Headliners and Legends* for MSNBC, 2000.

Ron Howard: Hollywood's Favorite Son segment of *Biography* for A&E, 1999.

DVD COMMENTARIES

A Beautiful Mind, Two-Disc Awards Edition, 2002
American Graffiti, Collector's Edition, 1998
Apollo 13, Collector's Edition, 1998
Backdraft, 1998
Dr. Seuss' How the Grinch Stole Christmas, Collector's Edition, 2001
EDtv, Collector's Edition, 1999
Eat My Dust, 1999
Far and Away, 1998
The First Nudie Musical, 26th Anniversary Special Edition, 2002
Grand Theft Auto, 25th Anniversary Special Edition, 1999
The Music Man, Collector's Edition, 1999
Parenthood, 1998
Ransom, 2002
The Shootist, 2001
Willow, Special Edition, 2001

INTERVIEWS CONDUCTED BY THE AUTHOR

Allan Arkush (June 27, 2001)
Whitney Bain (October 8, 2001)
Tim Brehm (June 16, 2001)
Steve Campbell (June 27, 2001)
Phyllis Cohen (August 7, 2001)
Rich Correll (September 5, 2001)
Joe Dante (May 30, 2001)
Warwick Davis (August 14, 2001)
Scott DeShields (July 9, 2001)
Frances Doel (June 1, 2001)
Miller Drake (July 23, 2001)
Fred Fox Jr. (October 1, 2001)
Gary Graver (October 12, 2001)
Eric Greene (October 28, 2001)
Gloria Greene (October 12, 2001 and October 22, 2001)
Natalie Gustafson (November 21, 2001)

Charles B. Griffith (November 7, 2001)
Tina Hirsch (July 17, 2001)
Kirk Honeycutt (July 20, 2001)
Ron Howard (January 29, 1999)
Shirley Jones (October 23, 2001)
Bruce Kimmel (June 8, 2001)
Doris Krutcher (June 16, 2001)
George Lindsey (August 22, 2001)
Ryan Malanaphy (January 7, 2002)
Pat Morita (September 5, 2001)
Howard Morris (November 5, 2001)
David Nowell (October 7, 2001)
Nancy Pierce (February 6, 2002)
Nancy Sackett (February 7, 2002)
Lenore Silverman (November 9, 2001)
Keith Thibodeaux (July 24, 2001)
Garv Thorp (November 9, 2001 and November 12, 2001)
Gedde Watanabe (September 13, 2001, and September 14, 2001)

DATABASES AND WEBSITES

The Alamo Movie Site	www.thealamofilm.com
The Andy Griffith Show Rerun Watchers Club	www.mayberry.com
A Beautiful Mind Official Site	www.abeautifulmind.com/main.html
The Clint Howard Variety Show	www.clinthoward.com
CountingDown.com	www.countingdown.com/theater
Happy Days Online	www.sitcomsonline.com/happydays.html
John F. Nash Jr. Home Page	www.math.princeton.edu/jfnj/
Imagine Entertainment Official Site	www.imagine-entertainment.com
Internet Movie Database	us.imdb.com

John Dagley's Ron Howard Fan Site	groups.yahoo.com/group/RonHowardfans
The Simpsons Archive	www.snpp.com/episodeguide.html
The Willow/Warwick Davis Web Site	www.behindthemasks.com/dawnatello/willow/

Index

About the Author

After completing her Ph.D. in Twentieth-Century American Fiction at UCLA, Beverly Gray was surprised to find herself working in the movie industry. Throughout her career, she has divided her time between academic settings and show business. While an assistant professor at the University of Southern California, she taught "Fiction into Film" courses. Later, as story editor for the legendary Roger Corman at Concorde-New Horizons Pictures, she developed scripts for 170 low-budget feature films with such titles as *Carnosaur*, *Stripped to Kill*, and *The Skateboard Kid*. Since 1995, she has covered the entertainment scene for the *Hollywood Reporter*, while teaching screenwriting workshops for the Writers' Program at UCLA Extension. Her widely acclaimed first book, *Roger Corman: An Unauthorized Biography of the Godfather of Indie Filmmaking*, was published in 2000.

Gray is a resident of Santa Monica, California. She enjoys salsa dancing, the alto recorder, and travel (the manuscript of this book has made numerous trips to China and back).